D0806130

THE RIGHT TO PARTICIPATE

The Law and Individuals With Handicapping Conditions in Physical Education and Sports

By

DR. HERB APPENZELLER
*Professor of Sports Studies
and Athletic Director
Guilford College
Greensboro, North Carolina*

Contributing Authors

DR. VICKI M. BAKER
*Assistant Professor of HPELS
Oklahoma State University
Stillwater, Oklahoma*

DR. TERRELL WEST
*Professor of Physical Education
Sandhills Community College
Southern Pines, North Carolina*

WITHDRAWN FROM
THE EUGENE SMITH LIBRARY
EASTERN CONN. STATE UNIVERSITY
WILLIMANTIC. CT 06226

THE MICHIE COMPANY
Law Publishers
Charlottesville, Virginia

J. EUGENE SMITH LIBRARY
EASTERN CONN. STATE UNIVERSITY
WILLIMANTIC. CONN. 06226

KF
4203
.A963
1983

Copyright 1983
BY
The Michie Company

Library of Congress Catalog Card No. 83-60385
ISBN 0-87215-620-6

For My Children

Thomas—A coach and a teacher;

Linda—who has taught severely retarded children;

Mary—who works with the hearing impaired.

With Affection and Admiration

144726

PREFACE

With the publication of *Sports and the Courts* in 1980, the Michie Company added a fourth book to its physical education and sports law series that includes: *From the Gym to the Jury* (1970), *Athletics and the Law* (1975) and *Physical Education and the Law* (1978).

It soon became apparent that an additional book was needed in the series since a new era has developed in physical education and sports for individuals with impairments, disabilities and handicapping conditions. Although federal legislation, notably the Rehabilitation Act (1973) and the Education for All Handicapped Children Act (1975), has created new opportunities in physical education and sports, the legislation has raised complex and confusing questions that often limit the potential benefits of the laws.

Because of this, litigation has increased dramatically in this area and judicial decisions are extremely helpful in interpreting the laws and setting parameters for compliance. This book attempts to review the legislation and subsequent litigation to help identify the issues and the courts' attitude toward them. In the text the Rehabilitation Act will often be referred to as section 504 and the Education for All Handicapped Children Act as Public Law 94-142.

The Physical Education and Recreation for the Handicapped: Information and Research Utilization Center and the American Alliance for Health, Physical Education, Recreation and Dance sponsored a publication: *Values of Physical Education, Recreation and Sports for All*. The publication defines the differences between the impaired, disabled and handicapped persons as follows:

> • *Impaired* individuals have identifiable organic
> or functional conditions — some part of the

v

body is actually missing, a portion of an anatomical structure is gone, or one of more parts of the body do not function properly or adequately. The condition may be permanent, as in the case of amputation, congenital birth defects, cerebral palsy, brain damage, or rectolinial fibroplasia. It may be temporary — functional speech defects, some learning disabilities, various emotional problems, certain social maladjustments, or specific movement deficiencies.

- *Disabled* individuals, because of impairments, are limited or restricted in executing some skills, doing specific jobs or tasks, or performing certain activities. Individuals with impairments should not be automatically excluded from activities because the condition makes it appear that they cannot participate safely, successfully, or with personal satisfaction. Some impaired persons attain high levels of excellence in activities in which they are not supposedly able to perform or participate.

- *Handicapped* individuals, because of impairment or disability, are adversely affected psychologically, emotionally, or socially. Handicapped persons reflect an *attitude* of self-pity. Some individuals with impairments and disabilities are handicapped; some severely. Others with severe impairments or disabilities adjust extremely well to their conditions and live happy and productive lives. In their eyes they are not handicapped though society continues to label them handicapped. Undoubtedly many persons in society with neither an impairment nor a disability are handicapped.

Since this book is written for people with impairments, disabilities and handicapping conditions, most references to athletes, individuals and students will refer to them. When references are made to the nonhandicapped they will be identified as such in the text.

Chapter One introduces the topic. Chapter Two highlights the possibilities that exist for achievement in sports, by not only the gifted athlete, but also for individuals with severe limitations for whom the mere attempt to participate in the simplest exercise or activity might represent a significant achievement and measure of success. Chapter Three reviews the important historical events and legislative background that led to the passage of the two most important laws for individuals with handicapping conditions: The Rehabilitation Act (section 504) and the Education for All Handicapped Children Act (Public Law 94-142). The chapter is divided into four eras: 1817-1950, 1950-1973, 1973-1975 and 1975 until the present. Chapter Four discusses the judicial process relating to civil cases and trials. It answers the questions: "What To Do If Involved In A Lawsuit" and "What To Expect At A Trial." It attempts to prepare the reader for the chapters that follow by presenting a typical case involving litigation of Public Law 94-142. Chapter Five reviews litigation involving the legal mandates of Public Law 94-142 that include: free appropriate education, least restrictive environment, due process and individualized education programs. Chapter Six examines court cases involving eligibility rules for participation in sports. Chapter Seven employs the case study method by reviewing a number of cases involving injuries to participants in physical education and sports programs. It gives attention to the liability of the administrator, physical education instructor, coach and school board. At the end of chapters two through seven is a brief summary of each chapter. Chapter Eight concludes the book and lists recommendations for those involved in physical education and sports programs.

The case study method is utilized whenever possible with the hope that the readers can identify and relate to situations that are familiar to them. It is important, however, to note that judicial decisions may be overturned at any time since the law is ever-changing. The reader should be aware of the fact that the decisions reported in this book deal with the law at a particular point in time and should review the state of the laws to be certain that they are up-to-date as they affect an issue.

ACKNOWLEDGEMENTS

Appreciation is due the following people who made this book a reality:

- Dr. Vicki M. Baker, contributing author, who had the original idea for the book and contributed material to various parts of the text.

- Becky Dye spent countless hours typing and retyping the manuscript in a caring and efficient manner.

- Nancy Frank devised a knowledge test covering selecting liabilities of physical educators and coaches. The self-test with answers is included in the text.

- Dr. James F. Gifford, Duke University, edited the text and provided helpful and valuable criticisms and suggestions.

- Dr. Pauline Loeffler, Director of Adapted and Special Education, Charles D. McIver School, read the manuscript and offered valuable suggestions.

- C. Thomas Ross, Attorney in the law firm of Craige, Brawley, Liipfert and Ross, wrote two sections in Chapter Four and helpfully discussed many legal interpretations in the book.

- Dr. Julian U. Stein, Professor of Physical Education, George Mason University and former Director of the Unit for the Handicapped, The American Alliance for Health, Physical Education, Recreation and Dance, went far beyond the "call of duty" in reading the many drafts of the text. His information and constructive criticism were always accompanied by a spirit of encouragement and support. His contribution to the text was invaluable.

- Jeaneane Williams, Guilford College, helped with many technical questions in the text.

- Dr. Terrell West, contributing author, furnished valuable material from his doctoral dissertation "Legal Aspects of Physical Education and Athletics Relating to Handicapped Children." In addition he has contributed research for the text.

YOUR GIFT

Your life has given me a time
To really see myself
To re-examine what I have
More valuable than wealth.

A body strong and full of life
To move and play and be
Was given by our mom and dad
Not to you, just me.

I do not understand it well.
I only wonder why.
The reason must be planned by one
Enlightened more than I.

So I will share the gifts you give
With those whose life I touch
Always thinking, all the while
Your life has meant so much.

Vicki McKeeman Baker

TABLE OF CONTENTS

TABLE OF CONTENTS

CHAPTER 1

Introduction

First came black power and brown power and red power.
Then came the women's movement, the white
ethnics, the gays and the elderly. Now the
physically and mentally handicapped are
emerging as one of the newest and most
aggressive political groups.[1]

A new day is dawning in America for individuals with handicapping conditions, and new opportunities in physical education and sports will be a big part of it. The new era began with the efforts of these individuals to make their presence known in society. Their success to date has come through the media, the Congress and the courts. The media have created a new public awareness both of problems and potential solutions in this area by highlighting the accomplishments of exceptional individuals. Congress has created a new political and administrative climate by enacting statutes mandating that new opportunities be available to all who can benefit from them. The courts increasingly are positive concerning the benefits of sports participation and the right of individuals to obtain them. The attitude of many Americans toward these changes, however, too often remains negative. Beyond providing relevant information, this book hopes to make a contribution toward changing these attitudes.

Media attention to exceptional achievement plays an important role in our understanding of what is possible. In 1981, for example, nine mountain climbers thrilled the world when they reached the summit of Mt. Rainier. The climbers, who reached the top of the 14,410 foot snow-capped mountain, included an epileptic, one man with an artificial leg, five blind climbers who traced the route

1

with Braille maps, and two deaf men. Richard Ross, an epileptic, shouted: "There's one for the epileptics!" when he reached the summit. Justin McDevitt, who is blind exclaimed:

> It was an exhilarating experience .... There were times when I just about gave up. The outcome of this climb will be felt by disabled people all over the new world to meet new challenges.[2]

This remarkable accomplishment followed the death of Terry Fox, Canada's most prominent hero, by just four days. Terry, a former high school athlete, had his leg amputated as a result of cancer. In 4½ months he ran 3,338 miles on his artificial leg to publicize the needs of cancer victims. Terry died but succeeded in gaining his nation's attention by raising over $20 million for cancer research. He was hailed as a "symbol of courage, of hope, and of unity" by his country.[3]

In another noteworthy endeavor, Phil Carpenter, crippled by a water skiing accident in 1972, and George Murray, disabled at age 14 from a hunting accident, departed in April, 1981, to travel from Los Angeles, California, to New York City. The two set a goal to cover 26.2 miles a day (a marathon a day) until they traversed the 3,400 miles to dramatize the International Year of Disabled Persons. Carpenter and Murray traveled in wheelchairs.[4] The two men met their goal and, in fact, exceeded it by averaging forty miles a day. One day they covered 101.2 miles including one stretch of twenty miles in which they averaged four minutes per mile.

These outstanding individuals join select world class athletes such as Wilma Rudolph and Harold Connelly who won gold medals for the United States in Olympic competition. Rudolph had birth defects which prevented her

2

from walking until she was four. She then contracted polio and could not walk again until she was eight. In the Rome Olympics, Rudolph captured the gold medal in the 100 and 200 meter dashes and anchored the 400 meter relay team to victory. Connelly ignored the disability of a withered left arm to win gold medals for the United States in the hammer throw.

The list of people who overcame their disabilities to succeed in sports is impressive and inspiring. Through sports, individuals are capturing the attention and admiration of a world desperately looking for heroes.

For too many years, however, these people as a group have been denied access to recreational and competitive sports opportunities. Prior to World War II, these children had little opportunity for recreation beyond resident segregated camping. The adult had even less chance for leisure activity or sports and most faced a solitary and sedentary life.[5]

Even more serious than the lack of recreational or sports-related activities was the tragic fact that many had little hope of living a long life. Victims of spinal cord injury, for example, seldom survived before World War II. During World War II medical technology improved so dramatically that life expectancy changed to a point where ninety percent of 4,000 spinal cord injury victims survived. The concept of rehabilitation through physical education, recreation and sports became a reality as the disabled not only survived but enjoyed the potential of good health. This new emphasis changed the focus from the quantity of the years remaining to one that stressed the quality of the years.[6]

John Bignall, a disabled sportsman, speaking about the effect of sports in the rehabilitation process declares that:

Sports can serve as a vehicle to bridge the conception one had of the self prior to the injury and incorporate this into the structuring of a new identity based on new physical conditions.[7]

Allan J. Ryan, a medical authority and editor-in-chief of *The Physician and Sportsmedicine,* recognizes this improvement in opportunities but feels that too few are able to assume a full part in the life of their community.[8] Ryan emphasizes the importance of sports when he remarks:

Since sports make up for such an important part of that life, even for those who are merely spectators, the disabled person's ability to play a part and achieve some recognition in sports can make a big difference in his or her acceptance in the community. The people who work with the disabled in recreational and competitive sports programs recognize this by always referring to them as athletes and carrying this attitude into the management of all their affairs.[9]

Ryan strongly urges physicians to take a vital role in the lives of the disabled by concluding:

The ability of a child with cerebral palsy, a young adult with paraplegia, or an older amputee to participate regularly in a suitable sports program may be the beginning of a new life for that person physically, mentally, and socially. All physicians should take every opportunity to see how this can happen and do what they can to make it happen for as many people as possible.[10]

Although many authorities in educational, medical and sports fields recognize the value and need of physical education, recreation and sports participation, the way has not been easy. Several years ago the American Medical Association strongly advised school officials to exclude

4

students with certain disqualifying conditions from participation in sports. The conditions included such things as inadequately controlled diabetes, jaundice, absence of one eye, active tuberculosis, enlarged kidney, renal disease and a variety of other conditions.[11] As a result, countless numbers of students were automatically denied the opportunity to participate in sports when school authorities accepted the American Medical Association's recommendations as an absolute mandate.

In many instances, individuals went to court to challenge the rules that denied them opportunities to participate in sports with little success. As late as 1976, John Columbo, a high school student with a hearing loss in one ear, was denied the opportunity to participate in interscholastic football, lacrosse and soccer.[12] The court felt that the risks involved were too high to overrule the school doctor's decision and it turned his petition down. Columbo's fate is repeated over and over again as athletes are consistently barred from sports competition.

It is clear that a revolution is taking place today which is unparalled in the history of American education; it is the revolution of rehabilitating individuals with handicapping conditions.[13] As the number of individuals increase, so does the concern to help them. In 1971 only fifteen states had laws providing these individuals an education,[14] while forty-six states adopted such educational provisions by 1974.[15]

In 1973, Congress enacted the Rehabilitation Act [16] and on November 29, 1975 passed the Education For All Handicapped Children Act [17] which placed certain mandates before educators across the nation for the over eight million students with handicapping conditions. (These laws are discussed in Chapter 3.) The Congress of the United States recognized the inherent value of physical education and sports and included these areas in its legislation.

5

Schools are now required to provide programs for students that will utilize equality in programs, equipment and personnel.[18] The impact of this legislation is just beginning to be felt by these individuals, and with the legislation has come an accompanying increase in litigation to enforce the laws.

Stuart Taylor, Jr., writing for the *New York Times*, attributes the recent rise in litigation in the United States to the increase in civil lawsuits filed each year in federal courts. Taylor notes that the population has only increased twenty-five percent from 1960 to 1980, but lawsuits have escalated by 185% with 59,284 suits in 1960 compared to 168,789 in 1980.[19]

Taylor reasons that:

> The dramatic increase in lawsuits in many areas, including civil rights, environmental law, medical malpractice and product liability, has resulted directly from the tremendous expansion of legal rights brought about by new state and federal laws and by evolving doctrines.[20]

He concludes:

> Underlying these developments has been a widely felt need to help innocent victims, to fix responsibilities for wrongs that in some societies might be attributed to the unscrutable workings of fate, to protect the public welfare against new dangers and, in some cases, to put an end to age-old injustices.[21]

When the laws were enacted to protect the rights of these individuals, predictions were made that the number of lawsuits would increase. The predictions have come true. The judicial interpretation of the legislation is beginning to establish guidelines that are essential to the development of sound educational programs. Three court cases, dealing with physical education and sports, illustrate the attitude of the court in cases of alleged discrimination.

INTRODUCTION

Ronald Suemnick was active in sports at Huron High School in New Boston, Michigan.[22] During the summer of 1972, he was injured in an accident and his lower limb was amputated between the ankle and knee. Ronald's doctors encouraged him to participate in football and he was fitted with an artificial plastic limb. Through "great desire, hard work and courage, and an abundance of intestinal fortitude," Ronald won a place on the varsity team as a first string offensive tackle.

Ronald played in the first six games without injury to himself or any opponent. No one complained about his participation until an official, after the sixth game, pointed to a rule that prohibited him from participating with an artificial limb. The rule stated:

> Art. 3 . . . illegal equipment shall not be worn by any player, this applies to any equipment which, in the opinion of the umpire, is dangerous or confusing. Types of equipment which shall always be declared illegal include: . . . i. Artificial hand, arm or leg.

The rule was found in the Football Rule Book which the National Federation of State High School Associations published. When questioned about the rule, the Director of the Michigan High School Athletic Association (MHSAA) replied that he did not know when the Association adopted the rule but that he was certain it had been in effect for some time. He indicated that he would impose sanctions on Huron High School, the coach and officials if Ronald played in future games.

When the team took the field in preparation for its next game, a football official informed Ronald that he could not play because of his artificial limb. Ronald sought an injunction to prohibit the MHSAA from enforcing the rule so he could participate in the final two games of the season.

He contended that the rule violated his right of equal protection and due process guaranteed by the Fourteenth Amendment of the United States Constitution. He argued that the rule arbitrarily presumed that he and others like him were unfit to play.

Several physicians testified that they had encouraged him to play football during his senior year and that denying him the opportunity to play in the final two games would cause irreparable harm. They declared that Ronald's artificial limb was not as dangerous to opposing players as the rigid plastic helmets or cleats on football shoes.

The United States District Court, Eastern Division, agreed with the plaintiff's argument and granted a permanent injunction on November 1 enabling him to play in the final two games of the season.

The mother of a blind student alleged that her son, Michael, was not permitted to participate fully in a game of "goal line soccer" during a physical education class.[23] An investigation revealed that Michael had fully participated in "goal line soccer" on Tuesday of the week in question without injury. His teacher moved him to the sidelines on Thursday to avoid possible injury.

Michael's Individual Education Program did not limit his participation in physical education activities but actually encouraged full participation in "daily games and activities to increase endurance, fitness and knowledge."

Michael's mother complained that the teacher's failure to permit her son to fully participate in "goal line soccer" violated Section 504 of the Rehabilitation Act. The complaint was upheld and the school notified that Michael must be allowed to take part fully in all physical education activities.

An outstanding Pennsylvania high school running back was recruited to play intercollegiate football at Columbia

8

University.[24] The University's physician recommended that he not be allowed to play since he had only one eye.

The court found the University's action in prohibiting the student from participating in football to be in violation of Section 504 of the Rehabilitation Act of 1973 and commented that his willingness to participate in sports by hard work was in the public interest. It granted his petition for a restraining order prohibiting the University from denying him the opportunity to participate in college football because of a visual impairment.

Although Congress has enacted legislation on behalf of individuals and the courts are beginning to interpret the legislation in a favorable manner in physical education and sports-related cases, problems continue to hinder the potential benefits of the programs.

Problems Confronting Individuals With Handicapping Conditions
Society's Negative Attitude

Eunice Kennedy Shriver, Director of the Kennedy Foundation, referred to the handicapped as the "bypassed millions in our nation" and urged the nation's leaders to use their efforts to benefit the cause of the people.[25]

The late Sir Ludwig Guttmann, a pioneer in his work with the disabled athlete in England, decried the fact that society has maintained a negative attitude toward disabled individuals for years. He pointed out that many relatives often hid them because they are viewed as "society's outcasts."[26]

Guttmann saw progress toward the disabled but felt that society still fails to meet their needs when he declared that:

> A whole new era in sport has been opened up by the achievements of all disabled sportsmen, sportswomen and children. Unfortunately,

9

society has failed to keep in step with the development of sport for the disabled in its duty to provide proper facilities, and the disabled are still confronted with architectural barriers and lack of understanding. Although there has been an awakening of the needs of the disabled in recent years, there is still much left to be desired.[27]

Steven Roberts writing for the *New York Times* agrees that there are still problems in the accessibility of facilities, transportation, equipment and services, but insists that the "main obstacle they must overcome are in people's minds, not in concrete." [28]

This feeling of rejection by society often creates tension between the disabled and the world around them and eventually leads to a loss of dignity and self-confidence resulting in self-isolation and antisocial behavior. An anonymous writer expressed these sentiments in prose and reveals the way many individuals perceive society's attitude toward them:

> The wheelchair I sit in is not made of steel. It's made of stares and whispers, closed classroom doors, inaccessible public buildings. And the wheelchair seems to get larger everytime I'm not allowed to enter a restaurant or movie theater; everytime people curse me in public or try to do their "good deed."

> Sitting in a wheelchair isn't bad. It is the mental wheelchair that makes me believe, I'm different, ugly. Not to be touched or loved. It's the mental wheelchair that isolates, confines and limits me. It's the mental wheelchair that makes me believe I'm defeated before I begin. The wheelchair I sit in is not made of steel. It's made of misunderstandings, ignorance, fear of the unfamiliar — prejudice.

10

Why must you help it grow? And don't you see
that you, too, sit in a mental wheelchair? So tell me,
how am I different.[29]

*Adversarial Attitudes of School and
Governmental Officials Toward Programs
for Individuals With Handicapping Conditions*

In recent years considerable legislation has been enacted
on behalf of these individuals. Laws such as the
Rehabilitation Act of 1973 and the Education For All
Handicapped Children Act of 1975 place additional
financial pressures on school systems and create tension
and animosity between school and governmental officials
and the recipients of the funds. The financial problem is so
great that one authority said that: "... aid for special
education is now the largest and most rapidly growing
element of state financial assistance to local schools." [30]
James Kauffman, a professor of special education at the
University of Virginia, agrees when he declares that the
new federal laws requiring that all children receive an
education is "putting enormous burdens on school
systems." [31] Kauffman opposes the new laws as they now
read because they do not allow exceptions to be made. He
contends that the courts are saying: "I don't care if you've
done everything you know how to do and nothing
works—or that you don't have the money or personnel." [32]

Kauffman argues that the original intent of the law was
to prevent discrimination; he believes that this goal has
been attained but we now have "lost sight of our original
goals." He observes that:

> Americans are a peculiarly anti-intellectual
> group. We wouldn't think of spending great sums
> of money to develop the skills of sub-par athletes
> for instance. Our school budgets develop the kids

11

with the greatest potential. We push them to see how far they can go.[33]

Kauffman believes that federal funding is designed to create similar populations while ordinary and gifted children are deprived of educational opportunities in favor of the "disadvantaged, the underprivileged and the handicapped." [34]

Roger Starr, author of an article in *Harpers* magazine criticizing the "high cost of building to accommodate the disabled" said:

> I'm all for the programs in concept and need, but who's going to pay for them and how? And where's the proof that additional expense for training and education will make the disabled independent when thousands of able bodied people in this country can't find a job?[35]

Starr declared: "When I read that a disabled activist group in New York wanted the entire subway system rehabilitated at a cost of $1.4 billion my teeth chattered." [36]

Frank Bowe, a leader in the disabled activitist movement, responded:

> Our country had been inaccessible to people with limitations, shutting out a section of the population. Of course there will be costs involved, but if you don't spend money to help people become independent, you are guaranteeing them a lifetime as wards of the state, a permanent subclass of society. Additional expense now would mean a savings in the long run.[37]

August Steinhibber of the National School Boards Association explained the dilemma that exists by stating:

12

We believe these children deserve the extra services. But we are caught in a balancing act between providing services for handicapped kids and providing for the rest of the educational programs.[38]

Still other administrators point to another problem as they declare' that the "government is welshing on its commitment." They point out that while the federal government, under the provisions of the Education For All Handicapped Children Act, agreed to provide forty percent of the cost of educating children, it only pays about twelve percent of the cost. This presents a critical problem when the cost of educating children with handicapping conditions is estimated to be rising twice as fast as the cost of a regular education.[39]

In Greensboro, North Carolina, Guilford County school officials are threatening to develop their own programs to educate seventy-nine students who attend the Greensboro Cerebral Palsy and Orthopedic School (CP&O) and eighty trainable and severely mentally handicapped students who attend the McIver School. In 1979 Greensboro citizens approved $5 million in bond money to build a new facility for "orthopedically handicapped children." The issue is the Greensboro City's plan to raise the cost of educating children at the CP&O school from $5,263 to $10,172 per child. The children are sent to the CP&O and McIver schools because the county schools do not have appropriate programs for the 115 students.[40]

County School Superintendent Rogert Boggs remarked that the county renews its contract with the City of Greensboro on a year to year basis. City School Superintendent Kenneth Newbold claimed that the county schools would be reneging on their commitment. He stated: "It wouldn't close the school, but it means the faculty wouldn't be fully utilized. We also couldn't justify keeping all the staff there." [41]

Newbold concluded:

> The Greensboro Schools have been putting a disproportionate amount of dollars into these schools for years and haven't been charging the county schools the actual amount because we had more money then and didn't want to drive them off.[42]

It seems that the questions of funding has serious implications on all levels.

Prior to 1973 each governmental agency devised its own regulations regarding physical access to its buildings. Congress established a board to develop uniform standards regarding access to the various agencies in an attempt to reduce "massive inconsistencies" because the regulations require that over 35 million individuals have access to their government. The board completed its task in January, 1981, with a twenty-page document of minimum standards for access to government buildings, bathrooms, telephones, parking and transportation.[43]

Vice-President George Bush predicted that compliance with the regulations would cost the taxpayer $800 million and labeled them as unnecessary governmental regulations. The twenty-two-member Architectural and Transportation Barrier Compliance Board voted the guidelines down and handed disabled individuals a devastating setback.[44]

Harry Krents, an attorney who founded Mainstream, reports that school and governmental authorities have nothing to fear from the disabled. He notes that twenty-two percent of all children with limitations never go beyond the eighth grade and the number who live beyond the poverty level is almost twice as high as that for the general population. He questions the reason for people feeling threatened by the laws.[45]

Merritt B. Low, M.D., the former president of the American Academy of Pediatrics, warns that the "handicapped child might turn out to be the tail that wags the dog." [46] Dr. Ed Martin, the former Deputy Commissioner of Education, vigorously disagrees with Low when he emphatically replies to that charge by saying:

> One of the great myths is that the handicapped kids are going to take dollars away from nonhandicapped kids. But we don't believe it. It never happens; minorities don't end up with more privileges than the dominant party of society. [47]

While legislation such as the Rehabilitation Act of 1973 and the Education For All Handicapped Children Act of 1975 recognizes the importance of participation in physical education and sports by these individuals, certain problems continue to frustrate educators. One problem is a lack of understanding of the legislation. For example, while the Rehabilitation Act was enacted in 1973, Congress did not issue the rules and regulations until 1977.

It is essential, therefore, to examine the educational and legal issues associated with legislation as it applies to disabled individuals in the public schools, colleges and universities so that decisionmakers can obtain appropriate information to facilitate decisions and policies that are both educationally and legally sound.

This book will summarize information regarding these federal laws for decisionmakers in the area of physical education and sports. It will attempt to provide physical educators and sports personnel with suggestions necessary to develop the best possible environment for individuals with handicapping conditions within the guidelines of the laws. It will also record the issues placed before the courts and the position of the courts toward them.

15

FOOTNOTES

1. Greensboro Daily News, June 25, 1978.

2. Washington Post, July 4, 1981.

3. Greensboro Daily News and Record, June 29, 1981.

4. PHIL CARPENTER & GEORGE MURRAY, "CONTINENTAL QUEST" L.A. TO N.Y. A MARATHON A DAY, (Tampa, Florida, 1981).

5. Stanley Labanovich, *The Psychology of Wheelchair Sports,* THERAPEUTIC RECREATION JOURNAL, Vol. 12, First Quarter, 1979.

6. John Bignall, *Wheelchair Athletes: Deviant Competence,* a paper presented at the Pacific Sociological Association meeting in San Francisco, California, April 9-12, 1980.

7. *Id.*

8. Allan J. Ryan, *Sports Opportunities for the Disabled,* THE PHYSICIAN AND SPORTSMEDICINE, Vol. 9, No. 12, December, 1981.

9. *Id.*

10. *Id.*

11. HERB APPENZELLER & THOMAS APPENZELLER, SPORTS AND THE COURTS, The Michie Company, Charlottesville, Virginia, 1980.

12. Columbo v. Sewanhaka Central High School, Dist. No. 2, 383 N.Y.S.2d 518 (N.Y. Sup. Ct. 1976).

13. David Savage, *Educating All the Handicapped: What the Law Says and What the Schools Are Doing,* National School Publications Association, Washington, D.C., 1977.

14. *Aid for Education of the Handicapped,* AMERICAN EDUCATION, July, 1974.

15. Joan Alschuler, *Education for the Handicapped,* JOURNAL OF LAW & EDUCATION, October, 1978.

16. Public Law 93-112, 87 Stat. 355 (1974).

17. Public Law 94-142, 89 Stat. 773 (1975).

18. *Federal Register,* XLII, No. 163 (Aug. 1977): 42479.

19. *Supra* note 3.

20. *Id.*

21. *Id.*

22. Suemnick v. Michigan High School Athletic Association, Civil No. 74-70592, U.S. District Court, (E.D. Mich. 1973).

23. OCR/Complaint LOFS, Supplement 34, Vol. 257, Page 147, October 17, 1980.

24. Wright v. Columbia University, 520 F. Supp. 789 (E.D. Pa. 1981).

25. Eunice Kennedy Shriver, *Recreation for the Mentally Retarded,* JOURNAL OF HEALTH, PHYSICAL EDUCATION & RECREATION, Vol. 36, May 1965.

INTRODUCTION

26. SIR LUDWIG GUTTMANN, TEXTBOOK FOR THE DIDSABLED, HM&M Publishers, Anglesbury, Bucks, England.

27. *Id.*

28. *Supra* note 1.

29. *Therapeutic Recreation Journal,* Vol. 7, Second Quarter, 1973.

30. William Wilken, *State Aid for Special Education Benefits,* a paper presented at the National Conference of State Legislatures in Washington, D.C., 1976.

31. Greensboro Daily News, Sept. 6, 1981.

32. *Id.*

33. *Id.*

34. *Id.*

35. Greensboro Daily News, February 27, 1982.

36. *Id.*

37. *Id.*

38. PEOPLE, July 12, 1982.

39. *Id.*

40. Greensboro Daily News, Sept. 16, 1982.

41. *Id.*

42. *Id.*

43. *Supra* note 3.

44. *Id.*

45. *Supra* note 1.

46. David Cushing, *Physical Education: Integrating the Handicapped,* THE PHYSICIAN & SPORTSMEDICINE, Vol. 8, No. 1, Jan. 1980.

47. *Id.*

CHAPTER 2

Achievement in Sports

One summer I had the rare opportunity of touring Southeastern Asia with a nine-man track and field team sponsored by the State Department and the Amateur Athletic Union. Our athletes conducted clinics, lectured, put on demonstrations and competed on a friendly basis with the outstanding athletes of Asia. Our young men were overwhelmed by the wonderful reception we received and by the enthusiasm and ability of the athletes with whom we worked.

In all of the countries, however, I felt a growing sense of frustration whenever I was asked how an athlete of small stature could compete against athletes of tremendous size found in other countries of the world. From Singapore to Thailand, Hong Kong, and the Philippines this same question was asked. Whenever our 262-pound Massachusetts weight man would put the shot or throw the discus, I found myself agreeing with the Far East athletes and coaches that the smaller in stature Asians couldn't compete in these events.

Harold James

Gradually, I began to recall my days as a high school and college coach and remember athletes with whom I had worked. Whenever the question concerning size and performance was asked and the Asian athletes shrugged their shoulders in apparent defeat, I searched more and more diligently for an answer. Certainly I had coached a 165-pound halfback who was turned down by the major colleges because of size; yet he battered his way to Little All-America status and a trial with the Green Bay Packers. Likewise, I remembered a 6′2″ pivot man turned down by

19

other colleges because of size who broke record after record at Guilford College and went on to win All-Conference honors in a conference of giants. Yes, and above all, how about Harold James, a young man who *really* had a handicapping condition?

As I lectured and talked with the wonderful athletes of Southeast Asia, I began to tell the Harold James story and found that his story began to have an amazing effect on all who heard it. Many athletes and coaches marveled at Harold's accomplishments in the face of a serious handicap and resultant frustrations; some seemed to take new hope from his life.

Harold James was the victim of polio while an infant and the aftereffect left him with a small, withered left leg which was the size of an average person's arm. As a young boy he refused to accept the decision of doctors to give up his desire to compete in athletics. Instead he grew more determined than ever to participate like his friends. He limped home night after night exhausted from trying to keep pace with his friends who could run faster, climb higher, and play games better than he. The harder he tried to keep up with his friends the more his small leg hurt. But one thing he refused to do was to accept defeat. Sympathetic teachers and friends merely spurred him on with a fierce determination to excel, and this carried him through grammar school. Soon the challenge of high school confronted him and the way was not easy.

Again Harold had to convince his parents, coaches, and doctors that he could, and, in fact, had to play high school athletics. His coach, a former college classmate of mine, had a reputation as an excellent coach but one who was demanding of his athletes. He would not pity this struggling athlete but would expect the same from him as any boy with normal legs. The price Harold would be called upon to pay

20

would be high if he were to play. Harold James played the game the only way he knew how, giving no quarter to anyone and in turn expecting none from anyone. His high school record was known all over the Tidewater Area of Virginia where he led his football, basketball and track teams to many great victories. To climax his high school career, he was honored by being named the outstanding athlete in Virginia Beach High School.

The future looked dark to Harold after high school graduation. He was only an average academic student, having spent more time and interest in athletics than in scholastic attainment. He decided to try to apply for an athletic scholarship on the basis of his high school record, but the college coaches lost interest when they saw his left leg. Today college athletics require speed, size, and agility; the risk was too great.

I first met him when one of our athletes who had been a teammate of his in high school asked me to give him a tryout. I still remember the shock I experienced when he took of his sweatpants and began to jump over the bar at the high jump pit. A crowd of curious students quickly gathered as he continued to clear the bar at regular intervals until he had defeated all of our varsity jumpers. When he talked to me about college football I was confident that he would be given a chance, but I was certain he would be discouraged if he attempted to play. I felt, however, that he would be an asset to us in track.

Harold's application to Guilford College was rejected and a letter was sent expressing regret that his grades were not acceptable. We soon discovered that he was not ready to give up. His mother called and told us he was almost completely demoralized by our letter because he knew he could do the work if we gave him a chance. "Don't turn him down," she pleaded. "He needs a chance, and he'll prove to

you that he can do it, if you just try him for a semester."
After a brief, hurried consultation, our Admission's
Director reviewed his case and agreed to give him a chance
for a semester on probation.

Misfortune plagued him for his first three years. He
dislocated his shoulder and broke his finger in football,
injured his knee in track, and even became scholastically
ineligible for a semester as a sophomore. His determination
to make the varsity team in football never wavered, and he
put all his energy toward reaching this goal.

During his four years at Guilford Harold broke may
existing records of both the school and the district. He
scored more points in a dual meet and for an entire season
than anyone before him at Guilford. In one meet when the
squad was limited in numbers he ran the high hurdles, high
jumped, broad jumped, pole vaulted, threw the javelin and
discus. It was in this meet with an arch rival that Guilford
needed a second place in the javelin to win the meet. Harold
did not appear to have a chance as his first two throws fell
pitifully short, but as he lined up for the final throw he
smiled at me and said, "Don't worry, coach. We'll win." He
helped us do just that as he found some hidden reserve
strength and threw the javelin far enough to capture second
place and a victory for the team.

In track he came back after two narrow misses to try for
the final jump in the conference track meet. The tension
was terrific as he walked to the bar time and time again to
get ready for the most important jump of his career. I prayed
that he could make the height and win in his last meet of
the year. I visualized the hours of work, the sacrifice and
self-denial that this young athlete had put in and decided
that win or lose he had been truly great. I could barely see
as the crowd closed in on the pit for the last jump. Suddenly
a tremendous roar was heard and I knew he had made the

jump and was the new conference champion. People left the track in disbelief at this young man with the withered leg who refused to believe he could lose.

He entered his senior year and starred as a defensive halfback. Harold had the knack for sensing plays and hit like a ton of bricks. In our opening game upset of our heavily favored rival, he played as we had never seen him play. It was in this game that he hurdled over an opposing blocker to make a vicious tackle. The surprised blocker looked up in bewilderment and shouted, "Hey you, are you some kind of a kangaroo?" The name stuck and his teammates affectionately referred to him as the "kangaroo kid." In the next game against a powerful opponent, our outmanned team entered the game as a five touchdown underdog. It was here that I felt he had finally earned his starting spot at quarterback. We did not win but he put on one of the greatest offensive shows to bring us within a one-touchdown loss.

Later during the season he scored against the nation's number one small college team and again made plays that were fantastic. During one game an overly aggressive lineman twisted Harold's little leg during a pileup, and as he limped off the field I saw a grin on his face. "Coach, don't get upset," he said. "I'm flattered that anyone would think that much of my ability." He climaxed a great personal year by being named to the all-conference team as a quarterback.

In his senior year he entered the conference meet undefeated in the regular season competition in the high jump. Harold had won a tremendous following of both Guilford students and admiring opponents. To him the conference championship was the biggest and most important event at this time. When I arrived at the jumping pit I found that he was visibly upset by the new

23

hard-surfaced approach area. "Coach," he pleaded, "do something about this pit. I can't get traction on it." I knew his entire season and hopes were wrapped up in the event but I was helpless to change things. He tried desperately to clear a height he could usually clear in warmup and was defeated early in the competition. I still remember the deep hurt in his eyes and body as he limped pathetically from the track, disappointed and humiliated because he felt that he had let his friends and school down.

This temporary defeat was forgotten at the end of the year when he was chosen Sportsman of the Year in Virginia, an honor awarded to the truly great in Virginia. Later a writer interviewed him and asked him to tell of his greatest thrill in sports. Was it the day you scored against the national champions? Was it the day you broke the district high jump record, won the conference high jump championship, the all-conference football selection, or the honor of being chosen Virginia's Sportsman of the Year? He was quick to answer and his answer surprised me. He said, "None of these. It was the time when we played East Carolina when my coach put his arm around me before the game and told me he had decided that I was his number-one quarterback. "For you see," he told the surprised writer, "I knew that in America, a handicapped boy could reach his goal if he wanted to badly enough."

I remembered Harold James during those hot days in the Far East and the words of his high school coach who told me to forget his withered leg because his heart was big enough to take care of his handicap.

I saw him recently at our homecoming game. Somehow words did not come to me as I really wanted to tell him that he had been a source of inspiration to me and all our players and even opponents. Someday I'll tell him that in far away Asia countless numbers of wonderful young athletes have taken new hope because of him and that his story will continue to live in their lives as they too try to overcome handicaps to reach their goals.

My experience with Harold James opened my eyes to the realization that many individuals with disabilities achieve success in sports without attention or fanfare. To these people the important thing is participation. John E. Bignall, a wheelchair athlete, observes that physicians along with physical therapists find that sports participation is "an invaluable therapeutic tool."[1] Bignall emphasizes the importance of sports participation for wheelchair athletes when he states:

> Participation in wheelchair sports helps to increase physical strength, coordination, and endurance, each of which is important to the individual who must make his or her way in a world that is not designed for a wheelchair.[2]

Bignall observes that serious problems can result when the individual does not have the opportunity to take part in some activity. He comments:

> Severe traumatic disability can result in a self-centered isolation, which results from loss of activity, loss of self-confidence and an almost monotonous regularity that is associated with a severe disability.[3]

Bignall believes that sports participation leads to a process of "social interaction between the disabled and the able-bodied community." He points out that the wheelchair athlete changes society's stereotyped view of the individual and increases the person's feeling of self-worth and self-confidence so essential in the rehabilitation process.[4]

Bignall concludes that participation in sports leads to many benefits that include:

1. Wheelchair sports can demonstrate that the disability does not render the individual totally useless or dependent.

2. It may show that the injury limits the persons only in specific functions but that he/she is capable of performing efficiently and effectively in other areas.

3. The emphasis is on ability, not disability, and is an invaluable educational tool in all spheres of social interaction.

4. It provides role models for individuals who have recently sustained a spinal cord injury.[5]

Donald Batelaan, born with spina bifida, organized the Palm Beach Wide Tracks, a team of athletes with handicapping conditions. Batelaan, a champion swimmer, wheelchair racer and basketball player, regards sports participation as a positive factor in the lives of many individuals when he declares that: "Sports for the disabled is extremely important. It's a self-image builder and teaches people how to get along in a team atmosphere."[6]

Leslie Milk, the Executive Director of Mainstream, deplores society's paternalistic attitude toward these people who want "respect and dignity" instead and the "right to take risks."[7] Harry Cordellos, the outstanding blind athlete, supports her statement. In 1981, in a speech to the American Alliance for Health, Physical Education, Recreation and Dance, Cordellos advocates that every person with a handicapping condition should have the "right to fail." He opposes the accepted attitude on the part of many people that one should only compete when success is expected. The value of sports, insists Cordellos, is taking part—win or lose.[8]

Many stories are written and many more can be told of individuals who through their efforts and determination overcame limitations to achieve success in sports. For many the accomplishments are unbelievable, but for others, the mere act of taking part in some physical activity, no matter how little, is in effect, the true measure of success. The stories are endless and inspiring and although many will go untold and often unpublicized, they exist nevertheless. The job and sense of fulfillment they give the participant will be reward enough.

A few examples illustrate the possibilities that exist for individuals with disabilities.

Charlie Boswell

Charlie Boswell holds a record for a score of eighty-one for eighteen holes of golf in national competition. His score may seem insignificant until you realize that his record came in a tournament sponsored by the United States Blind Golfers Association. Boswell has won twelve national titles in twenty years and scored a hole-in-one on a par three, 147 yard hole in Birmingham, Alabama.[9]

While Charlie Boswell's story is unique, his accomplishments are typical for many individuals who continue to overcome adversity to bring attention to the potential in sports for people with handicapping conditions.

Charlie Boswell was an All America football player at the University of Alabama in the mid-1930's with a future in professional baseball. He commanded a tank battalion in North Africa during World War II and was blinded when his tank took a direct hit. At Valley Forge Rehabilitation Hospital in Pennsylvania, Boswell exhibited a belligerent and negative attitude, feeling sorry for himself with a "what's the use of living" philosophy. He refused to take part in the sports program at the hospital until a staff member told him that he was going to play golf the next day. Boswell who had never played a game of golf, replied, "What in the hell can a blind man do on a golf course?" The staff member told him, "Shut up, we're going." [10]

Someone put a golf club in his hands the following day and guided him through some preliminary swings. Finally Boswell, after some practice swings on his own, hit his first tee shot ever. According to Boswell, "he hit the ball right between the screws and he could feel it going 250 yards right down the middle." Golf gave him a thrill he had never experienced and it became his rehabilitation and road back to an active life. He often questions what would have happened to him if he had missed his first swing.[11]

Bick Long

Bick Long, a Greensboro, North Carolina resident, lost his right leg after an automobile accident in 1970 and Corbin Cherry, of Mill Valley, California, lost his leg while serving with the military in Vietnam.

Long successfully defended his golf title for the fourth time in the National Amputee Golf Tournament at Tanglewood Golf Course, in Winston-Salem, North Carolina, in August, 1982. Long in a post-tournament interview remarked:

> I was a pretty good player before the accident. I just decided that I wasn't going to let the handicap stop me. My artificial leg doesn't cause me any problems while I'm playing. In fact, I've played better since the accident.[12]

Runnerup Corbin Cherry commented: "It doesn't affect me at all. I've found that I've been more consistent since the accident. It only bothers me as much as I let it." [13]

Ninety-two golfers competed in the 1982 national event which was divided into six divisions on the basis of the amputation sustained.

Julian Stein, who has had a tremendous impact on sports for individuals with handicapping conditions, headed AAHPERD's Unit on Programs of services for the handicapped. Stein lists the names of athletes whose names are familiar to sports fans and whose accomplishments are well-known in sports. These athletes competed at a different level of limitation than the wheelchair athlete, the mentally retarded, the blind and other severe disabilities but, nevertheless overcame problems to achieve success in sports.

Baseball

Pete Gray played the outfield for the St. Louis Browns although he was a single arm amputee while Monty Stratton, a single leg amputee, pitched for the Chicago White Sox. Several diabetics played outstanding professional baseball, such as Catfish Hunter of the Oakland A's and New York Yankees; Ron Santo, of the Chicago Cubs and White Sox. Tony Lazzeri, of the New York Yankees had epilepsy and Hal Lanier, who played for San Francisco and New York, had grand mal epilepsy. It was said that Micky Mantle, the New York Yankees great outfielder, was a candidate for a rehabilitation center rather than the Baseball Hall of Fame. Mantle had bone disease that required wrapping and taping each day. Doc Ellis of the Pittsburg Pirates had a bad case of sickle-cell anemia.

Football

In football, Tom Dempsey attracted the attention of our nation when he kicked a winning game field goal for sixty-three yards. Dempsey, a fine golfer, had a congenital foot deformity that left him with only half a foot on his kicking foot. He also has little of his right hand.

Larry Brown, offensive halfback for the Washington Redskins, Bonnie Rowland, middle guard for the St. Louis Cardinals, and Yancey Sutton, who played linebacker for the University of Florida football team, all had hearing impairments.

Raymond Berry, Baltimore's great receiver, had one leg much shorter than the other, while Rocky Blier lost a portion of a foot during the Viet Nam conflict. Kansas City's offensive end Danny Abramowitz lost one eye after he joined the Chiefs.

In professional tennis the name of Jimmy Connors is well known to all fans. Connors is an asthmatic. During the 1981 Wimbledon series, Connors was warned by officials to stop grunting during his matches. Newspaper reports attributed it to his asthmatic condition.

Track and Field

In track and field Jim Ryun, Kansas University's record holder and Olympic standout, was also an asthmatic. Glen Cunningham was severely burned as a child and was never expected to walk again, but he achieved great success as America's premier miler in his day. Harold Connelly overcame the limitation of a withered left arm to win gold medals in the Olympics in the hammer throw. Wilma Rudolph, a victim of birth defects and polio, blazed her way to gold medals in the Rome Olympics in the 100 and 200 meter sprints and anchored the 400 meter gold medal relay team.

Swimming

Rick Damont won the 100 meter freestyle in 1972 only to be disqualified because of a controversy over approval for his use of medication to control an asthmatic condition. Shelly Mann overcame polio to win a gold medal in the Melbourne, Olympics in the 100 meter butterfly event.

30

Ted Volrath lost both legs in Korea but overcame his handicap to obtain a black belt in karate.

Other achievements include the performance of Jim Maelstro, who was blind and wrestled in the finals of the tournament to qualify for the Olympics despite a broken arm. Because of his courage and determination he was taken to the Montreal Olympics as a member of the United States wrestling team. Jack Robertson, a paraplegic with no use of his legs, came within 800 meters of swimming The English Channel. Pete Dawkins became the first cadet at West Point to captain the football team, serve as brigade commander and be president of the student body. Dawkins, an All-America halfback, was also a Rhodes Scholar. As a child he had polio and doctors predicted that he would never walk. Lamar Lundy, a great end at Purdue and an all-professional defensive end for the Los Angeles Rams, had a variety of visual perceptual problems but overcame them to be a standout in football.

Stein notes that this list only scratches the surface of men and women who achieved success in sports although they possessed physical limitations during their lives and careers.

These examples illustrate the great potential for sports participation inherent in the lives of many individuals with handicapping conditions. Sports activities are not only available to the highly skilled and motivated athlete but to most individuals if allowed the opportunity to participate.

For example, seven-year-old Matthew Raley has been crippled from birth by cerebral palsy. Matthew's mother revealed that her son loved sports, but only as a spectator. An electrical engineer and several graduate students devised a mechanical bat that Matthew can control by moving his head. With the mechanical bat, the boy can: "hit a switch with his head, activating a plastic bat mounted on a stand next to his wheelchair." [14]

One of the graduate students is attempting to develop a device utilizing "electrical signals of the eye to control toys and communication devices for quadriplegics and others who cannot control their limbs' movements." [15]

It is apparent that Public Law 94-142 and section 504 of the Rehabilitation Act will give more students in elementary, secondary, college and university levels the right to participate in physical education, intramural, club and organized sports programs than ever before. Many stories will be written about individuals in sports who through courage and determination will overcome physical or mental disabilities to achieve success. For many with all degrees of handicapping conditions, the act of participation, not accounts of record-breaking performances, will be the measure of success.

Summary

A new era has arrived for individuals with impairments, disabilities and handicapping conditions. These exceptional people are climbing mountains, participating in grueling marathons and competing in practically every sports activity. Their efforts and accomplishments are gaining attention through the media and the media is highlighting their problems, but also giving attention to solutions and the possibilities that exist for participation in sports-related activities. Participation in sports can increase a sense of self-worth and dignity and help overcome a loss of self-confidence and self-centered isolation.

Public Law 94-142 and section 504 of the Rehabilitation Act will undoubtedly give more people the *right to participate* in physical education, intramural, club and organized sports programs, no matter what or how severe their disability. Many exceptional athletes will continue to serve as role models as they set outstanding record-breaking performances. The true hero, however, may be the severely disabled, unskilled and uncoordinated person for whom the mere act of participation in the most elementary exercise or activity will be the benchmark of achievement.

FOOTNOTES

1. John E. Bignall, *Wheelchair Athletics: Competent Deviance,* a paper presented at the Pacific Sociological Association's meetings in San Francisco, California, April 9-12, 1980.

2. *Id.*

3. *Id.*

4. *Id.*

5. *Id.*

6. Greensboro Daily News and Record, July 18, 1982.

7. Greensboro Daily News and Records, June 29, 1981.

8. Harry Cordellos, a speech delivered at the American Alliance for Health, Physical Education, Recreation and Dance, Boston, Mass., April, 1981.

9. Letter from Julian Stein, September 16, 1982.

10. *Id.*

11. *Id.*

12. Greensboro Daily News and Record, August 29, 1982.

13. *Id.*

14. Greensboro Daily News and Record, August 21, 1982.

15. *Id.*

CHAPTER 3

Legislative Background

Many important events, legislation and judicial decisions led to the enactment of the Rehabilitation Act and the Education For All Handicapped Children Act (Public Law 94-142).

This chapter will review these two major laws in addition to the events, legislation and judicial decisions that influenced their enactment. The legislative background will be divided into four periods: 1817-1950, 1950-1973, 1973-1975, and 1975 until the present. (For a synopsis of the laws, see Appendix A).

1817-1950

Claudine Sherrill, writing in *Adapted Physical Education and Recreation,* lists the important events in the history of assistance for individuals with handicapping conditions.[1] According to Sherrill, Thomas Gallaudet founded the first residential school for the deaf in Hartford, Connecticut in 1817. The first residential schools for the blind were founded in 1830 and 1833 in Boston, New York and Philadelphia. The Perkins Institution in Boston was the only school at that time to offer a physical education program for its students.[2]

The first residential facility for the mentally retarded in the United States was opened in 1848 in Massachusetts and the earliest residential facility in the United States for the orthopedically handicapped was organized in New York in 1863 and Philadelphia in 1877. In 1876 the American Association on Mental Deficiency (AAMD) was established to promote residential facilities for the mentally retarded. Twenty states opened residential schools for the retarded by 1886. By 1899 over 100 cities including Boston, Chicago,

Cleveland, Detroit, Milwaukee and New York had begun to educate individuals with handicapping conditions with special education classes.[3]

Prior to the twentieth century it was difficult to find material relating to persons with handicapping conditions. Beginning with the first publication of the *New York Times* in 1851, through the year of 1899, only nineteen articles appeared on the subject and none of the articles merited editorial comment. During the Civil War some articles appeared on the rehabilitation of wounded soldiers, but nothing was written about the education of people with disabilities.[4]

The United States Congress passed a bill in 1827 providing land for a seminary in Kentucky for the education of the deaf and dumb[5] and, thirty years later, established the Columbia Institution for the Deaf and Dumb.[6]

In 1902 a Department of Special Education was established by the National Education Association under the leadership of Alexander Graham Bell, a pioneer in the education for the deaf movement.[7]

The word "handicapped" first appeared in the *New York Times* in 1905 in reference to a football game between two Kentucky teams established for the blind — Crescent Hill and Kentucky Institute.[8]

In 1919, the "National Easter Seals Society for Crippled Children and Adults" was founded, and in 1922 the first organization for all groups with disabilities was founded — Council for Exceptional Children.[9]

In 1930 the Committee on the Physically and Mentally Handicapped wrote the Bill of Rights for Children with handicapping conditions, and the White House Conference on Child Health and Protection was held. In 1939 Title V, Part 2 of the Social Security Act authorized three important programs in every state that included:

36

1. Locating all crippled children and maintaining a state register.
2. Providing skilled diagnostic services by qualified surgeons and physicians at state clinics.
3. Providing skilled medical, surgical, nursing, medical-social, and physical therapy services for children in hospitals, convalescent homes, and foster homes.[10]

Public Law 113-78 was enacted in 1943 and, as the amended Vocational Rehabilitation Act, furnished disabled persons sixteen years of age and older with the services needed "to render them employable." [11]

The American Athletic Association for the Deaf was founded in 1945 and was the "first special population in the United States to form its own sports organization." It was followed in 1949 by the establishment of the National Wheelchair Basketball Association and the National Wheelchair Athletic Association.[12]

1950-1973

A mid-century White House Conference on Children and Youth was convened in 1950 with over 300 organizations attending. These organizations met to discuss the problems of children with handicapping conditions.[13] In the same year Howard A. Rusk, Director of the Institute of Physical Medicine and Rehabilitation, reported that money was available through the Social Security Act of 1935 for those individuals. Rusk urged Congress to enact legislation to provide benefits to children under seventeen years of age since the present act aided only those persons who had reached the age of seventeen.[14]

Congress enacted a number of laws that served as building blocks for each other. We review these developments because they led to the two most important laws for people with handicapping conditions: the Rehabilitation Act of 1973 [15] and the Education For All Handicapped Children Act in 1975.[16] (The text of a number of these related laws is found in Appendix A).

Public Law 815 (H.R. 2317, September 23, 1950)

This law was directed to the construction of school facilities in federally affected areas such as military installations, Indian reservations and other federally owned and operated property.[17] Although the law did not specify assistance to disabled persons, it became a stepping stone for later legislation that benefitted them. Public Law 815 set age limits for children who would receive a free public education. Congress adopted a cautious attitude toward athletics, preferring not to use federal funds to build athletic facilities to enhance althletics programs, by defining:

> school facilities as classrooms and other related facilities. Athletic facilities did not include ... athletic stadia, or structures or facilities intended primarily for athletic exhibitions, contests, or games or other events for which admissions is to be charged to the general public.[18]

Public Law 874 (September 30, 1950)

Seven days after the passage of Public Law 815 the same 81st Congress passed Public Law 874 which now is known as one of the most amended laws ever enacted. While its original version provided educational improvements for students, its main purpose was to provide financial aid for the education of children of employees on federal properties with the exception of Indian children. The original version also prohibited spending monies for the construction of facilities and for the purchase of land for later construction.

After the enactment of Public Law 815 and Public Law 874, a number of leaders began to promote the cause of individuals with handicapping conditions.

President Dwight Eisenhower focused on a program for the rehabilitation of the disabled in his State of the Union Address in 1952.[19] Editorials appeared in newspapers following President Eisenhower's plea for help and attention was drawn to his efforts to improve conditions for the 650 thousand Americans disabled each year. Editorials called for bipartisan support of the proposed budget.

In 1952 Congress responded to the mid-century White House Conference, attention from the media and President Eisenhower's plea for help by enacting the Cooperative Research Act, Public Law 85-531.[20] In 1954 the nation's first complete rehabilitation center for crippled children opened at Bellevue Medical Center co-sponsored by the Center and the Joseph P. Kennedy, Jr. Foundation.[21] The facility provided medical services for children with emotional, physical and mental problems.[22]

J. A. Fischer, an outstanding physical educator, reported the findings of a study that established the fact that physical education was excellent therapy for children who possessed disabilities since it relieved them of their fears, anxieties and rejections and enabled them to develop a positive self-image.[23]

Julian Stein, an instructor at Wakefield High School in Arlington, Virginia, emerged as a leader in the new field by offering practical suggestions for students in "adaptive physical education" and urging an emphasis on research to help teachers in their work with less fortunate students.[24]

A national effort was initiated to develop methods for helping the disabled in physical education since very few programs existed for the disadvantaged in education.[25]

Eunice Kennedy Shriver, Executive Director of the Joseph P. Kennedy, Jr. Foundation, considered mental retardation to be the number one health problem among children and a national problem.[26] Shriver believed that three revolutions were taking place in America. The first represented a new interest, hope and responsibility for the mentally retarded. The second was in the field of medical research, where diseases such as phenylketonuria were being discovered and treated at birth. The third dealt with prenatal and postnatal care which, Shriver noted, was lacking for thirty percent of all mothers.[27]

Shriver predicted that a fourth revolution was yet to come — the revolution for the mentally retarded in physical education and recreation. She cited studies that revealed that test scores improved as much as ten percent when mentally retarded children were given additional play time. Shriver declared: "The nation is looking to you for leadership. I can think of no worthier cause for you to spend yourselves in than the cause of the mentally retarded, the by-passed millions in this nation."[28]

A White House Conference on Education was called in 1965, and 700 education leaders considered a request from Congress to make recommendations to help them provide better educational services for America's students. The Conference leaders encouraged educators to make every effort to integrate the special student with the non-handicapped.[29] The Elementary and Secondary Education Act, Public Law 89-10, enacted the same year, incorporated many of Shriver's ideas and those developed at the White House Conference.[30]

Public Law 89-10 (H.R. 2362, April 11, 1965)

Public Law 89-10, known as the Elementary and Secondary Act of 1965, amended Public Law 874. It was intended to improve educational opportunities for low income families and meet the educational needs of deprived children.[31]

This law marked the first time since Public Law 815 was passed in 1950 that funds were available for the purchase of land and construction and remodeling of educational facilities. Congress continued to restrict funds for athletics by refusing to provide monies for any gymnasium or athletic facility that charged admission for athletic contests.

Public Law 89-10 is noteworthy for sections 303 and 504 which provide grants for the establishment and operation of primary and secondary schools for diverse educational experiences for students of various talents. Among the approved activities were health, physical education and recreation.

Congress first used the word "handicapped" in Public Law 89-10 in section 303 when it made specialized instruction and equipment available for: "students interested in studying advanced subjects which are not taught in the schools or which can be provided more effectively on a centralized basis, or for persons who are handicapped or of preschool age." [32]

Section 504 of Public Law 89-10 established the recording, collecting, processing and interpreting of local systems to the various state offices to help students determine their present level for future development. In section 504 Congress mentioned students with handicapping conditions by providing available monies for physical education. It also recognized the importance of school health, physical education and recreation in the lives of special students.[33]

41

Public Law 89-313 (November 1, 1965)

Congress amended Public Law 874 with Public Law 89-313 by adding a new paragraph listing various types of students that require special education. These included: "mentally retarded students, those hard of hearing, deaf, speech impaired, visually handicapped, seriously emotionally disturbed, crippled, or other health impaired children."[34]

Although the list has been more clearly defined, it still is applicable today.

Public Law 89-750 (H.R. 13161, November 6, 1966)

The 89th Congress, more than any previous session, assisted special students. Public Law 89-750 was the third law the 89th Congress passed in their behalf.[35] The law, known as the Elementary and Secondary Amendments of 1966, amended Public Law 874 by making money available to meet the special needs of the educationally deprived student on Indian reservations. This amendment reinforced the responsibility of the local education agency to provide free public education for deprived students and included neglected or delinquent children who are institutionalized. The types of handicapping conditions remained consistent with those identified in Public Law 89-313.

Public Law 89-750 granted fifty million dollars in federal funds in 1966-1967 and provided an additional one hundred and fifty million dollars for 1967-1968 to initiate, expand and improve programs for children. The term "handicapped children" remained unchanged although no specific definition clarified handicapping conditions.

Under Public Law 89-10 Congress has set an age limit of five to seventeen. It extended the age limit from three to twenty-one years in Public Law 89-750.

Congress issued several requirements for receiving federal funds, among them that:

1. The state must design a plan to meet the special needs of students with handicapped conditions.
2. The plan must be approved by the State's Commissioner of Education.
3. The plan must include certain criteria such as a procedure to locate all students in need of special help.
4. A record must be kept of these students.
5. A procedure must be developed for acquiring, distributing and up-dating essential information on the students for use by the teachers and administrative personnel.

The latter part of Title I established a National Advisory Committee on Handicapped Children. Title II, section 231, states that: "Any federal funds for the construction of school facilities be made accessible to and usable by handicapped students." [36]

This was the first attempt by Congress to provide federal funds for the construction of facilities as long as that structure was accessible to all students.

Public Law 90-247 (H.R. 7819, January 2, 1968)

The 90th Congress amended Public Law 89-313 by extending the dates of the original law and Public Law 874 by granting additional funds.[37]

Public Law 90-247 established regional centers for deaf-blind students but its major emphasis was the recruitment of new teachers, aids for students and the establishment of instructional media programs. It included provisions for parental involvement in the planning of their children's education.

Congress appropriated one million dollars to public and private educational agencies to encourage students to prepare for careers with the mentally retarded and individuals with visual impairments. Congress included teachers' aides and technicians, such as physical therapists, in the appropriation. For the first time libraries were encouraged to improve their facilities to accommodate special students.

Public Law 91-230 (H.R. 514, April 12, 1970)

This law was passed as an amendment to extend the programs already enacted by the Elementary and Secondary Education Act of 1965.[38] The main feature of the law is included under Title VI and is called "Education of the Handicapped."

Congress appropriated $200 million in 1971 and increased it over the next two years to $220 million. These funds were available to all public and private educational agencies offering programs for children. Monies could be used to buy equipment or to construct facilities. Incentive grants were available for teachers who spent extra time planning activities for these children. Individual states were eligible for monies where educational provisions were planned and approved. The educational plans, however, had to be new to receive the extra money and agencies with existing programs could not receive the additional income.

Public Law 91-230 defined "children with specific learning disabilities" as:

> those children who have a disorder in one or more of the basic psychological processes involved in understanding or in using language, spoken or written, which disorder may manifest itself in imperfect ability to listen, think, speak, read, write, spell or do mathematical calculations. Such disorders include such condi-

44

tions as perceptual handicaps, brain injury, minimal brain dysfunction, dyslexia, and developmental aphasia.[39]

Public Law 91-230 established the Bureau of Education for the Handicapped to carry out programs, test, locate and train students and personnel to teach and support the prospective students.

It mandated that federal monies were to be used as supplementary assistance but could not constitute the sole income to operate state programs. The states were given guidelines mandating that:

1. Policy and procedures to provide assurance that funds paid the state will be used as requisitioned.
2. The money will be used to initiate, expand or improve various programs including pre-school programs.
3. Programs will be designed to meet the special educational needs of handicapped students.
4. A program to locate and test the handicapped children in both public and private educational agencies will be developed.[40]

Public Law 91-230 gave support to physical education and recreation by granting funds to institutions of higher education to encourage and train physical education and recreation personnel. It also provided funds for:

research and related purposes relating to physical education or recreation for handicapped children, and to conduct research, surveys, or demonstrations relating to physical education or recreation for handicapped children.[41]

Landmark Judicial Decisions

Four court cases had a tremendous impact on the passage of the Education For All Handicapped Children Act (Public

Law 94-142). With the exception of *Brown v. Board of Education* [42] (1954), the three important judicial decisions were made in the early 1970's.

The *Brown* case has been described as a benchmark decision that began a judicial trend toward providing educational opportunity. Although *Brown* is best known for its importance to racial justice, it provides the groundwork for the right of all children to be educated and this includes children with handicapping conditions. In *Brown,* the United States Supreme Court declared:

> In these days, it is doubtful that any child may reasonably be expected to succeed in life if he is denied the opportunity of an education. Such an opportunity, where the state has undertaken to provide it, is a right which must be made available to all on equal terms. [43]

From *Brown* two issues emerged: the state's responsibility for educating its children, and the "due process" and "equal protection" clause of the amendments to the federal Constitution. [44] Three important cases, following *Brown,* reveal the supportive attitude of the court toward individuals who are denied equal educational opportunities and the right of due process and equal protection.

In *Diana v. Board of Education,* [45] nine Mexican-American students had been given intelligence tests in English, and as a result of their test scores, were placed in classes for the mentally retarded. The plaintiffs claimed that they suffered irreparable harm because they received an inadequate education along with the stigma of mental retardation. The case was settled out of court when the school district agreed to correct the existing problems by doing the following:

- Intelligence testing, through the use of interpreters, would be made in the student's native language.
- Mexican-American and Chinese students in the educable mentally retarded classes would be retested.
- A special effort would be made to help misplaced students to be relocated.
- An effort would be made to design an appropriate I.Q. test.

Two landmark decisions followed *Diana* that enabled the movement for equal educational opportunities for students with handicapping conditions to gain recognition. In the first, the Pennsylvania Association for Retarded Children (PARC) instituted a class action suit to prohibit the Commonwealth of Pennsylvania from denying a free public education to mentally retarded children.[46] The Association sought to accomplish the following:

- Secure a guarantee of a full due process hearing before the educational status of students could be changed.
- Provide the right to a free and appropriate educational program for each individual student.
- Secure the assurance that students who had been wrongfully excluded from any educational program would be provided with a compensatory program.

The court favored the Association with a consent agreement that obligated the defendants to "assign each mentally retarded child to a free and appropriate educational program."

Two years later the Pennsylvania Association for Retarded Children sought a permanent injunction against the enforcement of statutes that would exclude retarded children from educational programs in the public schools.[47]

47

The district court supported the plaintiff's claim and ordered the defendants to formulate and submit a plan designed to provide the following:

- Free public program of education for all mentally retarded persons.
- Availability to those between the ages of four and twenty one.
- A range of programs.
- Arrangement for financing.
- Recruitment, hiring, and training of personnel to help the mentally retarded.

Joseph Bryson and Charles Bentley, legal scholars, regard the decision as an extremely important one in the "area of classification of students" when they remark:

> While this case related specifically to mentally retarded children, later decisions used the language in PARC to extend educational benefits to all handicapped children. The PARC decision triggered a chain reaction of similar decisions in other states including Alabama, New York, Massachusetts, Tennessee, Georgia, Maine, South Carolina and Indiana. No doubt this decision, along with similar ones, was largely responsible for the eventual passage of the Education For All Handicapped Children Act of 1975 (P.L. 94-142).[48]

The third case that affected education for the special child also is considered to be a landmark decision. In *Mills v. Board of Education of District of Columbia*,[49] Peter Mills and six other children with a variety of handicapping conditions and disciplinary problems were representative of the more than 22,000 retarded, emotionally disturbed, blind, deaf, and speech and learning-disabled students in the District of Columbia. The parents of the seven children contended that because of labeling their children had been denied the opportunity for an education without the proper due process procedures.

48

Judge Waddy, of the District of Columbia Federal District Court, agreed that the rights of the plaintiffs had been violated and set guidelines for the school board to follow that included a mandate to:

- provide named-plaintiffs with a publicly supported education suited to their needs;
- provide plaintiff's counsel with a list of every school age child known not to be attending a publicly supported educational program because of supervision, expulsion, exclusion or any other denial of placement;
- initiate efforts to identify remaining members of the class not known to them;
- consider, with plaintiffs, the selection and compensation of a master who would determine the proper placement of children in contested areas.

In August, 1972, Judge Waddy issued a final judgment in which he declared that:

- The statutes of the District of Columbia, the regulations of the Board of Education, and the Constitution of the United States guarantee a publicly supported education for all children including "exceptional children."
- The denial of all publicly supported education to plaintiffs and their class, while providing such education to other children, was a violation of the plaintiff's rights to equal protection of the law.
- Any exclusion, termination, or classification into a special program must be preceded by a due process hearing procedure.
- The school system was ordered to produce a comprehensive plan for serving all handicapped children and for providing full due process procedures for all students before they could be excluded, suspended or reclassified.

49

Bryson and Bentley comment that the decision in *Mills* added to the legal principles established in *PARC* and set guidelines for "other school systems and states" in similar situations involving children with disabilities.[50] The decisions · in *Diana, PARC* and *Mills* significantly influenced the passage of the Rehabilitation Act of 1973 and the Education For All Handicapped Children Act of 1975.

One final law gave impetus to the passage of the Rehabilitation Act.

Public Law 92-318 (June 23, 1972)

Public Law 92-318 (Title IX) was passed by the 94th Congress to amend the Elementary and Secondary Act of 1965 and Public Law 874.[51] While Title IX gained national attention because of its sex discrimination prohibitions, it contained many other noteworthy provisions. It was intended to aid youths with academic potential from low-income families and students with physical handicapping conditions.

Public Law 92-318, like previous laws, prohibited federal monies for facilities where the public would be charged admission. Congress limited its funding to physical education by excluding:

> any gymnasium or other facility specially designed for athletic or recreational activities, other than for an academic course in physical education or where the Commissioner finds that the physical integration of such facilities with other academic facilities included under this title is required to carry out the objectives of this title.

An additional provision has gone virtually unnoticed that is important for students with impaired vision. Section 904 of the law states that:

50

No person in the United States shall, on the ground of blindness or severely impaired vision, be denied admission in any course of study by a recipient of Federal financial assistance for any education program or activity.[52]

1973-1975

Public Law 93-112, The Rehabilitation Act (September 26, 1973)

The Rehabilitation Act, hailed as the first federal civil rights law to protect the rights of people with handicapping conditions, was passed after two vetoes by President Richard Nixon.[53]

Section 504 of the law is of major interest to people with handicapping conditions and reads as follows:

No otherwise qualified handicapped individual in the United States, as defined in section 7 (6), shall, solely by reason of his handicap, be excluded from the participation in, be denied the benefits of, or be subjected to discrimination under any program or activity receiving Federal financial assistance.[54]

While the Rehabilitation Act originally defined a handicapped individual only as having "a physical or mental disability which ... constitutes or results in a substantial handicap to employment" and, therefore, "can reasonably be expected to benefit in terms of employability," subsequent amendments (and regulations) have expanded the definition to include:

• Any person who has a physical or mental impairment which substantially limits one or more major life activities. The term includes such disease and conditions as orthopedic, visual, speech, and hearing impairments, cerebral palsy, muscular dystrophy, multiple sclerosis, cancer,

51

diabetes, mental retardation, emotional illness, and drug and alcohol addiction.
- Any person who has a record of such impairment. (Congress seems to be saying that persons who once had impairments cannot be discriminated against on the basis of the impairment when they no longer are impaired.)
- Any person who is regarded as having a physical or mental impairment which substantially limits one or more major life activities.

Directives to the preschool, elementary and secondary school administrator provide that:

- Administrators should identify and locate all handicapped children within the recipient's home area who are not receiving a free appropriate public education.
- Local agencies should notify the parents of their child's opportunities under the new law.
- Schools should provide a normal as possible regular educational environment of combining handicapped children with their non-handicapped peers.[55]

The specific areas of physical education and athletics are referred to under "nonacademic services" in 34 CFR sections 104.37 and 104.47. Requirements of those sections have been stated as follows:

- In providing physical education courses and athletics and similar programs and activities to any of its students, a recipient to which this subpart applies may not discriminate on the basis of handicap. A recipient which offers physical education courses or which operates or sponsors interscholastic, club, or intramural athletics shall provide to handicapped students equal opportunities for comparable participation in these activities.

• Physical education and athletics activities offered to handicapped students may be separate or different from those offered to nonhandicapped students to the extent that separation or differentiation is necessary to ensure the health and safety of the students or to take into account their interest.[56]

In regard to athletic scholarships the section 504 prohibition of discrimination has been interpreted as not applying to the denial of a scholarship on the basis of an impairment to an athlete who cannot perform at a required level. For example, a wheelchair student desiring to play varsity football would not qualify for an athletic grant. However, to deny a deaf student a scholarship from the diving team solely because of his deafness, when the student merits such an award, is indeed discrimination and violates the law.[57]

Public Law 93-380 (August 21, 1974)

Public Law 93-380, known as the Education Amendments of 1974, was an extension of the Elementary and Secondary Education Act of 1965 and set the age limit for children to benefit from the law at three to twenty-one years of age.[58] Congress set the amount of money granted per student at eight dollars and seventy-five cents. The law gave parents the assurance that they would have decision-making power in the placement of their child. If the parents are not satisfied with the testing, evaluation or placement of their child, an impartial hearing is guaranteed and the results of that hearing binding, subject only to proper appeal by school authorities.

Public Law 94-142, The Education For All Handicapped Children Act (November 29, 1975)

Section 504 of the Rehabilitation Act of 1973 paved the way for Public Law 94-142 known as the Education For All Handicapped Children Act.[59] Congress overwhelmingly supported the law by voting 404 to 7 in the House of Representatives and eighty-seven to seven in the Senate for its passage.[60] Unlike section 504 of the Rehabilitation Act, funding is provided for students under this law. (For the formula see Appendix B). Regulations established to enforce the provisions of Public Law 94-142 define types of handicapping conditions as follows:

> Handicapped student: Those children who after adequate evaluation are shown to be mentally retarded, hard of hearing, deaf, speech impaired, visually handicapped, seriously emotionally disturbed, ortho- pedically impaired, other health impaired, deaf-blind, multi-handicapped, or as having specific learning disabilities and in need of special educational services.
>
> Deaf: A hearing impairment which is so severe that the child is impaired in processing linguistic information through hearing, with or without amplification, which adversely affects educational performance.
>
> Deaf-Blind: Concomitant hearing and visual impairments, the combination of which causes such severe communication and other developmental and educational pro- blems that they cannot be accommodated in special education programs solely for deaf or blind children.
>
> Mentally retarded: Subaverage general intel- lectual functioning existing concurrently with deficits in adaptive behavior and manifested during the developmental

54

period, which adversely affects a child's educational performance.

Multi-handicapped: More than one impairment which in combination causes such severe educational problems that they cannot be accepted in special education programs because of one of the impairments.

Orthopedically impaired: A severe orthopedic impairment which adversely affects a child's educational performance. The term includes impairments caused by congenital anomaly, impairments caused by disease, and impairments from other causes.

Other health impaired: Limited strength, vitality or alertness, due to chronic or acute health problems such as a heart condition, tuberculosis, rheumatic fever, nephritis, asthma, sickle cell anemia, hemophilia, epilepsy, lead poisoning, leukemia, or diabetes, which adversely affects educational performance:

- An inability to learn which cannot be explained by intellectual, sensory, or health factors;
- An inability to build or maintain satisfactory interpersonal relationships with peers and teachers;
- Inappropriate types of behavior or feelings under normal circumstances;
- A general pervasive mood of unhappiness or depression; or
- A tendency to develop symptoms or fears associated with personal or school problems.

Specific learning disability: This means a disorder or more of the basic psychological processes involved in understanding or in using language, spoken or written, which may manifest itself in an imperfect ability to listen, think, speak, read, write, spell or to

55

do mathematical calculations. The term includes such conditions as perceptual handicaps, brain injury, minimal brain dysfunction, dyslexia, and developmental aphasia.

Speech impaired: A communication disorder, such as stuttering, impaired articulation, a language impairment, or a voice impairment, which adversely affects a child's educational performance.

Visually handicapped: A visual impairment which, even with correction, adversely affects a child's educational performance. The term includes both partially seeing and blind children.[61]

Public Law 94-142 also established procedural safeguards for parents, students and the local education agency. The rights of parents are as follows:

- The parents have a right to be informed before any action is taken in behalf of their child's education regarding testing, evaluation, and placement.
- The parents have a right to be fully informed of all information necessary regarding the activity of their child. This information is given in the language which the parents understand. This is both written and oral.
  - This would also include the knowledge of voluntary parental consent for their child's testing and final placement.
  - The parents have a right to have independent testing done if they believe this necessary.
  - The parents have a right to keep confidential all records and evaluations of their child.
- If the parents choose to disagree with the local education agencies, they have a right to an impartial hearing.[62]

56

Regarding the parent, child and local education agency's impartial due process hearing, the rights are clearly delineated. All persons involved in the hearing have the right to the following:

- Be accompanied and advised by counsel and by individuals with special knowledge or training with respect to the problems of handicapped students;
- Present evidence and confront, cross-examination, and compel the attendance of witnesses;
- Prohibit the introduction of any evidence at the hearing that has not been disclosed to that party at least five days before the hearing;
- Obtain a written or electronic verbatim record of the hearing;
- Have the child present if they (the parents) desire;
- Have a public hearing;
- If the parents and child are not pleased with the decision of the hearing committee, the right to appeal to a higher authority is available to them. In fact, the appeal if properly channeled, could go to the United States Supreme Court.[63]

Students also have rights, particularly in regard to the individual educational programs. General rights include the following: First, should the child be orphaned, the state shall appoint a surrogate parent for the child.[64] Secondly, all information to the child shall be in the language of the child, if it is different from that of his or her parents. Regarding the right of educational records, these records and the rights to them are transferred from the parents to the child when the child reaches the age of eighteen.[65]

In the area of the individual education program the rights of the child are as follows:

- The student has the right to have his or her parents present when decisions are made regarding testing, evaluation, and placement;
- The student has a right to be present at an impartial hearing;
- The student has a right to be present himself or herself in the planning of the individual educational program;
- Within the individual education plan, certain criteria must be present:

  - A statement of present levels of education performance of the child;
  - A statement of annual goals;
  - A statement of short-term instructional objectives;
  - A statement of the specific educational services and instructional material, including physical education;
  - The extent to which the child will be able to participate in regular education programs;
  - The appropriate objective criteria, evaluation procedures, and schedules for determining, on at least an annual basis, whether the instructional objectives are being achieved.[66]

Also of legislative concern is the placement of the student in his or her least restrictive environment. Section 612 of Public Law 94-142 mandates

> that, to the maximum extent appropriate, handicapped children, including children in public or private institutions or other care facilities, are educated with children who are not handicapped, and that special classes, separate schooling, or other removal of handicapped children from the regular educational environment occurs only when the nature or severity

of the handicap is such that education in regular classes with the use of supplementary aids and services cannot be achieved satisfactorily.

Both houses of Congress were concerned about physical education services for handicapped children. The Committee on Labor and Public Welfare states

> that although physical education services are available to and, in most instances, are required of, all children within a school system, the provision of physical education services, which are highly important to the physical development and well-being of handicapped children, are often seen as services to be provided only as a luxury for handicapped children. While in some instances such services need to be specially designed for handicapped children, these services should be provided as a matter of course, and the Committee expects the Commission of Education to take such action as may be necessary ... to assure that physical education ... [is] made available for handicapped children.[67]

Likewise, the House Report emphasizes

> The Committee expects the Commissioner of Education to take whatever action is necessary to assure that physical education services are available to all handicapped children, and has specifically included physical education within the definition of special education to make clear that the Committee expects such services, specially designed where necessary, to be provided as an integral part of the educational program of every handicapped child.[68]

Since section 504 did not carry any funding, Public Law 94-142 apparently was funded to carry its own weight plus that of the Rehabilitation Act as well. In the first year, over

$100 million was made available. Two hundred million dollars was appropriated the following year.[69] Estimates put the appropriated funds by 1981 at more than $316 billion.[70] In addition to these funds, more money is available for states from incentive grants built into the law.[71]

For physical educators, this law has many implications. For some teachers, who may have felt that physical education was not receiving the national recognition commensurate with its worth, this law meant that credence is being shown at last. For other teachers, it means more preparation for classes since these teachers must provide for a wider range of abilities within their classes. Whatever it means to the instructors, congressional intent is quite clear that physical education, *specially designed where necessary, [is] to be provided [to] every handicapped child."*[72] (emphasis added). Some interpreters believe that in adopting this Act, Congress is saying to the nation that its belief in the value of physical education for individuals with handicapping conditions is so strong that, whether the nonhandicapped children have a physical education program or not, a program is necessary for the growth and development of students with a handicapping condition.[73]

In order to create some type of common definition of physical education, Congress, with the aid of many experts and consultants, interpreted physical education as the development of:

1. Physical and motor fitness;
2. Fundamental and motor skills and patterns; and
3. Skills in aquatics, dance, and individual and group games and sports (including intramural and lifetime sports).
   (The term includes special physical education, adapted physical education,

60

movement education, and motor development.) [74]

William Chasey, who wrote the section on physical education, emphasized that Congress did not include athletics in this law.[75] Although sports is not specifically defined in the law it has been included in the "nonacademic services" of the law.[76] Therefore, in sports programs throughout the United States, no person can be denied the opportunity to participate solely on the basis of limited physical, mental, or emotional impairment. Separate programs, such as wheelchair basketball and bowling for the blind, for example, are permissible when judged to be in the best interest of the persons involved. Individuals must have comparable programs and equal opportunities, whether in the physical education curriculum, intramural program or on the institution's sports team.

The effect of the new law is graphically described in the *Nolpe School Law Journal* by Elizabeth A. Kurker-Stewart and David G. Carter, Sr., as follows:

> With the implementation of the Education For All Handicapped Children Act, litigation has focused more directly on the issues of misclassification, misplacement, and miseducation. The latter issue confronts educators persistently and regularly. The school district's charge under Public Law 94-142 to provide an appropriate education for each handicapped child encourages educational malpractice claims and establishes a structured framework within which to bring such suits. The prescriptive nature of the law enables parents, via the courts, to affix specific educational responsibility on individual educators, thereby eradicating one of the major historical obstacles to recovery for educational malpractice.[77]

61

The writers offer suggestions for the special educator that includes the following:

> Special educators have the responsibility of working not only among themselves but also with regular educators to foster an understanding of the spirit and intent of Public Law 94-142. A superficial grasp of the letter of the law inadequately informs the task of providing handicapped children with a meaningful education. Inservice activities may include but not be limited to presentations by staff members, the parents of handicapped children, handicapped adults, university experts, state consultants, and other guest speakers. Expanding the scope of such activities to encompass the community at large is another step toward educating and involving citizens who may not otherwise be linked to special education. Their commitment and support can provide invaluable help in augmenting existing services and developing new programs.[78]

The writers conclude:

> Ultimately, the benefits of Public Law 94-142 must be transferred to all children, handicapped, "gifted," and "average." Title I's encouragement of school personnel to develop individualized education programs for "special" children illustrates this trend. Although special educators increasingly bear the heavy threat of liability for miseducating handicapped children, the responsibility for meeting the learning needs of all children is a responsibility shared by all educators. Accountability within the profession, accompanied by new prescriptive legislation, will continue to bring those other educators into the courts to face educational malpractice claims, and special educators will no longer stand isolated from the rest of the profession in this regard. The responsibility is, therefore, a

62

collective one, and it will soon have to be addressed in that light.[79]

Since the Rehabilitation Act of 1973 and the Education For All Handicapped Children Act of 1975 are the two most important laws for individuals with handicapping conditions, it is important to look at a brief comparison of both laws.

BASIC FACTS OF
SECTION 504 OF THE REHABILITATION ACT
(PUBLIC LAW 93-112)
AND
THE EDUCATION FOR ALL HANDICAPPED
CHILDREN ACT (PUBLIC LAW 94-142)

Section 504	*Public Law*
Civil rights legislation barring discrimination against individuals with physical or mental impairment by an agency receiving federal funds.	Formula grant legislation to provide state and local education agencies funds to implement educational programs for all handicapped children.
In addition to guarantee of a free and appropriate education, guarantees extend to preschool and postsecondary education, employment practices, and health, welfare, and other social service programs.	Guarantees a free and appropriate public education for every handicapped child regardless of where the child is housed.
Education at all levels is to be conducted to the maximum degree possible with non-handicapped children in the most normal setting feasible.	Education is to be conducted to the maximum degree possible with non-handicapped children in the least restrictive environment.

63

Section 504

Educational programs are to be individualized for each child so as to meet his/her specific and unique needs; the individualized educational program is one way of satisfying this requirement.

At the present time no financial assistance for implementing this legislation is provided.

Specific subsections deal with physical education and athletics and specifically prohibit discrimination in these areas. In addition, qualified teachers and individuals interested in pursuing these areas in personnel professional preparation programs must be considered on their competencies and qualifications, not disqualified on the basis of some handicapping condition.

Recipients of federal funds, including local education agencies, are expected to make minor adaptations immediately so that

Public Law

Each child receiving special education or special education and related services must be programmed according to the specific provisions outlined for an individualized educational program.

Increasing amounts of funds are provided state and local education agencies to implement provisions mandated by this law.

Physical education is the only curricular area identified and included as a part of the definition of special education, recreation is included as a related service; athletics are identified as an extracurricular area. Handicapped children are entitled to experiences in these areas comparable to those received by their non-handicapped peers.

Provisions are made whereby local education agencies can obtain funds to remove architectural barriers so that schools can

Section 504 | Public Law

facilities will be accessible. Major structural changes must be made within three years with a plan developed outlining procedures to be followed to be completed within six months of enactment of final rules and regulations. All facilities do not have to be accessible as long as all programs are accessible.

be made accessible to students with different mobility problems. To date no funding has been provided for implementing this provision.

No age limitations or restrictions are imposed — programs for participants of all ages administered by agencies receiving federal funds are governed by this law.

Provisions cover children three to eighteen years of age (by September 1978) and three to twenty-one years of age by September 1980.

Office For Civil Rights (OCR) is the responsible federal agency for administering Title IX of the Education Amendments of 1972 so that action is taken only after a specific complaint for noncompliance is registered.

Bureau of Education for the Handicapped (BEH) is the responsible federal agency for administering this law. As such, BEH is to monitor state education agencies, state education agencies are to monitor local education agencies, and local education agencies are to see that provisions of the law are fulfilled throughout the local system.

Public Law	*Section 504*
Final rules and regulations appeared in the Federal Register May 4, 1977.	Final rules and regulations appeared in the Federal Register August 23, 1977.[80]

1975 Until the Present

After the passage of the Rehabilitation Act (section 504) and the Education For All Handicapped Children Act (Public Law 94-142), final regulations to implement section 504 were issued on May 4, 1977. The Office of Education made some "clarifying and technical changes in the federal regulations for Public Law 94-142." [81]

It was estimated that the States and local school districts could conceivably spend over "6.5 billion" in addition to an appropriation from the federal government of 1 billion during the 1981-82 school year.[82] Angela Giordano-Evans writing for the Congressional Research Service notes that:

> the final responsibility for meeting both the State and Federal mandates for special education rests with the States and their local agencies. In the end, it is the States and their school districts that have the primary responsibility to provide free public education for all handicapped children.[83]

Giordana-Evans reports that there have been problems regarding funding in recent years when she declares:

> For each of school years 1977-78 and 1978-79, the first two years after implementation of P.L. 94-142, total part B appropriations were sufficient to pay the full authorization for the program. Beginning in school year 1979-80 and continuing through the current school year 1982-83, appropriations have been insufficient to meet the authorization of appropriation ceilings established by P.L. 94-142.[84]

As an example the following table below reveals the estimated number of children in the program and the various levels of federal assistance since Public Law 94-142 was enacted.

Fiscal Year	Children served	Federal funding	Funded % of APPE Authorized under P.L. 94-142	Actual funded % of APPE
1977	3,485,000	$251,769,927	5	5.1
1978	3,561,000	566,030,074	10	10.1
1979	3,700,000	804,000,000	20	12.5
1980	3,803,000	874,500,000	30	12.0
1981	3,941,000	874,500,000	40	10.0
1982	4,000,000	931,008,000	40	9.0[84.1]

(For additional information on funding see Appendix B)

It was emphasized by reports of the House of Representatives and the Senate that the priority for the funds would be for children with handicapping conditions that were still unserved. Senate Report 94-168 stated that:

> the bill requires that the States establish priorities for providing a free appropriate public education to all handicapped children and that these priorities shall meet the timetables of the bill, first with respect to handicapped children with the most severe handicaps who are receiving an inadequate education. The Committee stresses that the first priority must be given to meeting the timetable for handicapped children who are currently not receiving any educational services. This group of children is by far the most neglected in the educational process and must be the first priority for State and local educational agencies.[85]

The Committee estimated the number of unserved children to be four million.

Public Law 95-49 (H.R. 6692) July 17, 1977

The 95th Congress, in its first session, "extended the authorizations for the various project grant authorities under parts C, D, E and F of the Education For All Handicapped Children Act through 1982." [86]

The Act was referred to as the Education For All Handicapped Amendments of 1977 and includes the following provisions:

- training personnel for education of the handicapped
- instructional media for the handicapped.

Public Law 95-561 (H.R. 15) November 1, 1978

In the second session, the 95th Congress enacted Public Law 95-561, the Education Amendments of 1978. The law extends through 1983 Public Law 89-10, the Elementary and Secondary Education Act. [87] It extends programs for children with handicapping conditions in state-supported schools under ESEA Title 1. It adds impact assistance to "federally connected handicapped children for the annual state count of handicapped children." The law also provided funds by:

- special entitlement provisions for military and Indian land handicapped children under the Public Law 81-874 impact aid program.
- adding federally connected handicapped children for whom tuition is paid as eligible for funding.

Public Law 96-536 (1981)

This law, called the Second Continuing Resolution for 1981, gave the administration the authority to reduce the funding of programs authorized by the Education For All

Handicapped Children Act by twenty-five percent or approximately $270 million.[87.1]

Public Law 97-12 (June 5, 1981)

This law, referred to as the Supplemental Appropriations and Recissions Act, provided for the reduction of programs under the Education For All Handicapped Children Act by seven percent, or $76 million.[87.2] The budget authority for the states' grant programs, was reduced by five percent, from $922 million to $874.5 million. In addition, individual project grants were cut by sixteen percent representing a decrease from $180.1 million to $150.7 million (Parts C-F).

Public Law 97-35 (August 13, 1981)

Public Law 97-35 is known as the Omnibus Budget Reconciliation Act of 1981. The current programs under the Education For All Handicapped Children Act are not included in this Act.[87.3] The Act extended and placed a ceiling on the authorizations of appropriations for all programs under the Education For All Handicapped Children Act, provided $969.9 million for 1982 and $1,017 million for 1983 and 1984 for Part B-State grant program. The Act authorized "$25 million for (each of) 1982 and 1983 for the preschool incentive program; and $155 million for each of the 1982 and 1983 project grant programs."

It is especially important because it approved ceilings for the Education For All Handicapped Children Act under the Omnibus Budget Reconciliation Act of 1981 which reflects an increase of twelve percent over the 1981 appropriation figures.

Public Law 97-92 (December 15, 1981)

This law provided temporary funding through March 31, 1982 of all Department of Education programs including the Education For All Handicapped Children Act.[87.4]

Public Law 97-161 (March 31, 1982)

This law extended "further continuing appropriations" through September 30, 1982 and continued authorized levels of funding under Public Law 97-92 for all Department of Education and Education For All Handicapped Children Act programs.[87.5]

Public Law 97-257 (1982)

Public Law 97-257 provides $26.5 million in additional funds for programs of education for individuals with handicapping conditions.[87.6] As such the Act provides a $15.7 million supplement for special education personnel development, $7.2 million for early childhood education and $3.6 million for innovation and development. Under this Act and the provisions of Public Law 97-161, appropriations are available of $1,068,580,000; Part B funding of $931,008,000 which represents eighty-seven percent of the total 1982 budget available to the Education For All Handicapped Children programs.

Many educators contended that Public Law 94-142 was too prescriptive on states and local school districts. They did not imply that the programs were not desirable but questioned, instead, the feasibility of achieving them within the timetable established. The educators felt that the timetable was not practical for training teachers, developing and implementing IEP's, free appropriate education, least restrictive environment and due process procedures. As a result, the federal government proposed a number of changes in Public Law 94-142 regulations regarding the mandates for educating individuals with handicapping conditions.[88] The proposed changes are numerous but the most important are listed below by the North Carolina Governor's Advocacy Council For Persons With Disabilities:

70

PARENT INVOLVEMENT AND PARENT RIGHTS

- Parent consent would not be required for evaluation or placement.
- School districts would not have to notify parents of the evaluation results used to make placement decisions.
- School districts would not have to document efforts to involve parents in IEP meetings.
- Parents would not have to be provided interpreters at IEP meetings.
- Parents asking for a hearing would not have to receive information about advocacy services, or be informed of the school district's evidence prior to a hearing. Parents would not have the right to a hearing that is open to the public.

EDUCATIONAL SERVICES AND RELATED SERVICES

- Districts would not have to make sure that hearing aids function correctly.
- School health services, social work services, and parent counseling and training, all of which are presently included as related services, would be eliminated. This could hurt emotionally disturbed, retarded and autistic children whose parents frequently need help in behavior programming at home.
- Schools would not have to give medications, or to provide clean intermittent catheterization, or to do anything that might be considered medically related, such as giving shots. As a result, many children could be forced out of school to "home-bound" services.
- School districts could put "reasonable limitations" on the type and amount of related services offered.

71

- People providing related services would not have to be "qualified" under state standards.

EVALUATIONS

- School districts would not have to re-evaluate children every three years.
- Districts would not have to do "multi-disciplinary" evaluations of many children.
- Parents would not have the right to a free independent evaluation as they do now.
- Tests would not have to be validated for the purpose for which they are used.

LEAST RESTRICTIVE ENVIRONMENT/EQUAL OPPORTUNITY/EXCLUDING THE HANDI-CAPPED

- Different placement options, such as resource room, or self-contained class, would not be defined and districts would not have to offer the "continuum" of placements they now have to.
- There would no longer be a preference for educating the child as close to home as possible or in the school he would normally attend if not handicapped.
- Officials could weigh the "disruptive" impact a handicapped child might have on the non-handicapped in determining placement. This could result in too much segregation of handicapped children.
- Handicapped children could be suspended or expelled for lengthy periods without the involvement of a professional psychologist, a multi-disciplinary team, or an impartial hearing officer to determine whether the child's misbehavior and handicap are related.
- Handicapped children would have no specific guarantees that they would receive either regular or special P.E., or have access to extracurricular and nonacademic services.[89]

72

Public hearings were conducted nationwide by the Department of Education. The Department of Education set November 2, 1982 as the last day it would accept comments on the proposed changes in Public Law 94-142 regulations. A decision will be made in 1983 on the proposed changes.

Summary

Many important events, judicial decisions and legislation preceded the enactment of the Rehabilitation Act (1973) and the Education For All Handicapped Children Act (1975), called the two most important laws for individuals with handicapping conditions. From the founding of the first residential school for the deaf in 1817, until 1950, many residential schools for the blind, mentally retarded and orthopedically handicapped were established.

A mid-century White House Conference on Children and Youth was convened in 1950 and from that time until 1973 Congress enacted a series of laws that led to the passage of the Rehabilitation Act. In that period of time, Public Law 89-10, known as the Elementary and Secondary Act of 1965, was one of the most significant laws. Congress used the word "handicapped" for the first time in this law and made specialized instruction and equipment available to them.

Several landmark judicial decisions influenced the passage of the Rehabilitation Act that included: *Brown v. Board of Education* (1954), *Diana v. Board of Education* (1970), *Pennsylvania Association for Retarded Children v. Commonwealth of Pennsylvania* (1972) and *Mills v. Board of Education of District of Columbia* (1972). These cases revealed the supportive attitude of the court toward individuals with handicapping conditions who were denied equal educational opportunities and due process.

The Rehabilitation Act was the culmination of the efforts of many individuals, judicial decisions and congressional legislation. It was hailed as the first civil rights law to protect the rights of individuals with handicapping conditions. Section 504 of the law is of major importance to these individuals and provides that:

> No otherwise qualified handicapped individual in the United.States . . . shall by reason of his handicap, be excluded from the participation in, be denied the benefits of, or subjected to discrimination under any program or activity receiving Federal financial assistance.

34 C.F.R. sections 104.37 and 104.47 (regulations to enforce the Act) refer to physical education and athletics as "nonacademic services."

The Education For All Handicapped Children Act (Public Law 94-142) affirmed the provisions of the Rehabilitation Act. Unlike section 504 funding for students is provided under this law. It stresses the importance of physical education since it is the only curricular area identified in the Act. It includes athletics as an extracurricular activity.

At the present time the Department of Education has proposed changes in Public Law 94-142 regulations. The changes would affect parental involvement and rights, educational and related services, evaluations and least restrictive environment. Hearings have been conducted nationwide and negative criticism of the proposed changes has been reported.

The Department of Education is evaluating the results of the hearings before deciding on the direction it will go in its recommendations to Congress.

FOOTNOTES

1. Claudine Sherrill, *Adapted Physical Education and Recreation,* Wm. C. Brown, Dubuque, Iowa, 1982.

2. *Id.*

3. *Id.*

4. *Forward,* New York Times Index, Bowker Company, New York, 1966.

5. David P. Riley et al., *National Incentives in Special Education,* National Association of State Directors of Special Education, Washington, D.C., 1978.

6. Angela Evans & David Osman, *Education of Handicapped,* Government Printing Office, Washington, D.C., 1976.

7. *Supra* note 1.

8. New York Times, Oct. 12, 1905.

9. *Supra* note 1.

10. *Id.*

11. *Id.*

12. *Id.*

13. New York Times, May 27, 1950.

14. *Id.*

15. Public Law 93-112, 87 Stat. 355 (1973).

16. Public Law 94-142, 89 Stat. 773 (1975).

17. Public Law 815, 64 Stat. 967 (1950).

18. Public Law 874, 64 Stat. 110 (1950).

19. New York Times, Jan. 10, 1952.

20. New York Times, Feb. 1, 1952.

21. *Supra* note 6.

22. New York Times, Dec. 28, 1954.

23. J. A. Fischer, *Helping To Solve the Social and Psychological Problems of the Handicapped,* JOURNAL OF HEALTH, PHYSICAL EDUCATION & RECREATION, Vol. 31, No. 2, Feb. 1960.

24. Julian U. Stein, *Adapted Physical Education for the Educable Mentally Handicapped,* JOURNAL OF HEALTH, PHYSICAL EDUCATION & RECREATION, Vol. 33, Dec. 1962.

25. Robert H. Wyatt, *Critical Issues and Problems in Education,* JOURNAL OF HEALTH, PHYSICAL EDUCATION & RECREATION, Vol. 35, June, 1964.

26. Eunice Kennedy Shriver, *Recreation for the Mentally Retarded,* JOURNAL OF HEALTH, PHYSICAL EDUCATION & RECREATION, Vol. 36, May, 1965.

27. *Id.*

28. *Id.*

29. *White House Conference,* JOURNAL OF PHYSICAL EDUCATION, RECREATION & DANCE, Vol. 36, Sept. 1965.

30. Edwin W. Martin, *A National Commitment to the Rights of the Individual . . . 1776-1976,* EXCEPTIONAL CHILDREN, Vol. 43, Nov. 1976.

31. Public Law 89-10, 79 Stat. 27 (1966).

32. *Id.*

33. *Id.*

34. Public Law 89-313, 79 Stat. 1158 (1966).

35. Public Law 89-750, 80 Stat. 1191 (1967).

36. *Id.*

37. Public Law 90-247, 81 Stat. 783 (1968).

38. Public Law 91-230, 84 Stat. 121 (1971).

39. *Id.*

40. *Id.*

41. *Id.*

42. Brown v. Board of Education, 347 U.S. 483 (1954).

43. *Id.*

44. Tom O'Connell, *Sources of Law: Right to an Equal Educational Opportunity,* AMERICUS, Vol. 2, April, 1977.

45. Diana v. Board of Education, Civ. No. C-70-37, RFN (N.D. Cal. 1970).

46. Pennsylvania Association for Retarded Children v. Commonwealth of Pennsylvania, 334 F. Supp. 1257 (E.D. Pa. 1970).

47. Pennsylvania Association for Retarded Children v. Commonwealth of Pennsylvania, 343 F. Supp. 279 (E.D. Pa. 1972).

48. JOSEPH BRYSON & CHARLES BENTLEY, ABILITY GROUPING OF PUBLIC SCHOOL STUDENTS, The Michie Company, Charlottesville, Virginia, 1980.

49. Mills v. Board of Education of District of Columbia, 348 F. Supp. 866 (D.D.C. 1972).

50. *Supra* note 48.

51. Public Law 92-318, 86 Stat. 235 (1973).

52. *Id.*

53. Public Law 93-112, 87 Stat. 355 (1974).

54. *Id.*

55. PRACTICAL POINTERS: INDIVIDUALIZED EDUCATION PROGRAMS, AMERICAN ALLIANCE OF HEALTH, PHYSICAL EDUCATION, RECREATION AND DANCE, Vol. 1, No. 6, October, 1977.

56. *Id.*

57. *Practical Pointers: Implications of Section 504 of the Rehabilition Act as Related to Physical Education Instructional Personnel Preparation, Intramural Interscholastic/Intercollegiate Sport Program,* American Alliance of Health, Physical Education, Recreation & Dance, Vol. 3, No. 11, Feb. 1980.

58. Public Law 93-380, 88 Stat. 484 (1976).

59. Public Law 94-142, 89 Stat. 773 (1975).

60. Carol Ann Peterson, *Why We Can't Wait: Implications of Public Law 94-142 for Recreation and Park Personnel and Program,* WEST VIRGINIA RECREATION & PARKS REVIEW, Vol. 3, May/June, 1977.

61. Federal Register 42, No. 163, 23 August 1977, 42491-42494.

62. Federal Register, Vol. 42, No. 250 (December 1977).

63. *Id.*

64. *Evaluation and Assessment Procedures Pertaining to Individualized Education and Placement,* THE PHYSICAL ACTIVITIES REPORT, Vol. 433, (April 1978).

65. Family Education Rights and Privacy Act, 45 CFR § 99.4.

66. Sara Smith, A Comparison of Staff Development Methods for Training School Based Assessment Committees to Develop an Individual Education Plan in Guilford County, (Ed.D., dissertation, University of North Carolina — Greensboro, 1978.)

67. Senate Report No. 94-168, 94th Cong., 1st Sess., 1975.

68. House Report No. 94-332, 94th Cong., 1st Sess., 1975.

69. *Supra* note 55.

70. Leroy V. Goodman, *A Bill of Rights for the Handicapped,* AMERICAN EDUCATION, Vol. 12 (July, 1976).

71. *Supra* note 61.

72. *Supra* note 68.

73. Ed Keller, *Principal Issues in Public Law 94-142,* NATIONAL ELEMENTARY PRINCIPAL, Vol. 56, March/April, 1977.

74. *Supra* note 53.

75. Interview with William Chasey, National Association of State Directors of Special Education, Washington, D.C., November 27, 1978.

76. *Supra* note 61.

77. Elizabeth A. Kurker-Stewart & David G. Carter, Sr., *Educational Malpractice and P.L. 94-142: A New Dilemma for Educators,* NOLPE SCHOOL LAW JOURNAL, Vol. 10, No. 1, 1981.

78. *Id.*

79. *Id.*

80. *Physical Education, Recreation and Sports For Disabled People: Questions and Answers About Section 504 and P.L. 94-142,* American Alliance for Health, Physical Education, Recreation and Dance and Unit on Programs for the Handicapped, President's Committee on Employment of the Handicapped, Washington, D.C., 1977.

81. Angela Evans & David Osman, Education of the Handicapped Issue Brief Number IB78040, The Library of Congress, Congressional Research Service, November 16, 1978.

82. Angela Giordano-Evans, Education of the Handicapped Brief Number IB78040, The Library of Congress, Congressional Research Service, October 20, 1982.

83. *Id.*

84. *Id.*

84.1. *Id.*

85. *Supra* note 81.

86. Public Law 95-49 (H.R. 6692) July 17, 1977.

87. Public Law 95-561 (H.R. 15) November 1, 1978.

87.1. Public Law 96-536 (1981).

87.2. Public Law 97-12 (June 5, 1981).

87.3. Public Law 97-35 (August 13, 1981).

87.4. Public Law 97-92 (December 15, 1981).

87.5. Public Law 97-161 (March 31, 1982).

87.6. Public Law 97-257 (1982).

88. Governor's Advocacy Council For Persons With Disabilities, Raleigh, North Carolina, 1982.

89. *Id.*

CHAPTER 4
The Judicial Process

The courts in many states presume that teachers, coaches, administrators and school board members know the law. Unfortunately, this is rarely true as many school people lack a basic knowledge of the law as it relates to their profession. H. C. Hudgins and Richard Vacca, writing in *Law and Education: Contemporary Issues and Court Decisions* stress the importance of an understanding of the law in education when they state that:

> knowledge and acceptance of current legal decisions prevent litigation and lead to better administration and boardmanship. When teachers operate within acceptable legal boundaries, they are demonstrating a respect for law.[1]

It has been said that an awareness of the basic processes of the law can increase "sensitivity to the growing body of law surrounding one's occupation" and build confidence in the daily operation of the school program.[2]

Paul Proehl, an authority on tort law, makes an interesting observation regarding the conduct of laymen toward certain professions, such as law, when he says:

> There is much conduct in certain professions which seem a mystery to the laymen (including the judge) simply because it is beyond the scope of his knowledge or comprehension. The inability of the laymen to probe, to know, and to evaluate the conduct of this kind may indeed result in a greater margin of error unless the conduct is policed by the profession itself.[3]

The American Bar Association designed a layman's handbook on court procedures to provide information on the law. In its publication, *Law and the Courts,* it states that:

79

The processes of the law and the courts are baffling and mysterious to many laymen. Frequently, these processes are looked upon as "legal red tape"... Yet the so-called red tape operates to safeguard the rights of every citizen. It permits the due process of law which is an integral part of our system of justice — the greatest bulwark of our free society.[4]

This chapter will attempt to answer the questions: "What does one do if involved in a lawsuit?" and "What does one expect at a trial?" It will look at the various categories of the court system and review a typical court case involving Public Law 94-142.

The Judicial System

It is important to know the various categories of the court system in which school officials are involved. The authors of *Public School Law* reveal the judicial structure by explaining that:[5]

the power for the operation of the public educational system originates with the Constitutional delegation of power for the legislature to provide for a system of education. With legislative enactments providing the basis for public school law, it then becomes the role of the courts, through litigation, to interpret the will of the legislature. The combination of constitutions, statutes, and court or case law form the primary legal foundation on which public schools are based.[6]

The courts are separated by various duties that include:

• Courts of General Jurisdiction
These courts are referred to as district or circuit courts with the responsibility of handling all matters except those referred to special courts.

80

- Courts of Special Jurisdiction

  Litigation that deals with large numbers of cases is handled here. The most common courts include "probate courts, domestic courts, and juvenile courts."

- Small Claims Courts

  As the name implies, lawsuits that involve small amounts of money are settled here.

- Appellate Courts

  All states have appellate courts that hear appeals from trial courts. These courts are often called the Supreme Court or Court of Appeals. (Larger states such as New York and California may have intermediate courts.)

Frequently, litigation concerning athletics or physical education goes to the federal courts when the issue raises constitutional questions. The United States federal court system includes "district courts, courts of appeals, special federal courts, and the Supreme Court." [7]

Each state has at least one district court and often there are two or more. The federal district court is empowered to handle various types of litigation such as:

- cases between citizens of different states
- cases involving litigation of federal statutes or the federal Constitution.

The district court is usually a one judge court but "in cases of injunction against the enforcement of a state or federal statute, a three-judge court is required." [8] A district court decision can be appealed to the federal court of appeals and occasionally to the Supreme Court.

In the federal judicial system, the appellate courts are divided into eleven judicial circuits. In the Eighth Circuit, for example, North Dakota, South Dakota, Nebraska, Minnesota, Iowa, Missouri and Arkansas are included. [9]

Athletic and physical education cases go to the courts above. If a state or federal statute is in question, the plaintiff may obtain a writ of certiorari which, if viewed by the court to be valid, may proceed to the highest court of the land, the Supreme Court, from which there is no appeal.[10]

Finally, it is well to remember that each case is decided on its own merits. While certain principles may be established as well as precedents, the human element of the jury, the powerful persuasion of a lawyer, and other factors make decisions unpredictable at times. It has been said that:

> the rule of law is also the rule of men. Legal disputes involve conflicts between people; lawyers and judges, after all, are men possessed of opinions, prejudices and passions. Their arguments and conclusions will reflect not only the application of a legal principle to a particular set of facts; they will mirror their social attitudes and philosophies, as well as personal unspoken judgments on the merits of the case before them.[11]

What to Do if Involved in a Lawsuit [12]

The question must arise, "What do I do when something happens that may lead to a lawsuit?" The answer is simple —call your insurance carrier and your lawyer, in that order. This will permit a prompt investigation of the entire case when all events are still fresh in everyone's mind, so that the actual facts may be accurately preserved for presentation later, perhaps years later. It will also protect you against taking any action that could prejudice your position at a later date.

Be sure to keep detailed notes on everything that you know or can remember about what happened, including names and addresses of all potential witnesses, even those people who say they don't know anything. Many times, under skillful questioning, they know much more than they think.

Be reluctant to discuss any aspect of the case without the advice of your attorney, particularly to the news media. This should not imply that you are trying to "cover up" or "hide" anything, but merely that any public statement should be delayed until all the facts are known. Many times statements are made at or about the time of an incident which later turn out not to be the true facts at all after an investigation has been completed.

Trials resulting from lawsuits are actually relatively simple mechanisms to understand, but are difficult and expensive to use. Your chances of being involved in litigation are greatly reduced if you conduct your activities as carefully as possible, use safe, well-maintained equipment and disclose as much as possible to participants and parents.

Many people do not realize that anyone can file a lawsuit against anybody for just about anything, but before a recovery can be obtained liability must be proven. Before liability can be established in a typical case, a breach of duty or violation of a right must be proved by the allegedly aggrieved party. This proof comes in almost all cases at the trial of the lawsuit, anywhere from six months to five years after the lawsuit is started. Fortunately, in some respects, many legitimate lawsuits are settled before trial or even before a lawsuit is filed.

What to Expect at a Trial [13]

All jurisdictions, both federal and state, have rules which govern the procedures that must be followed in every civil lawsuit. These are commonly called Rules of Civil Procedure. They are very specific and sometimes can be very technical. However, these rules are extremely valuable and helpful in charting the course that a lawsuit will follow.

Many things happen in that six-month to five-year period. In order to file a lawsuit, a pleading, usually called a complaint, has to be filed. This document does nothing more than set forth the facts which the aggrieved party alleges gave rise to his or her injury. In all cases the party being sued, usually called the defendant, must get notice of the lawsuit and have an opportunity to respond and rebut the allegations. This responsive pleading is usually called an answer. If the defendant for any reason feels the plaintiff may be liable to him, he must also incorporate into the answer something which is very logically called a counterclaim. Sometimes it may be necessary to add additional parties so that all those people or institutions who may be liable are within the jurisdiction of the court.

Once the initial pleadings are filed and everyone is "in court," there follows a prescribed period of time, usually at least four months but sometimes longer depending on the complexity of the case, called the discovery period.

The purpose of the discovery period is for all the parties to "discover" as many facts as possible about the lawsuit, such as exactly how an injury occurred, who the witnesses were, how much damage has been sustained and similar matters of a factual nature. This can be accomplished through depositions, where the party to be questioned is physically present with attorneys for all parties. The attorneys ask questions which are answered by the witness and everything said is taken down verbatim by a court reporter and transcribed and added to the record in the court file. These documents can be used at the trial to refresh the witness' recollection or to attack the witness' credibility in the event the answers have changed.

After discovery has been completed, the trial lawyers are then confronted with several alternative courses of action. If it appears that the facts are not in dispute and the outcome of the case depends solely on which law is to be applied, then the lawyer may file a motion for summary judgment. This permits the judge to make final decision on the outcome of the case without a trial and a jury. In order for the judge to grant summary judgment, there must be no dispute over any genuine issue of a material fact.

If there is a genuine dispute over material facts, then summary judgment would be improper and a trial will be necessary. Prior to the actual beginning of a trial, the lawyers have the most important portion of their work to do — careful, detailed preparation for every contingency that could occur at the trial. It will be necessary to carefully review all the facts again, talk in detail to all witnesses and potential witnesses, complete the legal research necessary to permit the drafting of a trial brief to state the client's legal position as favorably as possible and to assist the judge in getting a grasp on the case as quickly and easily as possible.

Once all the preparation is complete, you are prepared to begin the trial of the case, the ultimate point towards which the filing of the suit has been leading.

Generally speaking, a trial has several distinct parts. A jury must be selected and many trial lawyers consider this to be one of the most important aspects of the trial. After a jury of twelve presumably disinterested and impartial jurors has been selected, the lawyers present opening statements to the jury, in which they tell the jury what they will attempt to prove or disprove. After opening statements, the plaintiff then presents his or her case. If the plaintiff can offer sufficient evidence to establish a *prima facie* case, then the defendant(s) must present evidence to prove non-

85

liability and/or that damages are not as large as they are claimed to be. After all the evidence has been presented, the judge still has the option of granting a directed verdict if it appears one party clearly is entitled to a verdict. If a directed verdict is not granted, the case then "goes to the jury." The lawyers make their closing arguments as to why their client should win and how much in damages should be awarded, if any. After the closing arguments, the judge then instructs the jury on the law to be applied to the facts as they were presented during the trial. The jury is solely responsible for finding the facts of the case and they must apply the law to those facts as the law is explained by the judge. The jury then retires to reach their verdict and report it to the court. The verdict of the jury is then reduced to a judgment, which is but an order of the court directing disposition of the case.

Obviously, the losing party in any trial has an automatic right to appeal the judgment to an appellate court, who will review the record of errors of law or abuse of discretion. Appellate decisions are written and reported and then become binding as a portion of the body of law of a jurisdiction.

It seems appropriate, therefore, that the sports administrator develop a close relationship with a legal counselor to prevent potential legal problems and thereby conduct the sports program in a safe and efficient manner.

A Typical Court Case Involving Public Law 94-142 and Section 504

Many states have adopted a minimum competency test that students must pass to receive a high school diploma. The areas of knowledge included on these tests often include mathematic skills, elementary grammar and language arts and reading. With the passage of Public Law 94-142, many educators question whether these competency tests can or should be modified to accommodate students with handicapping conditions. They question the legality of such tests and the attitude of the court when the tests are challenged in court.

In 1982 an Illinois case revealed the attitude of the court when such a test was at issue in a lawsuit. Educators can use the decision to help them make judgments in similar situations that are both educationally and legally sound.

Brookhart v. Illinois State Board of Education, 534 F. Supp. 725 (C.D. Ill. 1982).

The plaintiffs were eleven exceptional students of the Peoria School District No. 150 who were placed in the special curriculum based on individual educational plans because of individual learning disabilities or handicapping conditions. The plaintiffs met all regular requirements for graduation but failed the required minimal competency test (MCT). As a result they were awarded a certificate indicating that they completed the program but had not earned a high school diploma.

The plaintiffs named as defendants the State Superintendent of Education, the Illinois State Board of Education, the Peoria School District No. 150 and the Superintendent of the Peoria School District No. 150.

During the trial the State Superintendent testified that the school had the authority to impose reasonable standards for graduation. He stated that the standards did not violate the provisions of the Education For All Handicapped Children Act (Public Law, 94-142). He also declared that the school was not required to modify the MCT for students with handicapping conditions. He believed, however, that the school failed to notify the students as required by Public Law 94-142 that the test would be required for graduation

87

with a diploma. He therefore ordered the school to give the eleven exceptional students their diplomas since their right of due process had, in his opinion, been violated.

The plaintiffs agreed with the State Superintendent's decision but sought modification of the MCT for students with specific disabilities. They insisted that the test be eliminated unless it was modified.

The defendants contended that the State Superintendent's order directing the school to award diplomas was out of order and asked the court to rule in their favor.

The United States District Court decided that the school had the right to develop a reasonable test as a standard for graduation. It rejected the plaintiffs' claim that the test violated the provisions of Public Law 94-142. On this point the court remarked:

> Perhaps no test of human beings by human beings can always be scientifically exact, but that is not a measure. It is a reasonable test of the accomplishment of the school system in imparting basic knowledge to all its students, and unless some such measure is permitted, no certification of graduation from an educational program can have any meaning whatsoever, to the student or to others, as the notice of educational attainment it is meant to be.

In regard to the plaintiffs' contention that the test be modified for exceptional students or eliminated, the court made an interesting comment when it said:

> It is certainly true that giving a blind person a test from a printed test sheet discloses only his handicap and nothing of his knowledge. To discover a blind person's knowledge, a test must be given orally or in braille, if appropriate.

The court, however, did not advocate the modification of the MCT for exceptional children and it stated its position on the subject when it declared:

88

This, however, certainly does not mean that we can discover the knowledge or degree of learning of a mentally impaired student by modifying the test to avoid contact with the mental deficiency. To do so would simply be to pretend that the deficiency did not exist, and to fail completely to measure the learning. *A diploma issued as a result of passing such a modified test would be a pervasion of the program to lend meaning to the diploma as a record of educational achievement.* (emphasis added)

The court made it clear that its decision did not reflect a lack of compassion for the people living with serious handicaps but that it put a premium on academic integrity and what a high school diploma entails.

The United States District Court, therefore, reversed the administrative order of the State School Superintendent and refused to permit the awarding of diplomas to the eleven plaintiffs. While it cancelled the order to issue diplomas, it affirmed the other parts of the administrative order.

It is interesting to note that although the United States District Court refused to allow the granting of the diplomas to the eleven exceptional children, the School Code of Illinois was changed after the filing of the case to prohibit the denial of a general diploma on the basis of the failure of the MCT when the failure can be "directly related to the students handicapping conditions."

In the following three chapters, court cases such as the one reviewed above, will be used as examples of litigation affecting section 504 of the Rehabilitation Act and the Education For All Handicapped Children Act (Public Law 94-142). The cases will review litigation involving the legal mandates of this federal legislation, eligibility rules for sports participation and tort liability for injuries to participants of physical education and sports programs.

Hudgins and Vacca, two legal scholars, issue a word of caution when they warn that:

> Since a court holding today may be overturned tomorrow, law is never static. Thus law should be viewed as being controlling at a given point in time. It is consequently necessary for one to review constantly the state of law on an issue in order to be certain of being up-to-date.[14]

Summary

There is a presumption that most educators are familiar with the basic processes of law as it affects their profession. This may be the exception, however, rather than the rule. Many legal scholars agree that the law is baffling and, at times, mysterious to the layman. These same authorities declare that a basic knowledge of the law can prevent litigation, build confidence and set parameters that can develop programs that are sound educationally and legally. These positive aspects apply to the physical education teacher as well as the athletic coach.

The case study method can be helpful in revealing the attitude of the court in its interpretation of legislation, such as, Public Law 94-142. A word of caution is needed since judicial decisions are not static but often changing. The law should be viewed as controlling at a particular point and constantly reviewed to keep up-to-date on its latest status.

FOOTNOTES

1. H. C. HUDGINS, JR. & RICHARD S. VACCA, LAW AND EDUCATION: CONTEMPORARY ISSUES AND COURT DECISIONS, The Michie Company, Charlottesville, Virginia, 1979.

2. MICHAEL R. SMITH, LAW AND THE NORTH CAROLINA TEACHER, Interstate Printers and Publishers, Inc., Danville, Virginia, 1975.

3. Paul Proehl, *Tort Liability of Teachers,* 12 VANDERBILT L. REV. 739 (1959).

4. LAW AND THE COURTS, American Bar Association, Chicago, Illinois, 1980.

5. Alexander, et al. PUBLIC SCHOOL LAW, West Publishing Co., St. Paul, Minnesota, 1969.

6. *Id.*

7. King-Smith v. Aaron, 317 F. Supp. 164 (W.D. Pa. 1970).

8. P. K. Peterson, *Modern Approaches to Liability and Insurance,* Proceedings of the Third Annual NACDA Convention, Cleveland, Ohio, June, 1968, at 50.

9. *Id.*

10. *Id.*

11. Behagen v. Intercollegiate Conference of Faculty Representatives, 346 F. Supp. 602 (D. Minn. 1972).

12. C. Thomas Ross, who contributes this information is a partner in a Winston-Salem, North Carolina law firm specializing in litigation. He brings to the law profession a background in sports.

13. *Id.*

14. *Supra* note 1.

CHAPTER 5

Legal Mandates

Congress emphasized the importance of physical education since it is the only curricular area included in the definition of special education under the provisions of the Education for All Handicapped Children Act (Public Law 94-142) [1] Physical education is required when an individual has special physical and motor needs. (Without special physical and motor needs the student is governed by the same rules, regulations and laws as his/her peers).

Congress stipulated that physical therapy is a related service and cannot be substituted for physical education. Medical excuses from physicians attempting to waive the physical education requirement is technically and legally prohibited under Public Law 94-142. In states that do not require physical education for the nonhandicapped, physical education must, nevertheless, be provided for the special student. The emphasis is on the needs of the child, not the availability of services. [2]

Before programs of physical education can be implemented in the school's programs, four key and specific mandates must be included in the overall program. These mandates of the law provide for: (1) free appropriate education, (2) least restrictive environment, (3) due process and (4) individualized education program.

In this chapter, selected cases will be reviewed from numerous court cases litigated for alleged violations of the four key mandates.

The decisions that follow hopefully will serve as examples of judicial interpretations of the law and assist school officials in developing programs that are educationally and legally sound.

Free Appropriate Education

Lynn Erb and Cecil D. Mercer, writing in the *NOLPE School Law Journal,* declare that:

> All children must be provided with a free appropriate public education in the least restrictive environment. This means that each individual must be accommodated with regular or special education services which are specifically designed to meet his/her needs at no cost to the parents. If the student's needs cannot be met at a public facility, transportation and educational services must be provided for the student to the appropriate setting at no cost to the parent.[3]

While this statement seems clear enough, the definition of an "appropriate" education is constantly challenged in court as litigants seek a judicial interpretation in lawsuits. In *Rowley v. Board of Education,*[4] a New York court attempted to define what is "appropriate" for a free appropriate education by declaring that:

> An "appropriate education" could mean an "adequate" education — that is, an education substantial to facilitate a child's progress from one grade to another to enable him or her to earn a high school diploma. An "appropriate" education could also mean one which enables the handicapped child to achieve his or her full potential. Between these two extremes, however, is a standard which I conclude is more in keeping with the regulations, with the Equal Protection decisions which motivated the passage of the Act, and with common sense. This standard would require that each handicapped child be given an opportunity to achieve his full potential commensurate with the opportunity provided other children.[5]

94

This definition has been cited by parties in subsequent litigation when the term "appropriate education" is at issue. The following cases are typical of the many that come before the bar and indicate the judgment of the court toward this controversial question.

Sherry Grace had a hearing loss of ninety-five percent which rendered her almost completely deaf.[6] Her parents requested the school district to provide the "best" appropriate education for their daughter. The school district preferred to send Sherry to the Arkansas School for the Deaf but her parents wanted her to attend the local school. The United States District Court, Western District Arkansas, found that Sherry could attend the local school and receive an "appropriate" education. The school district disagreed and appealed the decision to the United States Court of Appeals, Eighth Circuit.

The appellate court considered the facts of the case and made some interesting observations.[7] It reasoned that the Arkansas School for the Deaf was in all probability the best school for her to attend because:

> [she] would be receiving instruction in reading, arithmetic, spelling, telling of time, health, social sciences and art by a certified teacher of the deaf along with instruction in manual communication, lip reading, writing and speaking.

The court also believed that various teachers, aides, cooks, grounds keepers at the Arkansas School for the Deaf who were profoundly deaf would serve as role models for Sherry. The appellate court reasoned that the determining factor in the district court's decision was the belief that Sherry would be in constant contact with nonhandicapped students in "physical education, library, and possibly penmanship, science, health, social studies, music and art." This would not be possible at the School for the Deaf.

95

While the appellate court agreed with the district court's contention that the girl would receive the "best" education at the School for the Deaf, it too concluded that the state's obligation was to provide an appropriate education, not the "best" education. It ruled that Sherry attend the local school where she could receive an appropriate education.

Robert Shanberg filed suit against the Commonwealth of Pennsylvania, the Secretary of Education and the Pennsbury School District on behalf of his son Mark.[8] The plaintiff contended that Mark, a paraplegic confined to a wheelchair with a speech impairment, was not receiving an education that made the best use of his abilities. Under Mark's individualized education plan, he was mainstreamed into the regular education program of the junior high school. (The Pennsylvania school code requires the school district to place an exceptional child into a regular class program if the child can profit by such a placement.) Mark's individualized education plan provided "support services such as adaptive physical education for his upper extremities and physical therapy for his lower extremities."

He also participated in a reading course for individuals with reading problems and a "handwriting program and itinerant speech program."

The Commonwealth Court of Pennsylvania considered the plaintiff's argument that his son's abilities were not being met by the public school's educational plan and commented that:

> the school district is not required to devise a program of education which makes the best use of a student's abilities. Instead, the school district must only identify exceptional children and develop educational programs appropriate for the needs of each child.

It affirmed the Secretary of Education's decision to keep Mark in the regular education program of the high school.

In North Carolina the residents of four centers for the mentally retarded filed suit against the State Board of Public Instruction, contending that they were denied access to a free appropriate education due to their retardation.[9] They argued that the denial of an appropriate education was a violation of section 504 and Public Law 94-142.

The court agreed with the plaintiff's claim and the Board agreed to locate all mentally retarded children in need of a free appropriate education and to conduct a public information program designed to focus attention on the rights of individuals with handicapping conditions and their educational opportunities.

Two years later, the district court in North Carolina found that the Pitt County Board of Education inappropriately placed a ten-year-old boy in a school with older children who ranged in age from eleven to seventeen years.[10] The boy had a history of emotional problems and an inability to relate to other children. After he was placed with the older children, he developed additional problems and his condition worsened.

The court located three places it considered appropriate for the boy; one public facility within the state and two private schools outside the state. It recommended that the boy attend the public institution within the State of North Carolina with the notation that his program be reviewed annually. In making its decision, the court referred to a regulation that applied to the instant situation which said:

> If placement in a public or private residential program is necessary to provide a free appropriate education to a handicapped person because of his or her handicap, the program, including non-medical care and room and board,

97

shall be provided at no cost to the person or his or her parents or guardians.[11]

The regulation also suggested that: "The placement of each handicapped child shall be based on his or her individualized education program and shall be as close as possible to the child's home." [12]

Many states have statutes that attempt to release the public school from any obligation to provide an education to students who have conditions that limit their ability to benefit from an education. When these statutes are challenged in court, the results usually favor the students.

Connecticut had a statute that released the public school from the duty to educate children who:

1. could not take care of their personal needs;
2. were not responsive to directions;
3. had no means of intelligible communication.[13]

The Connecticut Association for Retarded Citizens challenged the State Board of Education's policy of enforcing a statute that allegedly violated Public Law 94-142 since it discriminated solely on the basis of a handicapping condition. The court concurred with the plaintiff's arguments and the statute was changed to provide an appropriate education for all mentally retarded children in Connecticut.

Soon after the decision in Connecticut, the state of Michigan evaluated its policies in regard to the new federal laws. As a result of its evaluation, it revamped its pre-school program to provide individual assessments.[14]

Indiana experienced problems associated with the new laws. One hundred and thirteen severely retarded children claimed that the state failed to provide educational services as mandated by section 504 and Public Law 94-142.[15] The plaintiffs argued that the state also failed to provide

98

adequate finances or special education teachers to meet their needs. The court did not agree and denied the plaintiff's motion for injunctive relief.

Several months later, however, an Indiana court reversed the decision.[16] Stephen L. contended that the Indiana State Board of Special Education failed to establish a proper identification process and denied special education opportunities and placement for himself and others. The court, reversing its previous decision, agreed to comply with the new federal regulations.

The Maryland Board of Education held that the local education agency was not required to provide a severely disabled student with educational opportunities.[17] The plaintiff was a hydrocephalic, nonambulatory, blind and mentally retarded girl who insisted that her rights under Public Law 94-142 were violated by the Board's failure to provide her with educational opportunities. Within thirty days after she instituted the lawsuit, she received appropriate educational placement and she dismissed her complaint.

The Maryland Department of Education was named as a defendant by a mentally retarded student who was receiving only three hours of instruction per week.[18] The Education Department decided to initiate a daily program for her but at a non-public facility. Within thirty days after she filed the suit, she was assigned an appropriate educational program and she dismissed the claim.

It appears that litigation or the threat of litigation has brought about change by encouraging school officials to provide appropriate educational opportunities for individuals who previously were denied access to such programs.

Number and Length of Days Challenged

Most schools have a rule that school terms are funded for a specific number of days. The rule has been questioned by parents of special children who contend that the rule is in conflict with the provisions of the Education For All Handicapped Children Act.

The definition of a "free appropriate education" became the center of controversy in Pennsylvania when five children and their parents sued the Commonwealth of Pennsylvania for denying their right to a "free publicly funded education in excess of 180 days." [19] The plaintiffs contended that an interruption of educational programs for "severely and profoundly impaired children and severely emotionally disturbed children" supported findings that regression occurred.

The United States District Court, Eastern District of Pennsylvania, granted declaratory and injunctive relief and the defendants appealed the decision.

The case started as three class actions by the five children and their parents and these were consolidated for trial. [20] During the trial the term "free appropriate education" was defined to include special education and related services. The appellate court defined special education as found in Public Law 94-142 as:

> specially designed instruction at no cost to parents or guardians, to meet the unique needs of a handicapped child, including classroom instruction, instruction in physical education, home instruction, and instruction in hospitals and institutions.

The court considered "related services" to be those activities that might be needed to assist in a child's benefit from special education. It listed the services or activities as: "transportation and developmental, corrective, and supportive services such as speech pathology, audiology,

100

recreation, psychological services, certain medical services, occupational therapy, and counseling services."

The court noted that normal children are able to recoup losses in a few weeks and rarely require more than one month to regain their skills and behaviors. The court observed that much greater time is required by the severely and profoundly impaired (SPI) and the severely emotionally disturbed (SED) youth.

The court felt that the intent of Congress regarding an appropriate education was to:

> provide for that education which would leave children, upon school's completion, as independent as possible from dependency on others, including the state, within the limits of the handicapping condition.

It concluded that the 180-day rule is inflexible and hinders the appropriate education for the "individual members of the plaintiff class." It remanded the case to the district court for disposition consistent with this opinion.

The parents of a thirteen-year-old girl with exceptional needs sought to obtain a summer program for their daughter.[20.1] The United States District Court, Eastern Division, Wisconsin, recognized the need for year-round educational programming in some cases but determined that such a program's availability would depend on the particular needs of the child in question. In the instant case the court admitted that the girl would "suffer some academic regression during a break in her educational programming" but concluded that she did not need a year-round program nor was the school district obligated to furnish such a program. The parents appealed to the United States Court of Appeals, Seventh Circuit seeking compensatory damages and attorney's fees.[21] The appellate court affirmed the lower court's ruling and declined to award any fees to the parents.

Laura J. was diagnosed as a multiple-handicapped child with severe language learning and behavioral impairments symptomatic of childhood schizophrenia.[22] The school district believed that Laura was severely retarded and assigned her to a self-contained special education class in an elementary school. Laura was fifteen years of age and significantly older than the class of seven- and eight-year-old children. Her parents claimed that she regressed during her year at the elementary school and that a program of six hours per day was inadequate to meet her needs. Laura's parents sought year-round residential placement and the school district objected.

The district court heard testimony that Laura required professional services that included:

> a licensed psychologist or psychiatrist consultant, a qualified speech and language pathologist, a special education teacher trained and experienced in working with childhood schizophrenia, and a licensed occupational therapist.

The court praised the efforts of Laura's parents and the school district in their attempt to provide the necessary educational experiences for her, but it believed that she needed the services provided at a residential facility on a twenty-four hour basis. The court admitted that Laura might be "beyond the reach of our educational expertise," and that the financial burden upon the state and local educational agencies could be substantial. It felt, however, that Laura's future held little promise and hoped that residential care could "avoid this dismal prognosis." It concluded: "That hope — indeed, that expectation is the very foundation upon which Congress created the Education For All Handicapped Children Act."

Timely Hearing

Although all parties may agree to an appropriate placement, it is important that it be made as soon as possible. An interesting case in Pennsylvania resulted in a favorable ruling by the court for a student when a school district failed to hear an appeal within a reasonable time.

Minda Krawitz attended regular classes from kindergarten through the sixth grade. Minda was classified as "mildly learning disabled and mildly emotionally disturbed." [23] The school district did not have an educational program that could meet her needs so she received approval and funds to attend a private residential school in the state.

Minda outgrew the school after two years and her parents requested another placement. Her parents rejected the school district's recommendation and requested a hearing before the Secretary of Education. After a considerable length of time passed, Minda's parents believed that the delay in setting up a hearing indicated that the state did not have an appropriate place for their daughter. They, therefore, sent Minda to a private school in Massachusetts.

Fourteen months later, a hearing was held and the hearing officer reported that the school district or one of several private schools in Pennsylvania could meet Minda's educational needs. He informed her parents that the state could not refund the tuition spent for schooling and that the Department's failure to provide a timely hearing did not prejudice the parents in the action they took.

The Commonwealth Court of Pennsylvania disagreed and emphatically stated:

> We do not agree that the Department's failure to provide a timely hearing was without con-sequence. Had the matter been disposed of Minda's parents might have accepted placement

103

in one of the Pennsylvania schools offered by the Department. We believe they should be reimbursed for tuition paid for the 1966-67 placement in Massachusetts at an institution, we note, whose tuition was less than that of the Pennsylvania school most highly recommended.

It ordered the payment of tuition and maintenance costs to the parents.

Seven years after the *Mills* case was decided, attorneys for the Mental Health Law Project sought a court order against the District of Columbia's School Board alleging that the Board was violating the time-frame for evaluating and placing children in proper educational programs as ordered by the court.[24] In *Mills* the parents requested placement within a fifty-day period. The complaint made a valid point for timely placement when it declared that:

> While several months of waiting may be inconsequential in the worlds of law and business, in a school year that is only ten months long, even slight delays in providing services to handicapped children may cause regression that can never be overcome.[25]

Placement in the Least Restrictive Environment

One of the legal mandates of Public Law 94-142 is that all children should be placed in the least restrictive environment. For years children were labeled and placed into classrooms according to these labels. Research and teacher observations refute past practices since children with handicapping conditions tend to be heterogeneous rather than homogeneous in group action "with respect to their abilities and rates of learning." [26]

Public Law 94-142 required changes in programs designed to avoid negative labeling and placement that is inappropriate for the students. The new guidelines

104

associated with Public Law 94-142 call for a new approach in determining educational placement that includes:

(a) determining a child's educational needs irrespective of his or her handicapping condition,

(b) preparing an individualized educational program (IEP) for each handicapped child which is designed to meet the child's unique needs, and then

(c) placing the child into the least restrictive environment in which those needs can be met.[27]

The American Alliance for Health, Physical Education, Recreation and Dance published interpretations for implementing the mandates in a publication entitled "Practical Pointers" that has proved to be extremely valuable for all teachers and coaches. In the publication several suggestions are made regarding placement that includes the following:

Placing children in least restrictive environments does *not* mean mainstreaming or the placing of all handicapped children into regular classes. The law requires that these children be placed in the most normal environment in which they can potentially succeed. The least restrictive environment will be different for each child. Additionally, handicapped children can and should be placed into different environments for different subject matter and activities if these various learning environments are the best way to meet the child's educational needs.[28]

Several court cases illustrate the various situations that have been brought before the bar regarding placement.

Paul Kruelle was a profoundly retarded eleven-year-old child, whose parents challenged the New Castle School District's educational plan and placement as inadequate.

105

Paul's Individualized Education Program ("IEP") assigned him to a specialized school for individuals with handicapping conditions.[29] The school was able to provide a "variety of treatments" that included: "Speech therapy, occupational therapy and physical therapy."

Although his parents agreed with the contents of their son's "IEP" and the fact that the school could provide the necessary treatments, they rejected the "IEP" because they believed Paul needed residential placement to fully meet his needs. Paul's physical development was complicated by cerebral palsy. In addition, at age twelve he had other problems that included the fact that:

> he cannot walk, dress himself, or eat unaided. He is not toilet trained. He does not speak, and his receptive communication level is extremely low. In addition to his physical problems, he has had a history of emotional problems which result in choking and self-inducing vomiting when experiencing stress.

When Paul was placed in respite care at the home of a person trained to work with retarded children and attended school during the day, he showed observable progress.

A child psychiatrist testified that Paul needed around the clock residential care with people who were trained if he was to maximize his chances of learning. The defendants argued, however, that:

> Paul's need for residential placement, if such a need exists, is caused by social and emotional problems resulting from the home environment, and that inadequacies there must be met by other agencies, perhaps by a neglect proceeding against the parents.

The court responded:

> Whether that problem is classified as "physical"
> or "emotional," and whether it results from the
> transition from school to home or from home to
> school, it is evident that Paul will realize his
> learning potential only if he receives more
> professional help than the Meadowood School
> day program can offer him.

The court, therefore, concluded that the "least restrictive environment" would be where Paul could receive full-time care. It hoped that he could develop a "minimal level of self-help skills" that would enable him to return to his family and "continue his training in a non-residential facility."

A very unusual case concerning "least restrictive environment" involved a seven-year-old multihandicapped boy, Raul Espino, who had been injured in an automobile accident when he was eleven-months-old. Raul was "diagnosed as a quadraplegic and confined to a wheelchair."[30]

Due to the damage to his sympathetic nervous system, Raul had a problem related to body temperature that forced him to spend his early childhood indoors where the temperature could be kept between sixty-eight and seventy-two degrees. His condition was described as follows:

> If Raul is subjected to excess heat, his skin turns
> red and he begins to hyperventilate. His internal
> body temperature begins to rise, often higher
> than his external temperature. He feels ill,
> restless and weak, and has difficulty con-
> centrating. Subjection to significant variations
> in temperature causes Raul to accumulate
> mucus in his lungs and increases his
> susceptibility to respiratory infections.

Raul attended a kindergarten for individuals with handicapping conditions that was fully air-conditioned. As a result, he experienced very few temperature problems.

The school committee developed an individualized education program for Raul that placed him in a school with nonhandicapped students. The committee felt that the placement at the school for individuals with handicapping conditions was too restrictive to meet his "intellectual and social needs." The committee stipulated that he be placed in a classroom that was air-conditioned to accommodate his special need for stable temperatures.

When Raul reported for school he discovered that he would be placed in a specially-constructed plexiglass cubicle, five foot by five foot, with a window air conditioner. The cubicle was designed by the superintendent to avoid criticism from the parents of nonhandicapped children in the regular classes who did not have air-conditioned classrooms. The superintendent also reasoned that the school district could not afford to air-condition the entire classroom.

Raul's parents sought injunctive relief to require the school to provide a fully air-conditioned room. They argued that their son's ability to communicate with his peers in group activities was hampered by the cubicle. A psychologist testified at the trial that:

> the cubicle did not represent a full educational opportunity for Raul as it isolated him and tended to call undue attention to his handicap. It farther tends to remove him from an environment of stimulation and cuts him off from positive reinforcement.

It is noteworthy that the cost of air-conditioning the classroom was $5,700 per year. The school district's budget was thirty-nine million dollars; three million of the budget was federal funds and $250 thousand was allocated for students with handicapping conditions.

The district court considered the testimony of both parties and then made some observations relating to the situation:

1. The mainstreaming provisions of the EAHCA, as set out previously require that a handicapped child be educated with his non-handicapped peers "to the maximum extent appropriate."
2. The decision to provide air-conditioning for Raul in a plexiglass cubicle, and therefore at times segregate him from his non-handicapped classmates is *prima facie* a violation of the mainstreaming provision of the EAHCA.
3. A purely theoretical risk of parental or teacher complaints is probably insufficient to offset the countervailing needs of Raul Espino, Jr.
4. Full social interaction is an important part of today's educational curriculum and is even more vital to a child like Raul who necessarily suffers a certain degree of isolation as a result of this handicap.

The court ordered the defendants to provide Raul with an air-conditioned environment and enjoined them from requiring him to attend class in a cubicle or any other segregated environment. It concluded with words that expressed its opinion in a clear manner when it said:

If handicapped children are ever to become useful, productive citizens, they must be given the opportunity to experience the world they inhabit. With the possible exception of a child whose immunological system requires that he or she be kept within a sterile atmosphere, education within a cubicle will hardly ever be appropriate.

Six developmentally disabled residents of the Laconia School and Training Center (LSS) in New Hampshire

109

instituted a class action suit in behalf of all disabled persons presently residing at LSS or those who might be institutionalized there in the future.[31] The plaintiffs claimed that they were denied habilitation treatment such as physical therapy, occupational therapy and other essential services. Habilitation was defined as: "the term of art used to refer to that education, training, and care required by retarded individuals to reach their maximum development."

The plaintiffs sought habilitation in the least restricted placement, which they contended would be best achieved in community placement. The issue became the question of whether: "habilitation can ever be provided in the traditional institutional setting as opposed to a setting in the community."

The six developmentally disabled individuals testified that they had regressed and deteriorated physically from the lack of services at the institution. The trial lasted forty days. The United States District Court made an interesting observation when it commented on the importance of the issues and the difficulty of arriving at a decision. The court declared that:

> Institutional reform cases of this type require courts to venture in areas foreign to their traditional expertise — including the fields of medicine, sociology, psychiatry, and education — an excursion which this Court undertakes with some trepidation. However, the important constitutional and statutory rights invoked by the parties require that such concerns be addressed.

The court in strong language agreed with the plaintiffs' argument of neglect and ordered the defendants to provide the residents with the following:

110

1. an Individual Service Plan documenting the individual needs of such residents, and providing for the delivery of services necessary to fulfill same;
2. five and one-half hours of education for the 180-day school year and whatever number of days in excess of 180 are required for the proper education of that particular individual;
3. medical services;
4. recreational services, including off-campus field trips, summer camps, etc. to residents on an equal basis, and shall not exclude residents from partaking in same solely on the basis of their mental retardation or their physical handicaps;
5. the opportunity to live in residential buildings of equivalent quality and caliber and shall not relegate the most severely retarded to the least desirable living facilities.

The court then warned the defendants that any "former presumption against deinstitutionalization of severely and profoundly handicapped residents shall cease. Defendants shall make community placements on an individualized basis."

In addition, the court ordered periodic reviews of each resident, improved hygienic conditions for the residents, sufficient furniture, balanced diets, a qualified physician, a sufficient number of staff and those with the expertise to carry out the orders.

The court did not believe, however, that habilitation had to be carried out in community settings. The services could be administered in the institution. It also believed that the orders would be carried out in good faith, but it reserved the right to appoint a special master to implement the orders if the "parties prove in any way recalcitrant in their prompt compliance with its orders."

111

The Department of Education of the state of Hawaii (DOE) sought a judicial review of the decision of a hearing officer regarding the placement of a four-year-old girl who suffered from cystic fibrosis.[32] In addition, Katherine D. had a condition diagnosed as tracheomalacia, requiring a tracheostomy which is kept in place "by means of a fourteen karat gold chain approximately ¼ to ½ inch in diameter." The tracheostomy and tracheotomy tube allow Katherine to breathe and expel secretion from her lungs.

Katherine's only adverse condition relating to her educational performance was her inability to vocalize normally. Katherine could receive an education in a regular classroom if it were not for the potential danger that her tracheotomy tube might become dislodged.

During the 1980-81 school year, Katherine did well academically and socially in St. Philomena's Child Care Center, a school approved by the DOE. Katherine's mother taught at the school and was available to administer medication and suction out mucus in her lungs two or three times a day through the tracheotomy tube. The cost of tuition in 1980-81 amounted to $1,200 for the year and was estimated at $1,300 for the 1981-82 school year.

The DOE, as required by the Education For All Handicapped Children Act, conducted an evaluation of Katherine D. in the summer of 1980. The DOE recognized that she qualified for special education and offered an individualized educational program (IEP). They recommended placement at Jefferson Orthopedic School but then withdrew the offer "and offered Katherine a homebound program consisting of 1½ hours of speech therapy and 40 minutes of parent counseling per week."

Katherine's parents felt that their daughter needed to socialize with other children and "develop her speech vocabulary." They opposed the homebound program and

112

favored a public school education. They insisted, however, that the school provide medical personnel to administer her medication and tend to her health needs. They rejected the DOE's offer and initiated a due process hearing. The hearing officer subsequently ruled that the recommendation of the DOE failed to provide Katherine with a "free appropriate public education in the least restrictive environment."

The DOE then recommended placement at Moanalua Elementary School with special emergency procedures outlined for her protection. School personnel were given training in techniques to administer to Katherine's needs. The teachers were upset with the plan and along with the school's administrators, filed a grievance charging: "Violation of their contracts of employment by being required to perform duties of a medical nature outside the scope of their contractural duties."

During the trial the court noted that the teachers were not without feeling or callous but that:

> it becomes clear that they responded to the plan with fear and trepidation. Fear that they could not perform the medical procedures correctly and that the child might die at their hands; or fear of the personal aspects of the procedure itself; and/or the fear of being sued if something untoward occurred during the procedure. These are genuine and legitimate fears and understandably so.

The court observed that the attitude of the school's staff made the plan unworkable. It declared that "the plan self-destructed with the filing of the grievance."

The court considered the DOE's argument that it met its obligation under the law when it offered Katherine the homebound program and that it did not assume responsibility for her tuition costs since her parents

113

voluntarily placed her in a private school. The court, however, agreed with the hearing officer's rejection of the defendant's argument and concluded that the DOE's offer of a home program did not meet the requirements of the "least restrictive environment prescribed by the federal regulations."

The United States District Court of Hawaii remarked:

1. that but for the possibility of physically harmful problems with her tracheostomy Katherine D. should be in regular school;
2. that the aid Katherine D. needs can be — and for some years has been — provided by trained lay people;
3. that the necessary skills can be learned at no cost in a matter of hours; and
4. that if a trained person is at hand, Katherine can attend school — as she did last year and the year before — without any serious risk to her well being.

The court noted that Katherine was entitled to a "school-based education with special attendants at DOE expense." It believed that attendance at St. Philomena met her needs since her mother was employed there and could give her assistance when needed. The court concluded:

This being so, placement at St. Philomena's together with DOE — provided itinerant speech therapy is the least restrictive environment appropriate for Katherine. Anything more restrictive is unnecessary given the opportunity available at St. Philomena's.

It then favored the defendants by ruling that:

1. The administrative hearing officer's decision is hereby affirmed;
2. The Defendants are hereby awarded reimbursement for tuition paid for Katherine D. at St. Philomena's School; and

114

3. The Defendants are hereby awarded attorney's fees in the sum of $15,000 together with their costs as taxed.

Due Process

Due process, or the right of an individual to receive fair play, has been extolled by educators for years. Simply stated, the Bill of Rights promises each person the opportunity to be a first class citizen. Specifically, the Fifth Amendment of the United States Constitution states that: "No person . . . shall be deprived of life, liberty, or property without due process of law." The Fifth Amendment applies only to the federal government. The Fourteenth Amendment, however, extends this concept to cover the operations of state governments as well, in reading, "nor shall any State deprive any person of life, liberty, or property without due process of law." [33]

The Supreme Court historically has refused to define due process, preferring instead to consider it a "gradual process of judicial inclusion and exclusion." [34] The law distinguishes between due process as substantive and as procedural. Substantive due process protects each person by requiring that a state must have a valid goal before it can deprive an individual of his right to life, liberty, or property. To take one example, children may be required to have a vaccination to protect them from disease before attending school. The vaccination is, in this instance, employed to insure the objective of the state and meets the requirement of substantial due process. [35]

Procedural due process includes the following conditions:

1. an individual must have proper notice that he is about to be deprived of life, liberty, or property;

2. an individual must be given the opportunity to be heard; and
3. an individual must be afforded a fair trial or hearing.[36]

Not all due process rights have been accorded all educational institutions. A distinction has developed between public and private institutions because of the application and interpretation of the Fourteenth Amendment.[37] If an educational institution is classified as private, its students have no constitutional protections under the Fourteenth Amendment. Instead, the courts rely on a contract theory, as decided in *Dixon v. Alabama State Board of Education*,[38] to safeguard the right of private school students to the protection afforded by due process. Under this contract theory an agreement is presumed to exist which provides that an institution will not act in an arbitrary manner toward its students in disciplinary cases.

Due process rights are guaranteed to students who attend public schools under the Fourteenth Amendment. While the courts have traditionally supported the authority of school officials to set rules and maintain order, it does insist on rules that are reasonable.[39]

Public Law 94-142 protects the rights of children with handicapping conditions to a quality education. There are two important aspects of the due process provision of this law relating to education that includes implications for the parents and evaluation procedures. The American Alliance for Health, Physical Education, Recreation and Dance, in "Practical Pointers" describes the due process provisions of the law.

Implications for Parents

Parents, under the provisions of Public Law 94-142 are considered to be partners with school officials in

116

decisionmaking as it affects their child. School officials are obligated to notify the parents in writing of any recommended changes in placement or special testing of the child. The school officials are required to schedule a meeting for the parents. In addition, parents are given the opportunity to seek redress when they do not feel that their child is "being served adequately." Parents are urged not to sign an approval sheet if they are not in agreement with any aspect of the IEP or evaluation for their child.

AAHPERD suggests to parents that "you have a right to challenge the school's decision or quality of service provided . . . if you believe":

- The evaluation was not appropriate.
- Your opinions concerning your child's education were not considered or addressed in planning conferences.
- The IEP developed for your child is not appropriate based on the evaluation findings.
- The school is not implementing the special education services as specified in the IEP.
- The school has delayed implementation of any service specified in the IEP.
- Your child is not showing any progress in the educational setting or with the special services identified in the IEP.
- You feel racial, cultural, or disability biases have led to the development of an inappropriate IEP for your child.[40]

Six legal actions are available in challenging the school:

- appeal to the local school officials,
- request an independent evaluation,
- request a hearing from an independent and neutral hearing officer,
- file an administrative appeal,

117

- file a complaint to the Federal Office for Civil
  Rights,
- file a lawsuit.[41]

Parents are encouraged to attempt to work out any issues with local officials. In the event that this procedure is unsatisfactory, parents should request due process procedures from the school district.

Parents and the local education agency have the following rights at a hearing:

- You are entitled to have anyone you wish present at and involved in the hearing process.
- You can request the presence and question anyone involved in your child's education thus far.
- Your child can attend and be questioned.
- You can decide whether the hearing be open or closed to the public.[42]

Testing and Evaluation Procedures

The second provision of due process under Public Law 94-142 guidelines affects testing and evaluation procedures as follows, stating that they:

- be provided and administered in the child's native language or other mode of communication unless it is not feasible to do so,
- be validated for the purpose for which they are used, and
- be administered by personnel trained in testing procedures.

When testing and evaluation is administered for the purpose of considering changes in the educational placement several guidelines are recommended that include the following:

118

- the child must be assessed in all curriculum and ability areas to determine (their) educational need,
- no single procedure may be used as the sole criterion for determining an appropriate educational program for a child, and
- the evaluation must be a multi-disciplinary effort.[43]

Exclusion From School

Suspension and expulsion are the two terms which characterize the exclusion of a student from school. H. C. Hudgins, Jr. and Richard S. Vacca, writing in *Law and Education Contemporary Issues and Court Decisions,* discuss exclusion as follows:

> Suspension denotes the temporary exclusion from school and is the prerogative of a teacher or administrator, according to a given state's statutes. Expulsion denotes a longer term of exclusion, varying from a number of days to the end of a school term. A board of education is vested with the authority of expulsion.[44]

The authors continue:

> Through the years courts have not interfered with the substantive right of school officials to exclude students. Although in recent years many courts have increasingly recognized the value of children remaining in school and in acquiring an education, they also accept the necessity of suspending or expelling students for very serious misbehavior.[45]

While disruptive behavior is a potential problem in all areas of education, the chances for disruption among individuals with handicapping conditions are greatly increased simply by the nature of the handicap.

119

Under provisions of the Education For All Handicapped Children Act, a child involved in a disciplinary action will remain in his/her present educational environment until the placement status is decided.[46] The law, however, provides that "while the placement may not be changed, this does not preclude the agency from using its normal procedures of dealing with children who are endangering themselves or others."[47]

The types of misbehavior leading to exclusion may differ as the following court decisions reveal.

Kathy Stuart (a fictitious name) was described as a student of limited intelligence with emotional problems and a series of behavioral difficulties.[48] Kathy was involved in a school-wide disturbance and received a ten-day suspension. The school superintendent recommended that the school board expel her for the remainder of the year. She sought judicial relief to prevent an expulsion hearing by the board, claiming that expulsion would deny her rights under the Education For All Handicapped Children Act (Public Law 94-142). Her claim raised novel issues regarding disciplinary policies of local schools in relation to the regulations of the Act.

The United States District Court recognized that school officials need authority and discretion in matters relating to discipline but asserted that expulsion in this situation contravened the regulations of the Education For All Handicapped Children Act. The court declared that any change in placement must be made by a Placement and Planning Team (PPT) in consideration of the student's needs. Regarding the disciplinary process the court observed:

> Handicapped children are neither immune from a school's disciplinary process nor are they entitled to participate in programs when their

120

behavior impairs the education of other children in the program. First, school authorities can take swift disciplinary measures, such as suspension, against disruptive handicapped children. Secondly, a PPT can request a change in the placement of handicapped children who have demonstrated that their present placement is inappropriate by disrupting the education of other children. The Handicapped Act thereby affords schools with both short-term and long-term methods of dealing with handicapped children who are behavioral problems.

The school officials insisted that its disciplinary policies were beyond the control of the court. The court recognized that local and state authorities had considerable power to operate its schools but declared that "it is equally clear that even a school's disciplinary procedures are subject to the scrutiny of the federal judiciary." It granted the plaintiff's request for judicial relief by ruling that: "The Handicapped Act vests jurisdiction in federal district courts over all claims of noncompliance with the Act's procedural safeguards, regardless of the amount in controversy."

It ordered the board to undertake an immediate review by a PPT of the plaintiff's special education program and enjoined the board from conducting a hearing to expel her.

Dennis Doe (a fictitious name) challenged school officials who suspended him from school and sought to expel him for the remainder of the year.[49] The defendants claimed that Doe failed to exhaust his administrative remedies before going to court. The Massachusetts court, however, responded that the Department of Health, Education and Welfare did not set up administrative procedures to cover the situation and since local and state remedies were not available, his action was proper. The court remarked: "As HEW interpreted the Handicapped Act, schools were not to expel students whose handicaps caused them to be disruptive; rather schools were to appropriately place such students."

The court made a timely comment when it noted that schools can expel students from schools under the same disciplinary rules of nonhandicapped students without violating their equal protection. It declared:

> A disruptive student interferes with the education of other students in his school. It is quite rational for a school to reserve the option of expelling any student who is interfering with the education of other students. At least with regard to the handicapped, whatever dangers of invid-dous discrimination are presented by a policy of disciplinary expulsions, those dangers are outweighed by the rationality of disciplinary expulsions.

While the court acknowledged the right of the school to expel disruptive students, it concluded that the school in the present instance could only suspend Doe if it placed him in an "appropriate, restrictive environment." It therefore granted him relief from expulsion.

Seven students, classified as educatable mentally retarded (EMR), mildly retarded, or EMR/dull normal were expelled from high school.[50] The students were charged with misconduct that allegedly included behavior ranging from: "masturbation or sexual acts against fellow students to willful defiance of authority, insubordination, vandalism, and the use of profane language."

The plaintiffs were expelled for the remainder of the year and the following year which represented the maximum time allowed by Florida law. The plaintiffs were given their procedural right of due process but argued that they were unfairly denied educational services provided under Public Law 94-142 and section 504.

The court of appeals noted that:

> expulsion is still a proper disciplinary tool under
> EHA and Section 504 when proper procedures
> are utilized and under proper circumstances. We
> cannot, however, authorize the complete
> cessation of educational services during an
> expulsion period.

The court concluded that the lower court did not err in
granting the plaintiffs injunctive relief. It set the accepted
terms of expulsion under Public Law 94-142 and section 504
regulations as follows:

1. before a handicapped student can be expelled,
   a trained and knowledgeable group of
   persons must determine whether the
   student's misconduct bears a relationship to
   his handicapping condition;
2. an expulsion is a change in educational
   placement thereby invoking the procedural
   protections of the EHA and Section 504;
3. expulsion is a proper disciplinary tool under
   the EHA and Section 504, but a complete
   cessation of educational services is not.

A final case illustrates the confusion that often exists
among school officials regarding disciplinary action. An
Illinois court was called upon to decide whether the State
Superintendent of Education could reverse the decision of
an Impartial Hearing Officer who suspended a student for
five days.[51]

David Buckley, a seventeen-year-old eleventh grade
student, who was judged to have "learning disabilities" was
mainstreamed into a course in auto mechanics. David
strenuously objected to detention after school for disturbing
the class with several other misbehaving students and
verbally abused his teacher. The Impartial Hearing Office
suspended him for five days finding that David had

123

"violated school policy" and concluding that his abusive action toward his teacher was not "perpetuated by his handicap."

The State Superintendent of Education and the State Board felt that David was not dangerous and reversed the Impartial Hearing Officer's decision and ordered the withdrawal of the suspension with the stipulation that the suspension be expunged from the student's records.

The court considered the action to be the result of the Superintendent's "own fallacious equating of a brief, temporary suspension, with explulsion or termination of special education."

The court admitted that it had very few judicial decisions upon which it could base its decision. It noted that there were several cases involving expulsion or termination of educational services, but not suspension. It referred to a landmark Supreme Court case in which suspension was the key issue. In *Goss v. Lopez* the Supreme Court declared that: "Suspension is considered not only to be a necessary tool to maintain order but a valuable educational device." [52]

The Court was emphatic in its opinion that the five-day suspension did not violate the law since it represented a disciplinary attempt to teach a student who knew better to avoid a repetition of the flagrant offense he committed. It remarked:

> There can be no doubt whatsoever for David being in the 11th grade on any terms, he knew better, and that he needed to be brought up short for saying what he did to his teacher. Any theory that some harm of the brief interruption of classwork could outweigh the educational value of the suspension here can only be recognized as pure imagination or a feeble attempt at rationalization of a notion that handicapped students, whatever the degree of handicap, are free of classroom discipline. *That is not the law.* (Emphasis added.)

124

The Court believed that a five-day suspension was no worse than a brief absence due to a common cold. It felt that the short suspension would benefit the student. It therefore reversed the State Superintendent's order to reinstate the student and upheld the Impartial Hearing Officer's decision.

Exhaustion of Administrative Remedies

Under the due process mandate, plans are provided for the resolution of disputes at the local level. One plan provides parents with procedural safeguards, while the other requires the states that receive federal assistance to file compliance plans. The Commissioner of Education determines whether the plans comply with the statute and is authorized to withhold funds from the state education agency if the plans fail to comply. The state has the opportunity to challenge any adverse decision in the "court of appeals for the circuit in which the state is located." [53] It is clear that Congress intended to enforce Public Law 94-142 with the two detailed remedies.

In many cases, involving individuals with handicapping conditions, the defendants argue that the plaintiffs failed to exhaust their administrative remedies and therefore called on the court to dismiss the action. Under Public Law 94-142 the states are required to set up a plan for administrative remedies. In Virginia, for example, an emotionally disturbed child was expelled from school for alleged violent behavior.[54] The state's plan was as follows:

1. the plaintiff could seek an impartial due process hearing by the local educational agency conducted by an independent hearing officer,
2. an impartial review of the hearing could be held by the State Department of Education.[55]

The court ruled that the plaintiff failed to follow the accepted procedure and held that the suit could not be maintained until he exhausted his administrative remedies.

In *Board of Education of Hendrick Hudson Central School District v. Rowley* [56] referred to earlier in the chapter, the plaintiffs went through the specific procedure adopted by the State of New York until the case was heard by the United States Supreme Court. Amy Rowley's parents refused to accept the individualized education program furnished by the school district because the program did not include the services of a sign language interpreter. The plaintiffs went through the following steps that included the following:

- They commenced proceedings by requesting the District Committee on the Handicapped to reconsider its recommendations;
- When the District Committee refused they appealed to an Independent Hearing Officer;
- After the Hearing Officer upheld the District Committee's plan, they appealed to the Commissioner of Education for the State of New York;
- When the Commissioner's decision was unfavorable, they instituted a lawsuit in the Southern District Court of New York;
- The school district appealed an adverse verdict to the U.S. Court of Appeals, Second Circuit;
- It then appealed that decision to the U.S. Supreme Court which ruled in favor of the school district. [57]

The Supreme Court commented on the doctrine of exhaustion of remedies as early as 1938 when it declared: "no one is entitled to judicial relief for a supposed or threatened injury until the prescribed administrative remedy has been exhausted." [58]

126

In particular, where Congress has enacted a specific scheme for obtaining judicial review which includes a directive to the states to provide effective procedural safe-guards to protect the rights provided by the statute, a Federal court should be circumspect and not exercise its jurisdiction before the contemplated administrative mechanism has had an opportunity to address the alleged deprivation.[59]

In 1968 the United States Supreme Court once again stressed the importance the doctrine serves when it remarked in *McKart v. United States* that:

It allows the agency to develop a factual record, to apply its expertise to a problem, to exercise its discretion, and to correct its own mistakes before a court will intervene. The doctrine thereby promotes accurate results not only at the agency level, but also by allowing more informed judicial review.[60]

It pointed out that the doctrine of exhaustion of remedies was a specific intent of Congress when it commented that:

litigants are discouraged from weakening the position of the agency by flouting its processes, while court resources are reserved for dealing primarily with those matters which could not be resolved administratively. Thus, the doctrine serves interests of accuracy, efficiency, agency autonomy and judicial economy.[61]

In *Mayor and City Council v. Matthews,* the court seems to sum up the positive aspects of exhausting administrative remedies when it commented:

The exhaustion doctrine, which is founded upon such principles as respect for administrative autonomy; a desire that administrative "expertise and discretion" should first be brought to bear upon specialized problems; and conservation of energies and resources.[62]

127

There are times when the doctrine does not serve the best interests of the parties involved. Some examples are listed in *McKart* that include the following:

1. the issue may be a pure matter of law as to which specialized administrative understanding plays little role,
2. agency proceedings may be futile, only delaying ultimate resolution,
3. it may waste resources and also work harm on the litigant.[63]

In *McKart* the Court declared that the legislative history of the Act reflects the understanding that exhaustion is not a rigid requirement.[64]

Senator Harrison Williams, author of the Senate bill, declared during the Conference Report on the Education For All Handicapped Children Act:

> Mr. President, with regard to the complaints, I want to underscore that exhaustion of the administrative procedures established under this part should not be required for any individual complaint filing a judicial action in cases where such exhaustion would be futile either as a legal or practical matter.[65]

There are numerous cases in which the court has ruled that exhaustion of administrative review is not required under Public Law 94-142 because exhaustion would be futile.[66]

In *Fells v. Brooks,* the court held that it would be pointless to pursue administrative remedies since federal funds had been withdrawn from the program and administrative review would represent an empty formality.[67] In *Jose P. v. Ambach,* the court ruled that the plaintiff could waive the administrative proceedings because:

1. the inefficacy of the available administrative remedies has been demonstrated;
2. of absence of a meaningful administrative enforcement mechanism.[68]

The court concluded that when educational benefits are deprived, administrative review is not required.[69]

In *Camenisch v. University of Texas*,[70] a deaf graduate student at the University of Texas filed suit because the University failed to provide a sign-language interpreter. The University declared that it was not obligated to pay for auxiliary aid to graduate students and that Camenisch failed to exhaust his administrative remedies. The court held that extensive delays would cause irreparable harm to the plaintiff thus rendering the administrative remedies inadequate to help him. It ruled that the waiver of exhaustive remedies was justified.

While the question of exhaustion of administrative remedies continues to be a controversial and complex issue, the court in *National Bank of Commerce v. Marshall*[71] predicted that: "The United States Supreme Court may soon address the split between courts applying such an exhaustion rule and those applying an absolute non-exhaustion rule."

Individualized Education Program

Under the Education For All Handicapped Children Act one of the most important aspects in meeting the needs of the child is the provision of an individualized education program (IEP). The IEP is developed by a multidisciplinary team that consists of the following:

- an administrator of the school (usually a principal or counselor),
- the child's teacher or teachers,

129

- one or both parents, and
- the child when appropriate.[72]

The IEP is a legally binding document that must contain the following items:

- the child's present level of performance in each curricular area;
- long range goals and short term objectives;
- a specification of the special educational services and materials which will be provided to help accomplish these goals;
- a statement of the extent to which the child will be integrated with nonhandicapped children in regular school programs;
- a timetable of when special services will begin and how long each service or program will be offered, and;
- a statement of when and how the child's performance and effectiveness of the plan will be evaluated.[73]

(For three examples of IEP's see Appendix C).

Elizabeth A. Kurker-Stewart and David G. Carter, Sr. writing in NOLPE School Law Journal stress the importance of a periodic review of the IEP when they state that: "A review of each handicapped child's individualized education program must be held at least annually to assess the adequacy of services being provided and to consider the appropriateness of the child's placement." [74]

The writers caution that:

> While the individualized education program does not constitute a guarantee on the part of the school district or teacher that the child will progress at a specified rate, it does obligate the school district and teacher to make good faith efforts to help the child achieve the established goals and objectives.[75]

They also stress that the Committee developing the individualized education program keep in mind that: "The handicapped child must be educated 'in the school which he or she would attend if not handicapped' unless the child's individualized education program specifically requires another arrangement." [76]

In "Practical Pointers" several key points are emphasized regarding the IEP that include:

> Until an agreement is reached between the parent or the hearing officer and the school system, the child remains in his/her present educational program. However, once the agreement is reached, and the IEP is signed, the IEP must begin immediately. [77]

Several cases illustrate the attitude of the courts when individualized education programs were challenged by the parents as failing to meet the needs of their child.

The parents of a girl, who suffered severe head injuries when she was in an automobile accident at nine years of age, refused to accept the school district's individualized education program. [78] The parents insisted that the IEP failed to meet the needs of their daughter by not providing an appropriate education.

The United States District Court, Eastern District Virginia, recognized that the parents were attempting to obtain an ideal education for their daughter. It realized that however admirable this aspiration was on their part, it was not practical. The court observed:

> But neither they nor any other parents have the right under the law to write a prescription for an ideal education for their child and to have the prescription filled at public expense. The law requires an appropriate free education. Efforts to build this requirement into something more will threaten the substantial gains already made in the education of the handicapped.

131

The court declared that it found no one who could testify that the girl's program was not appropriate. While it might not be the best or maximum program it was, nevertheless, appropriate. It also took exception to a statement made during the trial that cost should not be a consideration. The court remarked that cost is a factor in determining what is appropriate education for the nonhandicapped child. It stated clearly that: "No language in State or federal law can properly be read as mandating that costs may not be considered in determining what education is appropriate for a child — handicapped or non-handicapped."

It observed that the girl had made consistent progress by performing at a level that was typical for her age, ability and handicapping condition. The court, in denying the parents' request for year-round schooling by changing the IEP, made several observations it felt needed clarification when it said:

> As with any new venture, an education of the
> handicapped in public schools is relatively new,
> there are errors and omissions. But the existence
> of imperfection in the education of Evelyn Bales
> does not mean she is not securing an appropriate
> education under the law.

The United States District Court deplored the fact that the parents took an adversarial position against the school district from the beginning. An atmosphere of "suspicion and mistrust with a decided emphasis on legal rights and entitlements" existed between the parents and school officials.

The court lamented the fact that: "counsel, for plaintiff argues that the parents' constant complaints, criticisms and intimidation led to improvement in plaintiff's education. *But we will never know what a cooperative, constructive, appreciative attitude may have wrought.*" (Emphasis added.)

132

A New York case illustrates once more the various issues that come into a lawsuit. In this case the parents of a fifteen-year-old tenth grade student with a "congenital limb deficiency" brought suit under section 504 of the Rehabilitation Act against the South Colonie Central School.[79]

The parents had accepted the district's individualized education plan but sued when the district refused to permit their daughter to participate in a school-sponsored trip to Spain.

The plaintiff was three and one-half feet in height and her physical makeup was described as follows:

> Her legs are approximately one foot in length; her right arm has been amputated above the elbow and fitted with a prosthetic device. At the end of her left arm, which is shorter than normal, are two partially functional digits.

The plaintiff's parents sought and obtained a special van to transport her to and from school and the services of an aide to protect her from "inadvertent harm from her fellow classmates." The aide would block her from students hurrying to and from classes and also keep her from slipping and falling on the stairways. The plaintiff walks at a speed of about one-half that of a normal student and has difficulty in keeping up with the members of her class. However, she is "above average in intelligence, friendly and highly motivated for a child of her years."

The plaintiff wanted to participate in a trip to Spain by members of her Spanish class. She met the necessary language requirements, obtained a medical release and paid her deposit of $100 for the upcoming trip.

Several months later she was informed by school officials that she could not make the trip without an aide. Her parents refused to provide an aide to accompany her and the school withdrew her from the program and refunded her deposit.

The United States District Court, Northern District New York, recognized that she had a handicapping condition and that the proposed activity came under section 504 guidelines since the school district received federal assistance and school personnel would be supervising the trip. It noted that the issue was the safety of the girl since she would be doing considerable walking on the tour. The court went to considerable lengths to analyze the entire trip and found that one entire day would be spent walking in a Spanish city. It remarked:

> Given her present physical limitations, Jean would be unable to maintain the brisk and physically demanding pace of the group's walking tours and would be unable to ascend and descend the myriad stairways, many of which, as part of historically preserved sites, do not contain bannisters or guardrails necessary for her locomotion and safety.

The court believed that the heavy city traffic and crowded sections of the cities, constituted hazards to her safety. It therefore supported the school district's decision to deny the plaintiff the opportunity to participate with her classmates in the trip to Spain. It commented:

> Since Jean is unable to fulfill the physical requirements of the trip, and since a substantial degree of physical risk to her safety has been demonstrated were she to participate in the program, plaintiff Jean Wolff is not otherwise qualified within the meaning of Section 504 of the Act.

Margaret Lang, an eighteen-year-old student and her parents sued the Braintree School Committee and the Massachusetts Board of Education for developing an individualized education program (IEP) they felt denied her an appropriate education within the guidelines of the Education For All Handicapped Children Act.[80] The plaintiffs wanted the Braintree School Committee to continue to finance Margaret's education at a private school (St. Coletta's Day School) which she attended since 1971.

The defendants developed an IEP that provided that Margaret receive an education in the public school with special educational components consisting of: "a special education classroom with qualified special education teachers, speech and physical therapy, art, music, physical education and other non-academic subjects, and a special summer program."

They contend that their IEP is educationally sound and will enable Margaret to receive a more appropriate education than the one offered at the private school. They felt that Margaret would be in a least restrictive environment which would give her the opportunity to interact with students of "similar or somewhat superior skills."

The plaintiffs admitted that the Braintree program is basically satisfactory but contended that there were several disadvantages that made the plan unacceptable. They listed them as follows:

(1) the change from the private school to the public school would be psychologically and developmentally devastating,

(2) the Braintree program posed a safety threat because of the numerous stairs Margaret would be required to use, and

(3) the IEP was procedurally defective because the addenda were prepared without the parents consultation.

Several experts and faculty members testified at the administrative hearing and stated that the Braintree plan,

135

while a good one, would create a "severe psychotic regression which might be irreversible" because of the transfer from one school to another. A neurologist reported that the trauma of the move would be no different for Margaret than any child who was required to change schools after eight years. He felt that the key to the transition would be the influence of the parents over the move. Several faculty members of the St. Coletta's School testified that they were concerned that Margaret might feel out of place in the public school and be humiliated.

A teacher at the public school spoke in behalf of the defendants and declared that: "she considers herself able to handle Margaret's intellectual level, and that she uses positive behavior modification methods."

The special needs teacher expressed the opinion that the interaction with "normal" children would be beneficial to Margaret.

The district court felt that the educational program planned for the plaintiff was appropriate and sound. It concluded that the Braintree's offering was satisfactory under Public Law 94-142. It questioned the defendants claim for the reimbursement of funds expended by the local committee to maintain the plaintiff in St. Coletta's School pursuant to the court order of April 15, 1980. It reasoned that the procedural requirements of Public Law 94-142 require the school district to include the parents attendance at the meeting to develop an IEP for their child. The court observed that the parents were not included in the long-range planning meeting. The defendants had argued that this was corrected when the parents were included in the administrative hearing.

The court concluded that since Braintree had failed to include the parents in the IEP meeting, the parents should not be required to reimburse the school for the amount needed to keep their daughter at St. Coletta's School. It denied Braintree's request for compensation from the parents and directed the plaintiff to attend the public school.

Although these four key mandates may continue to be challenged in the courts, judicial decisions such as those reviewed in this chapter will help school officials interpret the attitude of the court regarding their implementation. The physical education teacher and coach, along with all school people, need to understand these decisions so that they can develop the parameters by which they can operate their programs.

Summary

Public Law 94-142 emphasizes the importance Congress places on physical education by making it the only required area of the curriculum for exceptional children when a child has special physical and mental needs. The law discourages medical excuses intended to waive the physical education requirement and the substitution of physical therapy for physical education.

Public Law 94-142 has four key mandates providing for: a free appropriate education, least restrictive placement, due process and an individualized education program for all students.

The courts have interpreted an appropriate education to be one that meets the child's needs and enables that child to live as independently as conditions permit. At times an appropriate education requires around the clock residential care and year-round programs. The courts insist on timely hearings since delays of several months can often cause the student to regress in a way that may never be overcome.

The intent of Public Law 94-142 is to eliminate labels and the grouping of students according to labels. While placing students in the least restrictive placement does not mandate mainstreaming, it does encourage placing the student with the nonhandicapped whenever possible. The key to placement is the intent to place the child in an environment that best meets the needs of the child.

Under the provisions of Public Law 94-142, student, parent and the local education agency are guaranteed procedural due process to challenge a school's decision regarding appropriate education, placement and individualized education plans. Parents are urged, however, to attempt to settle disputes on a cooperative basis with school officials and exhaust administrative remedies before instituting judicial action.

The parent has six legal actions available to challenge the school that include:

- Appeal to the local school officials;
- Request an independent evaluation;
- Request a hearing from an independent and neutral hearing officer;
- File an administrative appeal;
- File a complaint to the Office For Civil Rights;
- File a lawsuit.

Regarding exclusion, the courts have been consistent in their rulings. Students involved in disciplinary action are required to remain in their present educational environment until the placement question is decided. Schools can use normal procedures of discipline with disruptive students. Suspension can be a valuable educational device as well as a necessary tool to maintain order, and temporary suspension should not be equated with expulsion. Any change in placement, however, must be made by a Placement and Planning Team that considers the child's needs. The intent of Public Law 94-142 is to appropriately place the disruptive student rather than

138

exclude him/her. While expulsion may be a proper disciplinary tool, complete cessation of educational services is not.

Under Public Law 94-142 an individualized education program (IEP) must be developed for each child by a multi-disciplinary team. The team consists of: an administrator (usually the principal or counselor), the child's teacher(s), one or both parents, and the child, when appropriate. Since physical education is required, a physical education teacher should be included on a voluntary basis. The IEP is a legally binding document and should be reviewed annually to assess the adequacy of the child's placement. The child must remain in his/her present program until the parent and school system reach an agreement on the IEP. Once agreement is reached and the IEP signed, it becomes effective immediately. While the IEP is legally binding, teachers and administrators cannot be held accountable if an individual student fails to achieve specific goals and objectives. Teachers are held accountable for failing to follow or implement procedures agreed in the IEP.

The State of Utah instituted a plan to develop an individualized education program for every student. Since 1974 nonhandicapped students as well as those with handicapping conditions are the recipients of an IEP. (See Appendix C.)

The effect of the courts in interpreting the mandates of Public Law 94-142 cannot be minimized. Judicial decisions are interpreting complex and often confusing provisions of the law and enabling school officials to develop sound educational and legal parameters for compliance.

FOOTNOTES

1. Public Law 94-142, 89 Stat. 773 (1975).

2. Interpretations of Section 504 and Public Law 94-142, the Unit on Programs for the Handicapped, American Alliance of Health, Physical Education, Recreation & Dance, Update, Washington D.C., 1977.

3. Lynn Erb & Cecil D. Mercer, *Legislation for the Handicapped in Brief,* NOLPE SCHOOL LAW JOURNAL, Vol. 7, No. 2, 1977.

4. Board of Education of Hendrick Hudson Central School District v. Rowley, 102 S. Ct. 3034 (1982).

5. *Id.*

6. Springdale School District v. Grace, 494 F. Supp. 266 (W.D. Ark. 1980).

7. Springdale School District v. Grace, 658 F.2d 300 (8th Cir. 1981).

8. Shanberg v. Commonwealth of Pennsylvania et. al., 426 A.2d 232 (Pa. 1981).

9. North Carolina Association for Retarded Citizens v. State of North Carolina Board of Public Instruction, C.A. No. 3050 (E.D.N.C. 1978).

10. Hines v. Pitt County Board of Education, 497 F. Supp. 403 (E.D.N.C. 1980).

11. 45 C. F. S. Sec. 121 a 552 (a) (2).

12. *Id.*

13. Connecticut Association for Retarded Citizens v. State Board of Education, H77-122 (C. Conn. 1977).

14. Michigan Association for Retarded Citizens v. Trasverse Bay Area Intermediate School District, CC No. 77-5812-C-2 (Grand Traverse County Circuit Court, 1977).

15. Doe v. Grile, Civ. No. F 77-108 (N.D. Ind. 1978).

16. Stephen L. v. Indiana State Board of Special Education Appeals, No. F-78-6 (N.D. Ind. 1978).

17. Saunders v. Prince Georges County Board of Education, No. 77-1882 (D. Md. 1977).

18. Pickett v. Prince Georges County Board of Education, No. 77-1883 (D. Md. 1977).

19. Armstrong v. Kline, 476 F. Supp. 583 (E.D. Pa. 1979).

20. Battle v. Commonwealth of Pennsylvania, 629 F.2d 269 (3d Cir. 1980).

20.1. Anderson v. Thompson, 495 F. Supp. 1256 (E.D. Wisc. 1980).

21. Anderson v. Thompson, 658 F.2d 1205 (7th Cir. 1981).

22. Gladys J. v. Pearland Independent School District, 520 F. Supp. 869 (S.D. Texas 1981).

23. Krawitz v. Commonwealth of Pennsylvania, 408 A.2d 1202 (Pa. 1979).

24. *School Law News,* Capital Publications, Inc., Washington, D.C., Vol. 7, 1979.

25. *Id.*

26. *Practical Pointers,* Physical Education, and Recreation for the Handicapped: Information and Research Utilization Center, Washington, D.C., Vol. 1, No. 6, 1977.

27. *Id.*

28. *Id.*

29. Kruelle v. Biggs, 489 F. Supp. 169 (D. Del. 1980).

30. Espino v. Besteiro, 520 F. Supp. 905 (S.D. Tex. 1981).

31. Garrity v. Gallen, 522 F. Supp. 171 (D.H.N. 1981).

32. Department of Education, State of Hawaii v. Katherine D., 531 F Supp. 517 (D. Hawaii 1982).

33. HERB APPENZELLER, ATHLETICS AND THE LAW, The Michie Co., Charlottesville, Virginia, 1975.

34. Davidson v. New Orleans, 96 U.S. 97 (1887).

35. K. ALEXANDER, R. CORNS, W. MCCANN, PUBLIC SCHOOL LAW, West Publishing Co., St. Paul, Minn. 1969.

36. *Id.*

37. 1972-1973 ANNUAL SURVEY OF AMERICAN LAW, New York University.

38. Dixon v. Alabama State Board of Education, 294 F.2d 150 (5th Cir. 1961).

39. *Supra* note 35.

40. *Supra* note 24.

41. *Id.*

42. *Id.*

43. *Id.*

44. H. C. HUDGINS, JR. & RICHARD S. VACCA, LAW AND EDUCATION: CONTEMPORARY ISSUES AND COURT DECISIONS, The Michie Company, Charlottesville, Virginia, 1979.

45. *Id.*

46. Federal Register, August 23 1977, p. 42491.

47. *Id.*

48. Stuart v. Nappi, 443 F. Supp. 1235 (D. Conn. 1978).

49. Doe v. Amrig, 500 F. Supp. 802 (D. Mass. 1980).

50. S-1, P-1, et al. v. Turlington, 635 F.2d ___ (5th Cir. 1981).

51. Board of Education of the City of Peoria, School District 150 v. Illinois State Board of Education, 531 F. Supp. 182 (C.D. Ill. 1982).

52. Goss v. Lopez, 419 U.S. 565, 95 S. Ct. 729, 42 L. Ed. 2d 725 (1975).

53. *Supra* note 1.

54. *Id.*

55. Harris v. Campbell, 472 F. Supp. 51 (E.D. Va. 1979).

56. *Supra* note 4.

57. *Id.*

58. Myers v. Bethlehem Shipbuilding Corp., 303 U.S. 41, 58 S. Ct. 459, 82 L. Ed. 638 (1938).

59. H.R. v. Hornbeck, 3 E.H.L.R. 553:139 (1981).

60. McKart v. United States, 395 U.S. 185, 85 S. Ct. 1657, 23 L. Ed. 2d 194 (1968).

61. *Id.*

62. Mayor and City Council v. Matthews, 562 F.2d 914 (4th Cir. 1977).

63. *Supra* note 58.

64. *Id.*

65. 121 Cong. Rec. 37416 (1975).

66. *See* Sessions v. Livingston Parish School Bd., 501 F. Supp. 251 (M.D. La. 1980); Monohan v. Nebraska, 491 F. Supp. 1074 (D. Neb. 1980); Doe v. Koger, 480 F. Supp. 225 (N.D. Ind. 1979); Armstrong v. Kline, 476 F. Supp. 583 (E.D. Pa. 1979); Harris v. Campbell, 472 F. Supp. 51 (E.D. Va. 1979); Longhran v. Flanders, 470 F. Supp. 110 (D. Conn. 1979).

67. Fells v. Brooks, 522 F. Supp. 30 (D.D.C. 1981).

68. Jose P. v. Ambach, 669 F.2d 865 (2d Cir. 1982).

69. Sessions, note 63.

70. Camenisch v. University of Texas, 616 F.2d 127 (5th Cir. 1980).

71. National Bank of Commerce v. Marshall, 628 F.2d 474 (5th Cir. 1980).

72. *Supra* note 49.

73. *Id.*

74. Elizabeth A. Kurker-Stewart & David G. Carter, Sr., *Educational Malpractice and Public Law 94-142: A New Dilemma for Educators,* NOLPE School Law Journal, Vol. 10, No. 1, 1981.

75. *Id.*

76. *Id.*

77. *Supra* note 40.

78. Bales v. Clarke, 523 F. Supp. 1366 (E.D. Va. 1981).

79. Wolff v. South Colonie Central School District, 534 F. Supp. 758 (N.D.N.Y. 1982).

80. Lang v. Braintree School Committee, 545 F. Supp. 1221 (D. Mass. 1982).

CHAPTER 6

Eligibility Rules For Sports Participation

Although federal legislation prohibits discrimination toward individuals with handicapping conditions, many athletic governing organizations have rules that prevent these individuals from sports competition. For years the various state high school athletic associations have implemented rules that deal with age requirements, good conduct codes, post season play, "redshirting," summer camps, and issues involving transfers. These associations have successfully enforced eligibility rules and seem to win the majority of their lawsuits.

The Supreme Court of Georgia made a comment in a case involving athletic eligibility that seems to sum up the attitude of courts toward governing organizations regarding the necessity of rules and regulations when it said:

> Although the rule appears harsh in this case, the general goals of keeping high school interscholastic activities competitive and safe by allowing children of relatively equal maturity to compete, of insuring that as many children as possible are able to participate by limiting the number of eligible years for each student, and of protecting students from exploitation by coaches seeking to obtain transfers, to "redshirt" or to delay a student's normal progress in school are met by the rule.[1]

Many individuals with handicapping conditions are no longer willing to accept exclusion from sports because of established rules and are now seeking redress in court in ever-increasing numbers.

One of the rules that is being challenged is the age requirement that prohibits participation in sports after a certain age. In most states the age limit is nineteen but in a few states such as Maine, North Dakota and Washington the limit has been extended to twenty years of age.[2]

Gregory Amrig, the Massachusetts Commissioner of Education, became aware of the seriousness of the age rule when two high school students in Newton with hearing impairments faced expulsion from the high school basketball program when they reached the age of nineteen. The boys had been retained in the lower grades because of their handicapping condition and, now as students attending special education classes, faced termination from sports.

Amrig expressed his concern in a letter of August 23, 1979 to Bertram Holland, the Executive Director of the Massachusetts Interscholastic Athletic Association (MIAA). Amrig questioned whether the age rule was in violation of section 504 of the Rehabilitation Act and Public Law 94-142 of the Education For All Handicapped Children Act. He applauded the MIAA's action in waiving the age rule for a student with a handicapping condition which enabled the student to participate in interscholastic swimming. Amrig urged the MIAA to pursue a flexible policy with its eligibility rules so that students with handicapping conditions could have their special needs met through participation in sports.

Two court cases illustrate the attitude of the court and the reason for concern.

Scott Chambers was afflicted with asthma and a condition known as dyslexia.[3] The pressure to read and keep up with his classmates increased his asthma attacks and hindered him in his school work. Scott's parents were encouraged to have their son repeat the second grade so that he could learn to cope with his learning disability. They were assured that their son would rejoin his regular classmates the following year. Instead, Scott was compelled

144

to repeat the grade a second time although the decision affected his emotional and physical well-being.

When Scott reached nineteen he sought an injunction so that he could compete in ice hockey. He insisted that participation in sports enabled him to release tensions and anxieties which helped his asthmatic condition and dyslexia. Scott claimed that the MIAA's rule regarding age was unconstitutional since Massachusetts law provided that individuals from ages three through twenty-one could not be denied the right of equal educational opportunity "on the basis of national origin, sex, economic status, race, religion and physical or mental handicap." He contended that sports participation is a "part of the total educational process."

The eligibility committee of the Massachusetts Interscholastic Athletic Council (MIAC) denied the plaintiff's request for a waiver of the age rule for the following reasons:

1. Individuals on reaching the 19th birthday are too mature physically, mentally, emotionally to compete against less mature school boys and/or school girls.
2. Age limits must be set somewhere.
3. His participation would prevent the participation of another eligible player.

Justice Samuel Adams reasoned that the age rule was not arbitrary, capricious, nor constitutionally invalid. He concluded:

Although special need students through ages twenty-one (21) cannot be denied the equal educational opportunities on the basis of a physical or mental handicap, age limitations on interscholastic athletics grounded on safety and fairness do not violate this principle. The denial of the educational opportunity based on age does not constitute a denial based on a handicap.

145

In a similar case, Jeffrey McNulty challenged the Massachusetts Interscholastic Athletic Association's rule regarding "age limits." [4] McNulty wanted to participate in football, but because he was held back in the lower grades because of his disability, he was in violation of the "nineteen-year-old" rule in Massachusetts.

Superior Court Justice Thomas R. Morse, Jr. remarked that the case was being considered for a second time because there was a question regarding the Eligibility Review Board's decision. The court had directed the Review Board to determine whether the rule in question accomplished its purpose, whether it imposed a hardship on the student and whether the granting of the waiver would result in an unfair advantage to other students.

The court felt that the Review Board "applied a different standard than set out above" and Justice Morse declared that:

> The Board's decision is significantly wanting in that kind of support one would expect under Chapter 30 A review of agency decisions. But this proceeding is in the nature of certiorari and the record is characteristic of what can reasonably be expected from persons who may not be lawyers, and who are called upon to administer an extremely difficult problem which frequently may have emotional overtones.

He then commented that he was concerned by the fact that the Review Board may have assumed that all nineteen-year-old students should be denied participation in contact sports such as football. Although Justice Morse expressed concern, he noted that the court should not attempt to "substitute its judgment for that of the board." He therefore refused to grant relief to McNulty by concluding:

146

I cannot rule that the Board was wrong as a matter of law in focusing as it did on height, weight and maturity — I am not persuaded of any likelihood of success on the merits, although there is support for a finding of irreparable harm.

While it appears that an overwhelming number of court cases involving challenges by athletes and their parents are decided in favor of defendant governing organizations, there are exceptions made to established rules under "hardship" petitions. Simon Terrell, Executive Director of the North Carolina High School Athletic Association, reported that student-athletes frequently seek exceptions to the rules on the basis of hardship. Terrell notes that approximately one-half of all hardship petitions heard in North Carolina are waived.[5] Courts in various states have considered petitions for hardship with different results.

In Georgia, an athlete was denied the opportunity to participate in football, soccer and track because he had completed eight semesters of school work.[6] The athlete based his appeal on the fact that he had dropped out of school to help his widowed mother who was ill. The Supreme Court of Georgia upheld the trial court's decision refusing him the opportunity to participate in the sports program.

While the Supreme Court of Georgia's decision is convincing and typical of most cases of this nature, courts at times take the other side of similar issues and favor the student-athlete.

Dennis Lee attended school in California until the eleventh grade when he moved to Florida.[7] Lee stayed out of school in Florida to support his family and, a year later, enrolled in Hialeah Miami Lakes High School. He was informed that he was ineligible for sports since the Florida High School Activities Association (FHSAA) rules limit

147

sport participation to four consecutive years in high school. Lee appealed to the FHSAA on the basis of hardship. He explained that he could earn a college athletic scholarship if he had the opportunity to participate in sports during his senior year. The FHSAA refused to grant Lee an exception but the Court of Appeals of Florida viewed the Association's rule as arbitrary and reversed its decision.

In like manner, the District Court of Appeals of Florida, affirmed a circuit court's order granting Aaron Bryant injunctive relief against the FHSAA's eligibility rule.[8] Bryant argued that participation in high school sports had improved his academic work and his "attitude, self-confidence, discipline and maturity." The court credited his participation in sports with his rehabilitation from past problems. It concluded that "redshirting" was not involved and therefore approved his participation in sports.

Dr. Julian U. Stein, conducted a survey for the American Alliance of Health, Physical Education, Recreation and Dance in 1967. Stein, at that time was the AAHPERD's Director of the Unit on Programs for the Handicapped. He surveyed the fifty states and the District of Columbia to determine the status of academic eligibility rules regarding mentally retarded students who wanted to participate in high school sports.[9] All but two responded with the following results:

Category	Number	Per Cent
Eligible	22	44.0
Eligible on the basis of broad interpretation of by-laws	10	20.0
Not Eligible	17	34.0
	49	98.0

148

Some specific rules regarding the academic eligibility of mentally retarded students were as follows:

1. If a student meets the qualifications of the state Department of Education for special education, the scholastic requirement of one and one-half units is waived in order that the student be eligible to participate in athletics.

2. Special classes, educable (I.Q. 50-80) must pass three fourths of the work assigned at their level. It is not the intent of the high school league to make a student ineligible due to lack of (scholastic) ability. We question whether any student working to capacity becomes scholastically ineligible.

3. Mentally retarded pupils classified as "ungraded" and enrolled in "special" or "opportunity" classes shall be eligible for interscholastic athletic competition when they are graded as "satisfactory" in three-fourths of their requirements and are approved by the principal as good citizens. The enrollment of a student in one of these classes must be approved by the Special Education Division of the Department of Public Instruction.

4. Students must be certified as doing satisfactory work in the special education classes to which they have been assigned.

5. Only an age requirement; most school districts feel that retarded children never fail.

6. A boy who is making satisfactory progress in a school prescribed course as a member of a special slow-learning class may be exempted from the normal scholarship requirement.

7. Programs for exceptional students are referred to the Executive Committee for interpretation. (The Committee has taken under advisement each such request and in

149

some instances has indicated that the course offered meets the intent of the League scholarship standard but in other situations they have not reacted favorably).

In the states that deny sports participation to the mentally retarded student, they made the following comments:

1. Inability to satisfy academic minimums required of all students.
2. Academic requirements in retarded curriculum are not in harmony with those who are forced to meet higher standards.
3. Not eligible on any level for any team if they do not meet our regular requirements.
4. Our eligibility rules make no differentiation between scholastic requirements for any pupil as they must all meet a passing standard regardless of their situation.
5. [A] passing average in each of at least three full-credit high school studies.
6. Our state association does not prohibit the mentally retarded from participating on athletic teams, provided they are carrying a sufficient academic load, and are receiving credits that count toward graduation.
7. Interscholastic athletics are for the privileged and the most highly skilled high school students. The privilege of participating must be earned by meeting minimum standards of eligibility. Only students who will receive diplomas are eligible. Special students as described do not receive diplomas.

Stein listed additional comments from respondents to the survey that include the following:

1. We certainly would be taking a step backward if we allowed students to participate who

were not even enrolled in regular academic courses.

2. Again, let me say we are not denying mentally retarded children the opportunity to participate because they are mentally retarded, but because they do not meet our eligibility standards.

3. ... I believe firmly that participation in the interscholastic program should be reserved for those who earn the privilege. I recognize that many times and particularly in the case of retarded youngsters, it is not possible for them to earn this privilege in competition with other youngsters. This is unfortunate, although in many cases, it would seem to me that a retarded youngster would not want to display himself in the interscholastic program.

As a result of the survey Stein commented that there are many values to be derived through sports participation by mentally retarded students. He decried the fact that many retarded students are prohibited from participation by rules of governing athletic bodies. He predicted that legislation would be forthcoming that would enable the mentally retarded students to earn their eligibility for sports participation. He made several suggestions regarding the existing problem such as:

1. In those states where the retarded are eligible; by-laws should be reviewed to evaluate their effectiveness and identify any problem associated with the rule and its implementation.

2. In those states where the retarded are now eligible on the basis of appeal procedures, consideration should be given to amending by-laws so that definite procedures are established whereby the retarded may earn eligibility without the necessity of insti-

tuting an appeal to the Executive Committee, Board of Control, or Legislative Council.

3. In those states where the retarded are considered eligible on the basis of a broad interpretation of existing by-laws, definite procedures should be considered for inclusion in the by-laws so that there can be no doubt as to the ways in which the retarded may earn eligibility.

4. In those states where the retarded are not now eligible, addition of appropriate sections to the by-laws should be considered so that the retarded may earn eligibility.

Stein made several additional recommendations that included:

1. The inclusion of procedures to inform those at the local level of the changes in the by-laws which will permit the retarded to earn eligibility for participation in the interscholastic athletic program. Procedures can include special notification from the executive secretary to principals, athletic directors and coaches, of appropriate changes in the handbook, information in periodic bulletins and newsletters, and any other method deemed appropriate by the respective state group.

2. The inclusion of procedures to interpret the rule to all concerned in those states where the retarded can now earn eligibility. Those connected with athletic programs in schools with special education units should encourage the retarded to try out for teams and carry them on squads when they make the team.

Stein concluded his report with the hope that the National Federation of State High School Athletic

Associations would consider the recommendations made in the study and help eliminate inequality in sports programs throughout the nation.[10]

A survey was taken in 1982 to determine whether recent federal legislation had changed the rules of eligibility for the mentally retarded in the various states. The following data was reported:

Category	Number	Per Cent
Eligible	28	66.6
Not Eligible	14	33.3
States Reporting	42	100.0[11]

Although fewer states returned the questionnaire in 1982, it is evident that there is little change in the number of states that permit the mentally retarded student to participate in sports. In states that are flexible regarding eligibility rules, many interesting comments were made that include the following:

1. Each school district determines eligibility according to our standards. In many special education programs students cannot fail.
2. The decision on eligibility is left to the discretion of the principal who decides on the progress the student is making.
3. In EMR-TMR and Certificate programs, students are graded S and U and this is acceptable for eligibility.
4. Most students with handicapping conditions are mainstreamed and the local school determines if the individual is making satisfactory progress to meet eligibility requirements.
5. All mentally retarded students are waived.
6. We require 15 hours in a curriculum specifically designed to meet their needs.

153

7. The Association has no academic requirements. Students must be bona fide enrollees only. Local academic requirements are reflected.

8. Academic athletic eligibility is determined at the local level. There has not been any problem with the mentally retarded students as they are academically assessed on the basis of achievement compared to potential.

9. Pupils enrolled in "exceptional students" classes shall be eligible for participation in interscholastic athletics . . . provided that in the opinion of the principal and teacher, such pupil is making "satisfactory progress." "Satisfactory progress" is interpreted to mean that the pupil passes at least one academic subject on his level and two non-academic subjects. All other regulations of this Association shall be met.

10. An exception shall be made for any student who made standard progress for his level in a special education program for the handicapped which followed standards set by the Special Education Service of the State Department of Education.

Medical Disqualification

Several years ago the American Medical Association (AMA) set guidelines for disqualification from certain sports for conditions that included uncontrolled diabetes, jaundice, active tuberculosis, enlarged liver and the absence of a paired organ. (See Appendix D).[12]

The AMA guidelines were merely recommendations but many school officials accepted and enforced them as mandatory requirements. Countless numbers of student-athletes were denied participation in contact sports such as football, hockey, lacrosse, baseball, soccer, basketball and wrestling because of these guidelines. It appears that the majority of student-athletes, with conditions specified in the AMA guidelines, reluctantly accepted the decision prohibiting them from sports competition without the threat of a lawsuit. Today, however, student-athletes with physical impairments often refuse such prohibition and seek judicial redress, insisting that federal laws guarantee them the opportunity to participate in sports on the club, interscholastic, intramural and intercollegiate level.

The following cases illustrate the problems that often confront athletes, parents, physicians and school officials when student-athletes with handicapping conditions are denied participation in sports.

The Physically Impaired Athlete

Visually Impaired

A case that has had a tremendous impact on student-athletes with physical disabilities took place in New York in 1973.[13] Joseph Spitaleri sustained a serious eye injury at the age of six that resulted in a complete loss of vision in one eye but was an outstanding athlete in all sports including football despite his impairment of vision.

Spitaleri was disqualified for competition in football at the high school level by the school physician. The physician referred to the criteria set by the American Medical Association, which recommends prohibition from contact sports when the athlete is without a vital organ such as a kidney or an eye. Spitaleri's father pleaded with the school authorities to permit his son to play football since he felt that refusal would damage his son's well-being. The father agreed to waive responsibility for the school authorities by assuming all the risks involved in his son's participation in football. The Commissioner of Education of New York ignored the father's petition and upheld the physician's ruling as did the New York Superior Court that reasoned that the rule was designed to protect the young athlete from possible injury.

As a result of the decision in the *Spitaleri* case, statewide attention was focused on the problem. The New York Legislature attempted to correct what it believed was an unjust situation by enacting Senate Bill 1440 which became known as the "Spitaleri Bill." The legislature explained its rationale for enacting the bill by declaring:

> Because the State Education Department has tied together the medical and legal issues, a student who has a disqualifying condition cannot expect to receive permission to play a contact sport, regardless of the fact that objectively he might be medically capable. In addition, such decisions are insulated by the procedure for appealing administrative determinations, this procedure does not afford to a petitioner the review of the merits of conflicting opinions. The concern of both the court and Commissioner is with the possible arbitrariness of a determination. If a school physician's decision has some basis in reason, it will be upheld. The conflicting opinion from a private physician is not reviewed or considered although it might be more reasonable.[14]

Soon after the bill was passed, two students in New York, each having one eye, were denied permission to participate in contact sports by the court.[15] The court decided that the danger of injury to their remaining eyes was just too great a risk to take. One of the students, Margaret Kampmeier, pointed to the newly enacted "Spitaleri Bill" which stated that:

> Upon the verified petition of a parent/guardian and affidavits of two licensed physicians, the court would weigh the merits of the conflicting opinion of the school physician and the private

156

physicians. A determination could be made as to which of the two opinions would be in the best interests of the student.[16]

The "Spitaleri Bill" also extended protection for the physician and school district by providing that: "This determination would release the physicians and school districts from liability for the students' participation in a sport since the court would be necessarily dictating what is reasonable and prudent under the circumstances." [17]

The Supreme Court of New York, County of Monroe, recognized the fact that Kampmeier had met the requirements of the Spitaleri law by furnishing the court with two affidavits from two physicians who expressed the opinion that she could engage in school sports. The physicians believed that the sports program would be "reasonably safe" for her.

The New York court was troubled by the fact that the statute insulated the school district in advance from liability. It was unhappy over this immunity and the possibility that the girl's parents might be unable to obtain insurance to protect their daughter if she sustained an injury. For these reasons the court ruled that it was not in her best interest to participate in a contact sport.

Margaret Kampmeier refused to accept the adverse decision and appealed to the Supreme Court of New York, Appellate Division. The court found that the plaintiff was an exceptional athlete who would profit from participation in sports. It believed that she would be reasonably safe in competition as long as she used protective eyeglasses. It, therefore, reversed the lower court's decision and granted her permission to participate in the junior high school's sports program.[18]

In a similar situation, the New York Supreme Court, Albany County, allowed a high school freshman to

157

participate in sports despite impaired vision.[19] Kim Swiderski had defective vision in her right eye since birth. The impairment was described as a "congenital cataract and an underdeveloped optic nerve."

Kim's mother sought a court order which would allow her daughter to participate in sports at Albany High School. She furnished two affidavits from licensed physicians who claimed that sports participation was in Kim's best interest. The school officials opposed the claim and chose to rely on the school physician's contention that an injury to Kim's eye could cause the school district to be held liable.

The Supreme Court, Special Term, Albany County, decided, however, that the girl's interest would be best satisfied by sports participation. It ruled that she be permitted to engage in sports as long as she used protective eye shields as recommended by her physician. The court then declared that the school district would not be held liable for injury to the plaintiff under a provision of the education law.

Mike Borden, an outstanding high school basketball player in Ohio, tried out for the junior varsity basketball team at Ohio University.[20] Borden made the team one day, was examined by the school physician the next and was subsequently dismissed the following day because he had only one eye. Borden's dismissal aroused support in his behalf on the Ohio campus and throughout the State of Ohio. Borden commented that all his life people had encouraged him because he had only one eye and now it was being held against him. He insisted that he was not materially handicapped since he had been blind in one eye from the time he was three years of age, yet had been successful both in academics and athletics. He declared: "I didn't know what it was like to have two eyes . . . that would be a dream . . . but I know I can compete with anyone." [21]

158

Borden sought and obtained an injunction from the court enabling him to rejoin the team with the consent of the university. In his first collegiate game he scored twenty-two points and pulled down eight rebounds. The following year, although the court order was no longer in effect, the university officials refused to pursue the issue and Borden was allowed to participate on the basketball team.[22]

In a similar situation Kinney Redding and Keith Evans, both outstanding athletes at Missouri Western State College, were told by the team physician that they could not play football because each one was blind in the left eye.[23]

A federal judge granted both players permission to play football as soon as they signed a waiver releasing the college from liability. The judge felt that the failure to play would cause them serious damage and that it would represent a violation of their constitutional rights.

Although section 504 of the Rehabilitation Act was in force, there was no mention of it in the preceding cases. It was the basis of a recent case, however, in which an outstanding athlete was denied participation in intercollegiate football because he had sight in only one eye.[24] Joseph Wright, a recipient of academic awards and an outstanding Pennsylvania high school running back, was offered a grant-in-aid to play football for Columbia University. Columbia's physician, after consultation with Wright and the university's legal counsel wrote to the athletic director and recommended that he not be permitted to play intercollegiate football.

The plaintiff sought relief through a temporary restraining order since the football season was scheduled to begin in one week. He claimed that the university's action deprived him of rights under section 504 of the Rehabilitation Act that stated:

159

> No otherwise qualified handicapped individual
> ... as defined in Section 706(7) of this title, shall
> solely by reason of his handicap, be excluded
> from participation in, be denied benefits of, or be
> subject to discrimination under any program or
> activity receiving federal financial assistance.

The plaintiff insisted that he was qualified "aside from the handicap" to participate in football and his coaches supported his contention. He also declared that he and his parents were fully aware of the consequences of an injury to his left eye and were willing to sign a waiver releasing the university from any possible liability that might arise.

Columbia University's officials referred to a Michigan case in which a judge ruled that Title IX did not apply to specific programs that did not receive federal assistance.[25] Therefore, a Michigan High School did not have to permit a girl to play on the all-male golf team or create a separate team for girls. Columbia University argued that the same principle applied to them since their athletic program did not receive federal assistance and was not, therefore, subject to section 504 of the Rehabilitation Act.

The court refused to accept this argument by stating that:

> True, some relationship exists among and
> between Title VI, Title IX and Section 504.
> However, Columbia's contention that such a
> kinship compels the conclusion that analysis
> under Title VI and Title IX must be adopted
> whole cloth and applied to Section 504 forces the
> kinship to an unwarranted degree of
> consanguinity.

It then pointed out the fact that the regulations of section 504 define a recipient of federal funds as: "any public or private agency, institution, organization, or other entity, or any person to which federal assistance is extended directly or through another recipient."

The court then made an important observation regarding federal funding when it declared:

> Moreover, to accept defendant's argument would allow major institutions receiving substantial amounts of federal aid to dissect themselves, at whim, into discrete entities, to allocate federal dollars into programs which cannot discriminate against handicapped persons, and to free privately obtained funds from those programs and instead to channel such money into programs purportedly immune from Section 504 strictures. Columbia's construction of Section 504 would sanction this circumvention of federal policy against discrimination for institutions benefiting from federal aid.

The court referred to a New Jersey case in which a high school student was denied the opportunity to participate in the wrestling program because he had only one kidney.[26] The New Jersey court found the school's decision to prohibit participation in the wrestling program to violate section 504 regulations. It also noted that Wright had furnished proof from a "highly qualified ophthalmologist that no substantial risk of serious eye injury related to football exists." [27] The court recognized the university's concern for the welfare of one of its students but once again referred to *Poole* in which the court declared:

> Such motives, while laudably evidencing Columbia's concern for its students' well-being, derrogate from the rights secured to plaintiff under Section 504, which prohibits "paternalistic authorities" from deciding that certain activities are "too risky" for a handicapped person.[28]

It reasoned that the plaintiff's desire to participate in sports and by hard work overcome "enormous odds" was in the public interest. It, therefore, granted the plaintiff his petition for a temporary restraining order enjoining the university from "denying plaintiff the opportunity of participating in the intercollegiate football program because of his visual handicap." [29]

Hearing Impaired

John Colombo had a marked hearing loss of fifty percent in his left ear and a profound loss of hearing in his right ear.[30] The hearing loss had existed since birth and he used a hearing aid in his left ear. The doctor who examined him reported that Colombo could hear normal conversation if he was facing the person who was talking, but little else. For this reason the doctor discouraged participation in sports such as football, lacrosse or soccer. The doctor described the boy's hearing defect as one that: "leaves him with a permanent auditory blind right side that causes him to be vulnerable to the risk of bodily injury when compared to students with a full sensory perception."

The New York State Department based its decision to deny Colombo participation in contact sports on the recommendations of the AMA regarding disqualifying physical conditions. His parents pursued the issue by pointing out that the school physician was not aware of certain relevant facts when he refused to permit their son to play. These included:

1. Both parents gave their son approval to play;
2. The boy was an exceptional and talented athlete;
3. The boy had competed successfully in sports without an injury;
4. The boy had played football with nonschool groups;
5. The ruling not to allow him to participate caused him psychological damage and resulted in a lack of interest in school because he felt inferior to his classmates.

162

The boy's father explained that the family lacked the finances to send John to college and hoped, instead, that he would win an athletic scholarship if allowed to play. The father promised to assume all risk of injury to his son, including total deafness.

The Assistant Director of Admissions at Gallaudet College, a school for the deaf, testified in behalf of the plaintiff. He reported that between 1200 and 1800 deaf athletes competed in the Deaf Olympics, and, of that number, 700 took part in contact sports. He noted that fifty-nine schools sponsored contact sports for the deaf and that Gallaudet competed against regular college opponents. In all of this competition, he knew of no injury attributed to a hearing disability.

Dr. Donald Kasprzak, Chairman of the Committee on the Medial Aspects of Sports, commented that he saw no danger to Colombo in contact sports, but did foresee serious emotional problems if he was prevented from participating in sports. He then criticized the AMA guidelines as outmoded and in need of revision.

An otologist advised the school's medical officer that while he supported the AMA's regulation, he thought Colombo could play with a protective helmet.

The New York Court made reference to a case that was decided against a boy with one eye, but ultimately led to legislation that will affect future cases. In *Spitaleri* the court remarked:

> Clearly, the concern of the AMA and of the school physician as well as those physicians who hold the view that he should be permitted to play, is the always present danger of injury to the remaining organ which, if it should occur, would result in irreversible and permanent injury.[31]

It was ironic that the only time a court reversed a doctor's decision, in a similar situation, occurred in the same school district as presented here. In *Pendergast v. Sewanhaka Central High School District No. 2,* the circumstances were quite different, however, since the plaintiff had one testicle. In that instance the court observed that:

> An exercise of discretion cannot be based merely on the nature of the disability, i.e., the fact that one of the paired organs is missing. The loss of a testicle is not comparable to the loss of one of other paired organs such as eyes, ears, or kidneys.[32]

It explained that:

> The disability which results from the loss of one eye is functional in terms of participation in athletics. Lack of depth perception can increase the risk of further injury not only to the remaining sight, but to the other parts of the body. The inability to hear strongly directional sounds on the impaired hearing side could have similar consequences in some sports.[33]

While the court in *Colombo* sympathized with the boy's disappointment and frustration, it believed that the doctor's action was neither arbitrary nor capricious. It observed that participation in sports presented the danger of three risks to the hearing-impaired athlete, namely:

1. The risk of injury to the ear in which there is only partial hearing and to which further injury could result in irreversible and permanent damage — in this case, total deafness;
2. The risk to other parts of his body by reason of his failure to perceive the direction of sound;
3. The risk of injury to other participants.

The court felt that the risks involved were too high to overrule the school doctor's decision. It denied participation in contact sports to Colombo.[34] It is interesting to note that the revised American Medical Association's guidelines no longer include impaired hearing as a disqualifying physical condition for sports participation.

The New York legislature has attempted to protect the rights of the individual with a handicapping condition or physically impaired athlete to participate in sports of all types. At the same time, the legislature tried to waive by statute the liability of the physicians and school district. The *Spitaleri* ruling may be questioned and tested in court in the future.

A new issue may be raised by the legislation, and that is the liability of the physicians who sign the affidavits supporting the impaired athletes request to play.

A university official commented in a letter that the *Spitaleri* ruling may, in fact, not protect the physician at all. He made the following observation when he said: "Despite the statement in the supporting memorandum that the physicians who provide supporting affidavits, would be released from liability, the bill as drawn does not provide any such blanket protection." [35]

He then expressed his concern for all such physicians when he warned that: "A physician who has been negligent in diagnosing a student's physical condition would not be immune from a malpractice action for injuries occurring as a consequence of his negligence." [36]

It is possible that various state legislatures will attempt by judicial fiat to enact statutes meeting the federal requirements for individuals with handicapping conditions and at the same time protecting school officials. It is also possible that the statutes may be confusing and unable to adequately protect those for whom they are designed. Further litigation may well set precedent and legal parameters for all to follow.

165

Single Kidney

Along with visual impairment, the single kidney is one of the major reasons for medical disqualification from certain sports. It is interesting to compare the attitude of the court in 1976 when compared to a similar case in 1981.

The parents of a boy, referred to as "P.N.," sued the Board of Education in Elizabeth, New Jersey because it refused to allow their son to participate on the high school soccer team because he had only one kidney.[37] "P.N." had been examined prior to the start of the soccer season during his senior year. He had been permitted to play the previous years and had won first place honors in a United States Marine physical fitness program. The medical inspector informed the school superintendent that he had discussed the boy's medical history with three urologists. The three urologists were in agreement that "P.N." could participate in noncontact sports, but not in contact sports, because of his condition. The medical inspector, on their recommendation, informed the superintendent that "P.N." should be excluded from football, wrestling and soccer, despite the fact that he had competed in football and wrestling during his sophomore year and soccer during his junior year. "P.N.'s" parents charged the school officials with discrimination. The Commissioner of Education reviewed all the facts and ruled:

> The interests of the pupil, his parents and the community at large are best served by permitting the Board to exercise its legal discretion in adhering to the advice of its own medical inspector, absent a clear showing that the medical inspector's determination was arbitrary or discriminatory. Petitioner has failed to make such a clear showing.

166

The New Jersey Commissioner was again called upon to consider a medical inspector's recommendation regarding an athlete with a single kidney prohibited from participating in the high school wrestling program.[38] "R.P." had taken part in the school's physical education and intramural programs and the boy's parents offered to sign any release the Board required to hold it harmless in the event their son was injured. They insisted that the Board's action deprived their son of a complete education as provided by the New Jersey Constitution.

The Board contended that the release suggested by the parents would not protect it from liability since the boy could institute a suit of his own when he reached the age of majority. It suggested that the boy consider a number of non-contact sports as an alternative to the wrestling program. The New Jersey Commissioner of Education agreed with the ruling of the medical inspector and the Board and supported their action in denying the student participation in the wrestling program. Julian Stein, a professor at George Mason University, formerly the Director of the American Alliance for Health, Physical Education, Recreation and Dance's program for individuals with handicapping conditions disagreed with the Commissioner. Stein responded to the decision in a letter to the editors of *Sports and the Courts Quarterly* in which he strongly opposed the New Jersey Commissioner of Education's decision denying "R.P." the opportunity to participate in the high school wrestling program.[39] Stein vigorously protested the decision, declaring that the action constituted a violation of section 504. Stein listed his reasons as follows:

1. the individual is being discriminated against on the basis of a handicapping condition or a perceived one whichever portion of the law is used;

167

2. an official policy paper from the Office of Civil Rights makes it clear that individuals with only one of paired parts cannot be withheld from contact sports because of the condition (one kidney is specifically mentioned in the discussion of the policy); and

3. the same policy paper provides major responsibility in these decisions upon the individual's personal or family physician (i.e. the physician who knows the individual best). (See Appendix E).

Stein noted that the American Medical Association has changed its position on paired parts to place the responsibility for the decision to participate on the individual as long as he/she is aware of the potential dangers of participation in a particular sport. Stein concluded that the key factor in the final decision to participate is the responsibility of the individual and the school to make sure the individual is aware of the potential dangers that participation in a particular sport could present, and on the physician who best knows the individual.

In light of these factors and section 504, Stein felt that the New Jersey decision was wrong. When the case was later tried in a court, the decision supported Stein's observations and his comments concerning the case.

Richard Poole wrestled in the eighth, ninth and tenth grades despite the fact that he was born with one kidney.[40] The school district's medical doctor disqualified him from competition during his junior and senior years in high school stating that:

> It is in the best interest of the students to bar them from contact sports despite the wrath from both students and parents. How can you justify and explain to the student who has one kidney and the other destroyed that his death or lifelong

168

attachment to a kidney machine was worth the "glory."

The school board's attorney supported the medical doctor's concern for the boy's welfare when he declared: "Although at first blush, a complete release and waiver would appear to resolve the problem at hand, such an approach side-steps the basic question of responsibility."

He pointed out that the Board stood *in loco parentis,* (in place of the parents) and could not abrogate its duty by placing the burden of responsibility upon the boy and his parents. The attorney believed that the decision, as to the boy's participation in wrestling, was the ultimate responsibility of the Board, not the parents.

The court disagreed with this position and declared that the board "stands the doctrine of *in loco parentis* on its head." It felt that the board acted contrary to the wishes of the boy and his parents who considered all the potential risks and dangers and then made a rational decision for the benefit of the boy. The court referred to *Parham v. J.R.,* 99 S. Ct. 2493 (1979) in which it was said that: "Simply because the decision of a parent . . . involves risks does not automatically transfer the power to take that decision from the parents to some agency or officer of the state."

The court then considered whether the Board violated the boy's rights under section 504 of the Rehabilitation Act of 1973. It made some comments and observations that are noteworthy when it said: "life has risks and hardly a year goes by that there is not at least one instance of the tragic death of a healthy youth as a result of competitive sports activity."

It observed that section 504 is intended to enable individuals with handicapping conditions to "live life as fully as they are able, without paternalistic authorities deciding that certain activities are risky for them."

The court then addressed the question of a minor executing a waiver as stated by the board. The board argued that a minor cannot enter into a contract, making the waiver worthless. The court noted, however, that the consent form relieving the Board from responsibility was not a contract. It emphatically declared:

> This is a young man who, with his parents' support and approval, wishes to live an active life despite a congenital defect. The Board's responsibility is to see that he does not pursue this course in a foolish manner. They therefore have a duty to alert Richard and his parents to the dangers involved and to require them to deal with the matter rationally.

The court then commented that: "Whatever duty the Board may have toward Richard was satisfied once it became clear that the Poole's knew of the dangers involved and rationally reached a decision to encourage their son's participation in interscholastic wrestling."

It denied the school district's motion for summary judgment by stating that "the mandate of Section 504 must prevail" and declared "that if the plaintiff can prove the facts" as referred to in the court's opinion, he would "be entitled to a judgment that the Board violated Section 504."

A federal judge ruled that "Sparky" Grube, a seventeen-year-old senior at Freedom High School in Bethlehem, Pennsylvania could participate in football.[41] Grube was born with a malfunctioning kidney that was removed when he was two-years old. Grube had been prohibited from participating in football during his senior year although he played on the team during his freshman, sophomore and junior years.

The judge stated that the boy's rights as guaranteed by federal legislation were being violated since "he is a collegiate-caliber football player who hopes this talent will be his entry to college."

170

The school district argued that it was concerned for the liability that might be imposed if the boy loses the use of the remaining kidney. Grube's parents agreed to take responsibility for any injury their son suffered while playing football. They contended that to deny their son the opportunity to play the game he loves would cause him irreparable harm.[42]

The Emotionally Impaired Athlete

While the majority of cases deal with the individual with physical impairments, a Texas case illustrates the potential for litigation by the emotionally impaired participant.

John Doe spent several days in a psychiatric ward of a hospital for violent behavior which his parents could not control.[43] During 1977 he lived at home with his parents and played football at Friendswood High School. Later that year, physicians diagnosed his father's condition as terminal cancer, and from that time on John became unusually violent toward his parents. He even threatened them with a loaded shotgun. John received psychiatric treatment but his emotional problems increased until his therapist recommended that he live with his maternal grandparents.

His grandparents were named "managing conservators" and he enrolled at Alvin High School for his senior year. John's therapist strongly urged him to play football at Alvin, not Friendswood, because she felt it was essential for his emotional health. Both school principals agreed with the therapist, but the University Interscholastic League ruled that John was not eligible to play football that year. They cited the rule that stated:

    a. a student changing schools whose parents or
        guardians do not reside in the school district
        is ineligible for varsity contests,

171

    b. a student living with a guardian is eligible
       only if the guardianship is of one year's
       standing, and
    c. where both parents are still alive, the UIL
       will not acknowledge the existence of a legal
       guardianship.

The rule was designed to prevent athletes and coaches
from "shopping around for a school or a coach."

John's attorney alleged that the regulation was a
violation of section 504 of the Rehabilitation Act that
prohibits federally funded programs from discriminatory
practices against the handicapped.

A survey was taken to determine the number of state
high school athletic associations that waive rules regarding
individuals with handicapping conditions.[44] The survey
revealed that only six states of the forty that returned the
questionnaire waived any rules for such individuals.

While the majority of states do not make exceptions for
individuals with handicapping conditions in their rules, the
State of Virginia has met the changing times by
implementing a flexible rule that reads as follows:

> The Executive Committee shall be empowered to
> initiate such action as it may deem necessary or
> advisable in the best interests of the League for
> Group Board of Legislative Council con-
> sideration .... It is also authorized to make
> necessary exceptions to the Bona Fide Student
> Rule and the Enrollment Rule to permit
> compliance with state and federal regulations
> governing the education of handicapped
> children.[45]

The National Federation, a governing organization for the
various state high school athletic associations replied to the
question of rules or standards regarding the individual with
handicapping conditions by stating:

172

The National Federation does not have a recommended eligibility standard pertaining to the various types of "handicapped" students. As you have indicated, the issue is quite complex and is affected by a number of things including the different types of handicaps to which such a standard might apply. Accordingly, the National Federation's position to date has been to rely on state associations to handle this question in their respective states . . . . The National Federation's recommended eligibility standards are advisory only and each state association adopts its own rules which are enforceable upon member high schools and the students enrolled therein.[46]

It is obvious that the various state high school athletic associations are responsible for enacting eligibility rules for the high schools in their respective states. In states in which there are rigid rules, litigation is likely when an individual with a handicapping condition is prohibited from participation.

C. Thomas Ross, a trial lawyer and co-editor of *Sports and the Courts Quarterly* describes the situation confronting an athlete with a physical or emotional handicapping condition who wants to participate in sports as a dilemma that raises legal and ethical issues. Prior to the *Poole* case in New Jersey and the *Wright* case in Pennsylvania, Ross observed:

The trend seems to be as illustrated by the New Jersey case, that in cases where the handicap or impairment involves a vital organ, the athlete or student should not be permitted to engage in contact activities because of the risk of life threatening or permanent injury such as blindness. This seems to be the most reasonable course of action to follow. If the athlete or student still wants to participate, the courts are available to resolve the issue, and if the court orders the school to let them participate, the

173

school system coaches and P.E. teachers will be protected from liability for any injury which may arise solely due to the handicap or impairment.[47]

Herb Appenzeller and Thomas Appenzeller in *Sports and The Courts* discuss the dilemma that often faces the athlete, coach and school official when they comment: "It is clear, however, that Public Law 94-142 and Section 504 will require every institution that engages in physical education, athletics and intramurals to permit any student with a handicapping condition to try out and participate in the activities."

They conclude:

> It is apparent that state high school athletic associations will revise their regulations regarding the athlete with a handicapping condition and that more states will follow the example of the New York State Legislature in enacting statutes that permit participation in sports by protecting the school official and coaches from liability.[48]

The Appenzellers suggest that school officials consider each case on its own individual merit. This is the intent of federal legislation and may offer a possible solution for each student. They advise the following course of action in similar situations:

> Have a conference with all the people involved, including the athlete and parents, the team and family physicians and the coach of the sport in question. Discuss the consequences of participation and possible injury and consider alternatives such as non-contact sports or an association with the sport such as a student manager or trainer.
>
> If the athlete and the parents are in agreement with the opinion of the physicians and it is determined that the athlete can benefit from

174

participation in sports, sign a statement to that effect. Keep the notes of the meeting on file stating that such a meeting was held and that all parties were aware of the situation and possible consequences resulting from injury and still chose to participate. It will be helpful to have all the parties present sign the statement and keep the record on file for future reference in the event of a lawsuit.

If the athlete and parents do not agree with the opinion of the school officials against sports participation and still want to participate, the school officials should keep a record in writing of the meeting and all of the discussion for future reference in the event an injury occurs and a lawsuit follows.

Above all, suggest the Appenzellers, school officials and coaches must use sound judgment and extreme care to avoid negligent conduct. They issue a word of caution when they declare that these suggestions are not intended to offer absolute solutions to a controversial and difficult problem, but should illustrate an area that needs additional study and research.[49] It appears, however, that recent judicial decisions such as those given in *Poole*[50] and *Wright*[51] are helping to clarify the attitude of the court and aiding in the resolution of the problem.

Summary

The Supreme Court of Georgia in *Smith v. Crim* declared that rules and regulations promulgated by state high school athletic associations are designed to keep sports competitive and safe. However, more than ever before, students are challenging rules that deny them sports participation. A new group has emerged: students with handicapping conditions who insist that federal legislation prohibits discrimination against them. One rule that has drawn considerable attention deals with the age of the participant. In a large number of states, nineteen years of age is the cut off point for sports participation although a few states extend the age requirement to twenty years of age. Students with disabilities, that kept them back in their early school years, argue that the age rule violates section 504 and Public Law 94-142. The courts, however, are consistent in ruling that a student of nineteen or over is too mature physically, mentally and emotionally when compared to less mature students. The courts also point out that the older student deprives a young student the opportunity to participate in sports. The courts answer the charge of discrimination by holding that rules based on safety and fairness do not violate equal protection safeguards.

In 1967 Julian Stein, AAHPERD's Director of the Unit on Programs for the Handicapped, surveyed the state high school athletic associations to determine academic eligibility requirements for sports participation for the mentally retarded student. Stein found that thirty-four percent of the respondents failed to enact rules to permit the mentally retarded student to compete in high school sports. Stein predicted that future federal legislation would liberalize the rules.

In 1982, nine years after the passage of section 504 and seven years after Public Law 94-142 was enacted, another survey reported that forty-two percent of the state high school athletic associations did not permit sports participation for the mentally retarded. Federal legislation has not liberalized the rules. In fact some states that previously permitted participation reversed their policy and now deny such participation.

For years school officials on the secondary and collegiate levels adopted the American Medical Association's recommendations for disqualification because of physical disabilities as absolute policy. The lack of a paired organ, particularly an eye or kidney, seems to be most involved in this type of litigation.

In 1980 and 1981 two cases, *Poole* and *Wright,* one of the secondary level involving a student with one kidney and the other regarding a university student with one eye, established important guidelines. The courts in New Jersey and Pennsylvania clearly interpret section 504 and Public Law 94-142 to cover both student athletes. The key appears to be the question of what is best for the student rather than an arbitrary rule directed against every individual with a disability.

FOOTNOTES

1. Smith v. Crim, 240 S.E.2d 884 (Ga. 1977).

2. Herb Appenzeller, *Rules Affecting the Eligibility of the Mentally Retarded and Individuals with Handicapping Conditions in Interscholastic Sports: A Survey of State High School Athletic Associations,* 1982.

3. Chambers v. Massachusetts Secondary School Principals Association, Inc., Superior Court, No. 9641, Jan. 1978.

4. McNulty v. Massachusetts Interscholastic Athletic Association, Superior Court, No. 37053, Jan. 1979.

5. Greensboro Daily News, Nov. 2, 1978.

6. *Supra* note 1.

7. Lee v. Florida High School Activities Association, Inc., 291 So. 2d 636 (Fla. App. 1974).

8. Florida High School Activities Association, Inc. v. Bryant, 313 So. 2d 57 (Fla. App. 1975).

9. Dr. Julian U. Stein, *Rules Affecting the Eligibility of the Mentally Retarded for Interscholastic Athletics: A Survey of State High School Athletic Associations,* Project on Recreation and Fitness for the Mentally Retarded, AAHPERD, (Mimeographed), 1967.

10. *Id.*

11. *Supra* note 2.

12. Disqualifying Conditions for Sports Participation, Medical Evaluation of the Athlete — A Guide (Reprinted with the permission of the American Medical Association, Chicago, Illinois 1977).

13. Spitaleri v. Nyquist, 345 N.Y.S.2d 878 (N.Y. Sup. Ct. 1973).

14. Kampmeier v. Harris, 403 N.Y.S.2d 638 (N.Y. Sup. Ct. 1978), *rev'd,* 411 N.Y.S. 744 (N.Y. App. Div. 1978).

15. *Id.*

16. *Id.*

17. *Id.*

18. *Id.*

19. Swiderski v. Board of Education, City School District of Albany, 408 N.Y.S.2d 744 (N.Y. Sup. Ct. 1978).

20. The Post, Athens, Ohio, Nov. 1975.

21. *Id.*

22. The Columbus Dispatch, Ohio, Dec. 7, 1977.

23. Evans & Redding v. Looney, No. 77-6052-CV-SJ, U.S. District Court for the W. D. of Missouri, Sept. 2, 1977.

24. Wright v. Columbia University, 520 F. Supp. 789 (E.D. Pa. 1981).

25. Othen v. Ann Arbor School Board, 507 F. Supp. 1376 (E.D. Mich. 1981).

26. Poole v. South Plainfield Board of Education, 490 F. Supp. 948 (D. N.J. 1980).

27. *Id.*

28. *Id.*

29. *Supra* note 24.

30. Colombo v. Sewanhaka Central High School Dist. No. 2, 383 N.Y.S.2d 518 (N.Y. Sup. Ct. 1976).

31. *Supra* note 13.

32. Pendergast v. Sewanhaka Central High School, Dist. No. 2 (Supreme Court, Nassau County, 1975).

33. *Id.*

34. *Supra* note 30.

35. Letter from Louis Welch, The State Education Department of the University of the State of New York at Albany, March 10, 1977.

36. *Id.*

37. "P.N." by his parents v. Board of Education of the City of Elizabeth, Union County (Decision of the New Jersey Commissioner of Education, 1975).

38. "R.P." and "F.P." as parents and guardians ad litem for "R.P." v. Board of Education of the Borough of South Plainfield, Middlesex County, (Decision of the Commissioner of Education, 1979).

39. Letter from Julian Stein, August 5, 1980.

40. *Supra* note 26.

41. Raleigh News and Observer, October 7, 1982.

42. *Id.*

43. Doe v. Marshall, 459 F. Supp. 1190 (S.D. Texas 1978).

44. *Supra* note 2.

45. *Id.*

46. Letter to Herb Appenzeller from Warren S. Brown, Assistant Director, National Federation, Kansas City, Missouri, April 13, 1982.

47. *Student With One Kidney Denied Participation in Varsity Wrestling Program,* SPORTS AND THE COURTS QUARTERLY, Vol. 1, No. 3 (1980).

48. *Id.*

49. *Id.*
50. *Supra* note 26.
51. *Supra* note 24.

CHAPTER 7

Injuries To Participants

Stuart Taylor, writing in the *New York Times*, recognizes that litigation is at an all-time high as Americans prefer to "sue rather than settle."[1] Taylor notes that legal authorities agree that the record number of lawsuits has created a litigious society. He concludes that:

> The American lust for justice; by most accounts, has produced more laws, lawyers, lawsuits, legal entanglements and a more powerful judiciary than the world has ever seen. Surely Americans must be unrivaled in sheer audacity in litigation.[2]

Legislation such as section 504 of the Rehabilitation Act and the Education For All Handicapped Children Act, Public Law 94-142, will undoubtedly increase participation in physical education and sports for individuals with disabilities. The increase in participation, in all probability, will lead to an accompanying rise in litigation.

It is unfortunate that while many administrators, coaches, teachers and school board members are vulnerable to litigation, they often lack the knowledge of liability that is essential to protect the students entrusted to their care.

Nancy Frank, a former physical education instructor and coach, recommends that everyone involved in the operation of a physical education and sports program take and score a self-test she designed. Her questions come from eight content categories that include: (1) terminology and principles, (2) equipment and facilities, (3) injuries and first aid, (4) activity preparedness, (5) travel and transportation, (6) insurance, (7) civil rights, and (8) supervision. Frank suggests if the score on the self-test is low that the reader obtain material on the legal aspects of physical education and sports from periodicals and books. She also encourages attendance at in-service workshops in the area of liability to keep abreast of current trends in the law as they relate to physical education and sports. Frank believes that a basic knowledge of the elements of law is necessary in the daily operation of physical education and sports programs. (See Appendix F for the self-test and answers).

This chapter will review court cases that represent litigation against administrators, teachers, coaches and school boards. The cases will involve individuals with handicapping conditions as well as nonhandicapped participants since the court makes little, if any, distinction between them in litigation dealing with injuries in physical education and sports programs.

Most of the cases in sports law deal with what is known as negligence. For this reason a brief discussion of the elements of negligence and the defenses against it will precede the court cases.

Elements of Negligence

William Prosser, John W. Wade and Victor E. Schwartz, in *Torts, Cases and Materials,* describe four elements that must be present in a cause of action as follows:

1. a *duty,* which is an obligation recognized by the law, requiring actor to conform to a certain standard of conduct, for the protection of others against unreasonable risks;
2. breach of duty, a failure to conform to the standard required;
3. proximate or legal cause, a reasonably close causal connection between the conduct and the resulting injury; and
4. damage, actual loss resulting to the interests of another.[3]

182

There are no sure criteria for determining what is negligent action and what is not since each case stands individually on its own merit. The key to liability is the presence of negligence since a school and its staff owe their students the duty of care that is required to save them from foreseeable harm.[4]

The American law of negligence is not to be found in a written code of laws. It is based upon the theory of precedent, or upon established modes of legal procedure. A previous judicial decision is used as a basis for subsequent decisions. Negligence must be viewed against this background. The fact that an accident occurs does not necessarily mean the teacher or coach is negligent or liable for damages. It must be proved that the injury is reasonably connected with negligence.[5] Bolmeier gives reassuring encouragement to all teachers and coaches when he writes:

> Before a school employee can be held liable for an injury sustained by a pupil there must be sufficient evidence that the alleged negligence is the proximate cause of the injury. Perhaps in the majority of all liability court cases charging negligence of some school officer or employee as the cause of the injury, the defendant has been found to be not liable. *In fact, no court has held a defendant liable where there was substantial evidence that the defendant acted with prudence and caution in the performance of his duties.* (emphasis added).[6]

Defenses Against Negligence

The best defense against a claim of negligence is to prove that one of the elements required for negligence is not present. Other defenses that can result in a "nonliability verdict for the defendant" include contributory negligence, comparative negligence and assumption of risk.

183

Contributory negligence prevents a person from recovering from damages if he is at fault to even the slightest degree in causing his own injury. A court will consider what standard of conduct is required for someone of the person's age, physical capabilities, sex and training before it makes a decision as to fault.

An example of a case in which contributory negligence was used as a defense took place in North Carolina. Roger Clary, a seventeen-year-old senior at Stoney Point High School, sued the Alexander County Board of Education for serious injuries he received in the school's gymnasium.[7] Roger had participated on the school's basketball team for three years and was aware of the glass windows which were located three feet from the end of the basketball court. He was running wind sprints at the end of practice as directed by his coach and he failed to stop or slow down and crashed into the glass window, shattering the glass and cutting himself severely. He sued the school for maintaining a negligent and unsafe facility. The school board responded that the plaintiff was contributorily negligent and that it could not be responsible for the player's liability.

The plaintiff testified during the trial that: "I didn't have any trouble seeing the window and I knew it was there — I knew I had to stop or run into something."

The plaintiff argued that he was not guilty of contributory negligence since his coach had ordered him to run wind sprints. The Court of Appeals of North Carolina disagreed however and declared:

> The rule with respect to acting in obedience to the rules of a person in authority requires that such orders be disregarded when a reasonable man under similar circumstances would know that his compliance with such orders would result in his injury.

184

The court was of the opinion that the athlete was guilty of contributory negligence since he was familiar with the conditions of the gymnasium, but ignored his own safety by refusing to use reasonable care. It held that while the injuries were regrettable, the trial court did not err in favoring the school board.

Comparative negligence means that the fault for a given circumstance is prorated. Most states are concerned that an injured party under a contributory negligence defense cannot recover damages because that party was negligent in some degree. Some states, such as California, North Dakota and Virginia, now permit an individual who is partially at fault to receive compensation on a prorated basis. Experts in tort law predict that many legislatures will follow California, North Dakota and Virginia's example and enact legislation permitting the use of the comparative negligence theory.

A case involving a tragic accident on a trampoline illustrates comparative negligence. Fourteen-year-old Alan Meharey and his friend Richard Hagler went to the Minot Air Base Recreation Center on a Sunday afternoon to play on the trampoline.[8] Alan, who was described as a "good trampoline performer" by his friends, attempted a one and a half flip twice without success and on the third try sustained a crippling injury when he landed. His friends dragged him from the trampoline and placed him on the floor until help could arrive. As a result of the injury Alan is a permanent quadriplegic.

Alan and his father, who was a sergeant in the Air Force, sued the United States under the Federal Tort Claims Act, 28 U.S.C. § 2674, alleging that it was liable for the injury because it failed to provide supervision for a dangerous apparatus.

185

The court agreed that the failure of the recreation center officials to furnish supervision was the proximate cause of the plaintiff's injury and constituted negligence. It noted that additional injury resulted when he was pulled from the trampoline to the floor by his companions.

North Dakota has a statute regarding comparative negligence which provides that a plaintiff whose negligence exceeds that of the defendant will not be entitled to damages. In this situation, however, it determined that the plaintiff was forty-five percent to blame compared to fifty-five percent negligence on the part of the defendant. It found the total damage to the plaintiff to be $2,300,000 but because he was guilty of negligence by forty-five percent, it reduced his award to $1,265,000.

Assumption of risk occurs when a person assumes the responsibility of his/her own safety. John C. Weistart and Cym H. Lowell in *The Law of Sports* comment that the assumption of risk doctrine states that: "a party who voluntarily assumes a risk of harm arising from the conduct of another cannot recover if harm in fact results." [9]

The Supreme Court of Pennsylvania commented on the assumption of risk doctrine in *Rutter v. Northeastern Beaver County School District* when it said: "The standard to be applied is a subjective one, of what the plaintiff sees, knows, understands and appreciates. In this it differs from the objective standard which is applied to contributory negligence." [10]

While the Pennsylvania court agrees with the statement of Weistart and Lowell regarding the doctrine it discusses the limitations as follows:

1. If by reason of age, or lack of information, experience, intelligence, or judgment, the plaintiff does not understand the risk involved in a known situation; he will not be taken to assume the risk.

186

2. A plaintiff does not assume a risk of harm unless he voluntarily accepts the risk.
3. The plaintiff's acceptance of a risk is not voluntary if the defendant's tortious conduct has left him no reasonable alternative course of conduct in order to . . . exercise or protect a right or privilege of which the defendant has no right to deprive him.[11]

A New York case that attracted nationwide attention because of the nature of the lawsuit and the enormous amount of damages initially awarded the plaintiff illustrates the assumption of risk defense.[12]

Ray Passantino had participated in baseball from the age of eight until his junior year in high school when he was crippled by an unfortunate injury. Passantino was on third base when his coach signalled for the squeeze play which required him to break for home plate as soon as the opposing pitcher committed himself. The batter was supposed to bunt the ball so the runner could easily score when the ball was thrown to first base. Passantino broke for home, but unfortunately the batter missed the ball and the catcher blocked the plate and waited for the runner. Instead of retreating back to third base, Passantino tried to run over the catcher. Both went down but only the catcher got up. Passantino was completely paralyzed and is now a permanent quadriplegic.

The injured plaintiff sued the City Board of Education and his baseball coach for negligence and the Supreme Court of Queen's County awarded him $1.8 million in damages. The appellate division of the supreme court considered his award excessive and reduced it to $1 million.

One of the justices objected to the verdict and voted in a powerful dissent to dismiss the case and reverse the previous decisions. The justice stated that he sympathized with Passantino but insisted that the boy was to blame for his actions. He asserted that the plaintiff assumed the risk of the sport when he volunteered for baseball and was responsible for the injury he sustained.

The justice's strong dissent was later affirmed by the action of the New York Appellate Court that reversed the previous decisions and upheld the defense of assumption of risk and dismissed the charges against the City Board of Education and the baseball coach.

Dr. Kenneth Clarke, the Director of Sports Medicine for the United States Olympic Committee, summed up an appropriate and practical defense against negligence when he stated that: "The principal defense against a complaint of negligence is a clear conscience that all reasonable measures were taken to minimize the risk inherent in that sport." [13]

Clarke then lists several essential guidelines for the safety of the sports participant that include the following:

Preparticipation Medical Exam — The school should be reasonably aware of the health status of each athlete. When the athlete first enters the athletic program, a thorough medical exam should be required. Subsequently an annual health history update with perceptive field observation and use of referral exams when warranted is sufficient. Federal guidelines now forbid disqualification of atypical persons from participation even in contact sports, but any such basis for disqualification should be registered and recorded if the athlete chooses to overrule the medical recommendation.

Acceptance of Risk — A "waiver of responsibility" by athletes should be based on an informed awareness of the risk of serious injury being accepted by participation in that sport. Not only does the individual share responsibility in preventive measures, but he or she should appreciate the purpose and significance of these measures.

188

Planning and Supervision — Those responsible for organized sport programs know where, when and to whom an athletic injury could occur. Consequently, planning for anticipated programs is an expectation, whether such requires general observation or specific intervention capability.

Equipment — Appropriate equipment recommended by rules or authoritative groups must be utilized by substitutes as well as regulars and in practice as well as games.

Facility — The adequacy and conditions of the facilities used for particular activities should not be overlooked, and periodic examination of the facilities should be conducted. Inspection of the facilities and their traffic patterns of use should include not only the competitive area, but warmup and adjacent areas.[14]

Who Is Responsible for Negligence?

In most cases that go to court, the plaintiff generally names as many individuals as defendants as possible. The most common defendants, however, are the teacher and coach, the administrator and the school board or district. The plaintiff hopes that someone will be found negligent and subject to damages. It is important to consider the position of each person or class of persons frequently accused of negligence.

Court Cases Involving the Physical Education Teacher and the Coach

It is important to reemphasize that the fact that an accident occurs does not necessarily mean the teacher or coach will be held liable for damages. It must be proved that the injury is proximately caused by the teacher or coach's negligence. The same standards apply to teachers and

189

coaches regarding negligence as to private individuals. In like manner, the same defenses used by all defendants are available to them.[15]

This section will review recent judicial decisions that come before the court. In this way the reader can study the decisions that typify the situations that arise in the daily routine of the physical education teacher and coach.

Cary Schumate was a mentally retarded student in Texas.[16] His teacher directed her aide to take the class to the playground for recess. Although the teacher's aide was also mentally retarded, she was allowed to choose the activity for the children. The teacher's aide held one end of a stick while a student held the other end and Cary was told to jump over the stick. He tripped and fell and injured his head, and also sustained a fractured vertebrae of the neck.

Cary's parents sued the teacher for negligence but the court favored the teacher, finding no negligence. This decision is unusual in the fact that most states do not protect the teacher or coach with immunity from suit. The Texas Education Code has a provision, however, that protects teachers from liability unless they use "excessive force in the discipline of students or negligence resulting in bodily injury to the students."

The decision was appealed and the Court of Civil Appeals of Texas upheld the lower court's verdict by ruling that the statute protecting the teacher did not violate the Fourteenth Amendment of the United States Constitution nor the Texas Constitution.

The court approved the desirability of providing limited protection to teachers and freedom from being placed in the position of an insurer against the injury of each child placed directly or indirectly in their care.

The State of Illinois has a statute that grants teachers and coaches immunity from liability for injuries to students under their direction unless their conduct can be proved to be "wanton and wilful." An interesting case came before the Illinois court to challenge the statute.

A fifteen-year-old girl suffered a severe neck injury during a tumbling exercise in a physical education class.[17] The girl was one of forty students preparing for a unit in gymnastics. The teacher used a student to demonstrate the stunts to the class before the students attempted them. After class the girl told her teacher that she was afraid to try the backward somersault since she injured herself as a child trying to perform it. She was also extremely overweight. The teacher volunteered to help her after school but the girl could not stay because she rode the school bus.

The next day when the teacher told the girl to try the backward somersault, the girl reminded the teacher of their conversation the previous day. The teacher directed the girl to get a fellow student to assist her with the stunt. Although the girl was afraid of the stunt, she tried, and in the middle of the somersault she "heard her neck snap." An orthopedic surgeon operated on her and performed "posterior cervical fusion, grafting a bone from the plaintiff's hip onto four vertebrae in the neck."

The injured girl sued the school district for the alleged "wanton and wilful misconduct" of her instructor who was aware of her obese condition and fear of the stunt. During the trial a gymnastic coach testified that a person who is overweight and lacks arm strength is vulnerable to injury in such a stunt. He added that "fear itself presents a danger of neck injury in the performance of the backward somersault."

The Appellate Court of Illinois, Fifth District, commented that the teacher was aware of the girl's excessive weight and inherent fear of the activity. It observed that the

191

teacher failed to help the girl with instruction but left it to another student. It concluded that the teacher was guilty of "wanton and wilful misconduct" and awarded the girl $77,000.

In another Illinois case, a student claimed that his physical education instructor was responsible for his injury because of "wanton and wilful misconduct." [18] Michael Montague sustained a broken arm attempting to vault a horse during a tumbling class in physical education. Michael sued the school district and his instructor for negligence but the Circuit Court of Cook County granted the defendants summary judgment. Michael appealed to the Appellate Court of Illinois.

During the trial, testimony revealed that Michael had performed over 30 vaults prior to the day of the accident, and on that day had already completed five vaults successfully. Michael claimed that he made the vaults without spotters, while the instructor insisted that he used spotters during the vaulting exercises.

The Appellate Court observed that certain facts were undisputed such as:

1. Before the start of the unit, the instructor taught his class the proper method of using the horse.

2. The instructor gave each student individual instruction on the use of the horse.

3. The instructor warned the students about the dangers of the horse before each class.

The court concluded that while the instructor might be guilty of negligence, the plaintiff failed to prove that he was guilty of "wanton and wilful misconduct." It therefore

192

upheld the lower court's decision in favor of the instructor and school board.

Patricia Stineman, a member of Fontbonne College's intercollegiate softball team, was struck in the eye during practice with a ball thrown by a teammate.[19] Witnesses reported that the impact of the ball striking her eye was heard over 100 yards away. Two of Patricia's coaches heard her cry out in pain and applied ice to the injured eye, assured her that her eye would be all right, and sent her to rest in her room in the dormitory.

Patricia had been deaf since infancy and relied on lip reading to communicate. Although the coaches knew that Patricia was "especially dependent upon her eyesight," they did not advise her to see a doctor.

Several days later Patricia experienced dizziness, severe blurring and coloring of her vision. Her parents directed her to an internist who recognized the seriousness of her injury and referred her to an opthalmologist at once. The opthalmologist reported that there was "blood in the anterior chamber of the eye, a condition called hyphema." The opthalmologist began immediate treatment but infection developed and she lost the vision in her eye. Medical authorities testified that prompt treatment to the eye in similar circumstances usually results in a "ninety percent or greater success rate."

The plaintiff filed suit against her teammate who threw the ball and the college for failing to provide medical assistance. The trial court dismissed the complaint against the plaintiff's teammate but found the college guilty of negligent conduct and awarded her $800,000. Fontbonne College officials appealed the decision arguing that the college had no obligation to provide medical services and that the $800,000 award was excessive.

The United States Court of Appeals, Eighth Circuit, upheld the trial court's judgment in determining that the college was negligent for failing to provide medical assistance. It agreed, however, with the defendants that the amount of damages was excessive. It declared:

> Viewing the evidence on economic loss in the light most favorable to the plaintiff and allowing for substantial pain and suffering damages because of the multiple handicaps present here, a total award of $600,000 could be sustained on the record.

It remanded the case back to the trial court with instructions that if the "plaintiff does file *remittitur,* the reduced award of $600,000 shall be satisfied . . . and the district court shall enter a conforming judgment."

Judge Nicols vigorously opposed the reduction of the award and commented that Patricia's loss of vision was devastating. He pointed out:

> She now wears glasses to protect her seeing eye as well as relieve the strain on it. She must be careful to always position herself against blows to her seeing eye by sitting with the eye facing the wall. She can no longer participate in any sports. Further Stineman suffers from the disfigurement which accompanies her injury. Her blind eye is shrinking and will continue to do so until it becomes the size of a pea. Therefore she must now wear a prothesis on her eye.

Judge Nicols concluded: "Stineman, as a woman of twenty-three, is now suffering from three disabilities; her deafness, her partial blindness, and the further disfigurement. In view of this I cannot say that the damage award was excessive."

David Brahatcek, a fourteen-year-old student, was fatally injured during a physical education class when a fellow student accidently struck him with a golf club.[20] David missed the first day of a unit in which the rules of safety in golf were discussed. When the class met for the second lesson, a student teacher replaced one of the regular teachers who was absent. The other full-time teacher repeated the instructions and divided the class into small groups to practice the grip and swing. Since the weather was inclement, the class was held in the gymnasium.

David had never swung a golf club and when his turn came to practice, he asked for help. A student volunteered to demonstrate the proper stance and grip and offered to take a few practice swings. David moved close to the student who was unaware that anyone was standing near him. David was struck in the head by the golf club and died soon after the accident.

The student teacher was working with a student in another area while the regular teacher was supervising a group of girls. She testified that she was unaware that the student teacher was devoting his time to one individual or she would have attempted to supervise the entire class.

The other regular teacher, who was absent on the day of the tragic accident, reported that he and the other teacher enforced the safety rule of the school curriculum prohibiting more than one student on the mat at a time. The student teacher testified, however, that he had been at the school for five weeks and did not receive directions from the regular teachers regarding the class or activity, nor did he have a lesson plan.

After a suit was filed against them, the defendants insisted that the action of the fellow student who struck the plaintiff was the intervening cause of the accident and thereby relieved them of any negligence. In addition, they argued, David was guilty of contributory negligence.

The Nebraska Supreme Court disagreed reasoning that David was unaware of the existing danger of a golf club since he was not familiar with the sport. It believed that the physical education teachers had a duty to foresee the danger that could result from such an activity with a group of ninth graders who were unfamiliar with golf. It observed that David had not received instructions from either teacher prior to his fatal injury.

The court found the school district guilty of negligence because the teachers failed to provide proper supervision. It judged the lack of supervision to be the proximate cause of death and awarded David's parents $3,470.06 in special damages and $50,000 in general damages.

Proper Standards

In many states physical education departments follow a syllabus that has been established for the use of its teachers. Occasionally the question is raised concerning the proper standards of a particular activity. In many instances when teachers and coaches are challenged in court proper standards become an issue.

Three cases illustrate the problem that exists when the court attempts to determine whether proper standards existed in a particular activity that were violated by negligent action on the part of the teacher or coach.

Thomas Fantini was a college student participating in the activities of a karate club.[21] He had received about twenty hours of instruction in karate and was injured when he was kicked in the head by a more advanced student during a "free fight" staged for demonstration purposes. He filed suit against the karate instructor alleging that the instructor was guilty of negligence for failing to properly instruct and supervise the class. He insisted that the instructor should have known that, as a complete novice, he could not compete against a person with considerable experience.

196

During the trial, the plaintiff had called upon an instructor who owned and taught in a karate school to serve as an expert witness. The trial court judge held that the expert witness did not establish any generally accepted standard in this type of situation and dismissed the case. The higher court overruled the decision of the lower court by ruling that there was a clear abuse of discretion on the part of the trial court in dismissing the case. It held that a standard did not mean a principle which every practitioner in the applicable profession would follow. It held that it only must be a generally recognized standard and that there will always be people in every profession who do not follow what the vast majority recognize as proper conduct. The New Jersey Superior Court, Appellate Division, found that although the expert witness's testimony on behalf of the plaintiff was weak, it was sufficient to constitute a question of fact which should have been submitted to the jury. It, therefore, reversed the trial court and remanded it back for trial.

The trial court entered a judgment for the defendant and the plaintiff appealed to the Superior Court of New Jersey, Appellate Division. On appeal the court declared that the applicable rule for measuring the defendant's conduct is set forth in Second Restatement of Torts, § 299 A as follows:

> Unless he represents that he has greater or less skill or knowledge, one who undertakes to render services in the practice of a profession or trade is required to exercise the skill and knowledge normally possessed by members of that profession or trade in good standing in similar communities.

Donna De Mauro, a Tusculum College freshman, was struck by a golf ball during physical education class and suffered painful injuries that resulted in two surgical

197

operations.[22] The court attempted to apply proper standards to the situation but found that it was difficult to do so.

The law court of Greene County awarded damages but the court of appeals reversed the decision and the plaintiff appealed to the Supreme Court of Tennessee.

Donna had never received instruction in golf, nor played a game of golf. She was enrolled in a golf class that met for two hours one day a week. After several sessions in the gymnasium, and one at a driving range, the class went to the local golf course to play a practice round. A senior, who was majoring in physical education, was assigned to the class as a teaching assistant. He was expected to serve as a practice teacher who would take charge of the class when the regular instructor was absent. The senior was a scholarship athlete who participated in basketball but had little experience in golf. He was with the plaintiff and two other freshmen at the time of the accident. He drove a ball off the tee and struck the plaintiff in the face causing severe injury to her face.

The Supreme Court of Tennessee referred to a previous Tennessee case in which an unqualified instructor taught in a wrestling class.[23] A student was permanently crippled and the instructor's failure to properly supervise and instruct the student was deemed to be the proximate cause of the paralyzing injury. The jury awarded the boy $385,000 which was reported to be the largest award by a federal court in Nashville, Tennessee, in more than a decade.[24] In *Stehn* the court commented that:

> students who are novices and are receiving courses of instruction in sports held out and offered for credit by an educational institution, a duty of supervision and instruction rises from the relationship which is not terminated or abrogated merely by reason of the fact that one student participant injures another.

198

The court admitted that it was difficult to find "hard and fast criteria" to apply to this case. It noted that the court frequently resorted to the testimony of experts in the field of physical education and sports to determine proper standards for an activity. It reasoned that the previous court erred in dismissing the case since there were many questions that needed consideration by a jury. It reversed the lower court's decision and remanded it back for a new trial.

Nathaniel Greene sued his physical education teacher after he was injured in a wrestling class.[25] Nathaniel contended that he was subjected to activity that was below an accepted reasonable standard of care. The court was called upon to decide the reasonableness of the teacher's action.

Nathaniel failed the school board's vision test so he was limited to non-contact activities during football practice. Two weeks after spring practice ended, his physical education class began a unit in wrestling and weightlifting.

The instructor devoted the first three classes in wrestling to physical conditioning drills with instructions on basic moves and positions. He taught three or four basic moves and on one occasion permitted the members of the class to wrestle at less than half speed. On the fourth day of wrestling, he directed the class to wrestle hard for thirty seconds after they loosened up. He instructed them to use any move they wanted to try in addition to the basic moves they knew, and assigned a varsity wrestler to officiate while he sat six feet from the mat.

Nathaniel was seriously hurt during the thirty second drill and is now permanently paralyzed. Nathaniel charged his instructor and the school board with negligence for allowing him to wrestle hard for thirty seconds when he was not in the proper physical condition for such a strenuous

199

activity. In addition, he claimed that he lacked proper instruction in wrestling and should not have been directed to use moves other than those taught in class.

The Court of Appeals of Louisiana, Fourth Circuit, heard different testimony from experts in wrestling. The experts agreed that the first requirement for wrestling was physical conditioning along with basic moves. They disagreed over the appropriateness of the thirty second drill. The witnesses for the injured plaintiff insisted that it was too early in the unit to require hard wrestling while the defendant's witnesses argued that the members of the class had just completed football drills and were in good shape and capable of participating in the thirty second drill. The court noted that certain sports, such a wrestling, require adequate instruction and supervision to limit the possibility of injury. It pointed out, however, that there are no national or local guidelines for wrestling in physical education classes. The standard of care, it reasoned, is one of reasonableness. As such, it found that the instructor's standard of instruction and supervision conformed to local or national reasonable standards of care for instructors in similar situations. It affirmed the lower court's decision in favor of the defendants.

Court Cases Involving the Administrator

Administrators, like teachers and coaches, are liable under the general principles of tort law for their own personal acts of negligence and wrongdoing. In the past, fewer administrators (athletic directors, principals and superintendents) were named as defendants in cases involving injuries to students than were other individuals. This has been attributed to the fact that they are generally removed from direct contact with the students. Several recent cases may signal a new attitude by the court and give administrators little reason for complacency in regard to their liability or that of their subordinates.

Supervision and Instruction

Administrators are required to furnish supervision for their students on the school premises. Recent court cases point out that the administrator is expected to provide adequate supervision of students in their physical education programs. Once again, judicial decisions reveal the court's position regarding the administrator's role in supervision.

Donald Cook was injured during recess in a game called "kill" which was described as "ultra dangerous." [26] One player would try to keep possession of a football while the rest of the participants would tackle or jump on the individual in an attempt to take the ball away. Donald and his parents sued the teacher and the elementary school principal for alleged negligence. The plaintiffs insisted that both defendants had observed the students on the playground playing "kill" on several occasions, but never furnished supervision or tried to stop the game.

The teacher argued that he was absent from school on the day the plaintiff was injured and a substitute was in charge of his class. He questioned how he could be guilty of negligence when he was not present at the time of the accident and placed the responsibility for the plaintiff's injury on the substitute teacher. The trial court supported the teacher's argument and dismissed the complaint against him. It also ruled that the principal was protected from liability by the doctrine of governmental immunity.

The plaintiffs appealed to the Court of Appeals of Michigan and it affirmed the lower court's verdict in favor of the teacher by stating that while a teacher is normally expected to "exercise reasonable care over students in his or

201

her charge," the duty depends on the teacher's presence at school.

Regarding the principal, the court of appeals commented that the State of Michigan gave it little practical guidance with the question of governmental immunity for principals in like situations. It reasoned, however, that the principal in this case failed to promulgate rules against dangerous games such as "kill" or provide supervision to lessen the danger of injury to the students on the playground. It concluded that the principal ignored her responsibility to protect the students under her care and could not claim protection under the doctrine of governmental immunity. It therefore reversed the trial court's judgment and found the principal negligent.

Steven Larson's eighth grade physical education teacher was ordered to report for military duty and a first year teacher replaced him.[27] Steven suffered a crippling injury when he broke his neck attempting a "headspring over a rolled mat" during physical education class. Steven and his father sued the new teacher, the principal and the school superintendent for alleged negligence that caused the injury.

The trial court dismissed the complaint against the superintendent because it felt that he was a level removed from direct contact with the student and could not be held responsible for the injury. It found the teacher ninety percent negligent and the principal ten percent negligent and awarded Steven $1,013,639.75 plus costs and disbursements. It awarded Steven's father $142,937.89 plus costs and disbursements. The court also held that the procurement of liability insurance in the sum of $50,000 by the school district waived its absolute defense of governmental immunity for torts committed by its employees. It found the school district jointly and severally

202

liable with the teacher and the principal in the sum of $50,000 to each plaintiff.

The teacher and principal appealed the trial court's decision.

The Supreme Court of Minnesota commented that several expert witnesses testified that the principal had an obligation to work closely with the inexperienced teacher to:

> exercise reasonable care in supervising in the development, planning, and administration of the physical education curriculum within the school; in supervising and evaluating the work of teachers within the school, and maintaining conditions conducive to the safety and welfare of students during the day.

The court observed that the principal chose to let the departing teacher meet with his replacement to discuss the transition process. The meeting between the two physical education teachers lasted a mere thirty minutes. The court reasoned that this was not enough time for the orientation of an inexperienced teacher and therefore supported the trial court's judgment against the principal. It agreed that the principal's conduct was: "unreasonable and that his failure to reasonably administer the curriculum and supervise the teaching of an inexperienced instructor created the opportunity for Steven's accident to occur."

The court supported the plaintiff's allegations that the teacher directed the members of the class to perform the headspring well before they progressed through a series of preliminary exercises. In addition the teacher added running to the mat to the exercise which increased the danger of the activity. It also agreed that the teacher was not properly "spotting" the exercise when Steven was hurt.

203

Both defendants insisted that they were protected from liability by a common-law doctrine of "discretionary immunity" but the court refused to uphold their claim and found them both guilty of negligence.

Two justices concurred with the trial court's judgment regarding the superintendent and principal but opposed the verdict against the principal. Justice Wahl approved the principal's decision to leave the transition to the two teachers involved who had the expertise he lacked in physical education. He believed that the principal was protected by the doctrine of "discretionary immunity."

Justice Otis argued that the principal was not qualified in physical education and used good judgment when he chose to leave the "details to the experts — the teachers — as an efficient administrator should." Otis questioned what the court would expect administrators to do when they lacked competence in certain subjects. He warned the court that its drastic decision could have serious ramifications because it could:

> Shift much of the responsibility for the safety of the students from the personnel best suited to handle such problems to an administrator who is not an expert in every area of teaching and cannot be in all places at all times. It would compel principals out of an abundance of caution to impose restrictions and restraints on subordinate teachers which might well be inappropriate and wholly inconsistent with sound teaching practices.

Otis ended his vigorous dissent by pointing out that:

> except in the rare case where the principal is negligent in selecting a teacher or fails to respond to actual notice of a potential hazard, I would limit the liability of the principal and impose it on where it belongs — on the negligent

204

teacher and on the school board which is vicariously responsible under principles of *respondeat superior.*

In Michigan, Gregory Vargo, a fifteen-year-old boy, attempted to lift 250 pounds of weights when he fell and sustained serious injuries that resulted in paraplegia.[28] The boy sued the athletic director, coach, principal, superintendent and school district and all claimed that they were protected by the doctrine of governmental immunity. The trial court upheld their plea with the exception of the coach who, it ruled, did not enjoy immunity.

The plaintiff appealed and the court of appeals reviewed the facts of the case.

Gregory reported that he was lifting weights, in preparation for the upcoming football season, because the principal had pressured him into participating in the weight program. He charged the principal with negligent conduct for:

> inducing, suggesting, encouraging ... intimidating and coercing plaintiff Gregory Roy Vargo ... to attend the weight lifting session and to attempt to lift and lower weights without having inquired as to his experience or capabilities to lift such weights without properly instructing him and other members of the class as to techniques of safety that would avoid injury and without providing proper mechanical and/or human safeguards.

The plaintiff charged the athletic director and principal with the failure to supervise the football coach who allegedly threatened, pressured and pushed his athletes beyond their capabilities. In addition, he declared that the principal ignored a Michigan High School Athletic Association rule that prohibited organized summer programs for football players.

Finally, he claimed that the room in the gymnasium, in which they lifted weights, was improperly ventilated and contributed to his injury.

The court of appeals referred to the *Cook* decision and stated:

> As in *Cook,* Principal Mayores had a duty to reasonably exercise supervisory powers so as to minimize injury to his students. The principal of the school maintains direct control over the use and conditions of the facilities. Therefore if the weight lifting room was, in fact, improperly equipped and designed for that use, the defendant principal would bear direct responsibility.[29]

The court continued by observing that: "Moreover, if the summer weight lifting program was, in fact, a violation of MHSAA rules and regulations, it would be the principal, Ernest Mayores, who would be in charge of such a program."[30]

The court made an interesting comment when it stated that it had not previously considered the liability of a school athletic director regarding the doctrine of governmental immunity. It was emphatic in its belief that the same reasons for assigning liability to the principal should apply to the athletic director. It felt that the summer weight-lifting program was his responsibility since he had the authority to eliminate any unsafe practices. The court recognized that the athletic director, because of his specialized training and position, had more obligation to enforce rules of safety than the principal.

The court concluded that the superintendent and the school district were protected from liability by the statute of governmental immunity, but it reversed the lower court's decision regarding the principal and athletic director and added their names to that of the coach for trial.

206

An interesting case took place in Illinois as a principal was sued because he refused to let a women's softball coach leave school early to begin practice.[31] Kathleen Pomrehn was a member of the Crete-Monee High School Softball team that practiced at an elementary school one mile from the high school. Freshmen and sophomores were driven by bus to the field while the upperclassmen furnished their own transportation for the after school practices.

Julie David taught at the high school in a "split shift attendance procedure" and at 5:45 p.m. would leave for her 5:50 p.m. practice. It was common practice for many teachers to leave school at 5:30 p.m. On the day before the injury to Kathleen, Coach David had left school at 5:30 p.m. to begin practice.

Her principal directed her to remain until 5:45 p.m. on the day the accident occurred. (It was reported that the principal was harassing the coach because she had instituted several discrimination suits against the school district). When Coach David asked her principal, "What happens if one of my kids get hurt?", he answered, "It won't happen."

Kathleen arrived at the field prior to the start of practice and one of her friends had locked her keys in her car. Kathleen accompanied another friend as the friend drove to her home a block away to get a coat hanger to open the door.

On the way back to the softball field, Kathleen rode "on the outside of the auto, atop the trunk." When the driver of the car turned off the road onto a grassy area near the field, Kathleen fell off the car and sustained serious head injuries. Her medical bills exceeded $25,000 and her earning capacity was reduced considerably by the accident.

Kathleen sued the driver of the car, and the driver's father, who owned the car, along with the Crete-Monee High School District for "wilful and wanton misconduct" alleging that the principal refused to let her coach get to practice before the players arrived. She claimed that he realized that the girls gathered at the field by 5:30 p.m. and allegedly singled Coach David out to remain until 5:45 p.m. She charged the principal with "intentional action in preventing the designated supervisor from being present at practice when the girls arrived prior to the scheduled practice." The court stated that:

> To sustain a claim of wilful and wanton misconduct the plaintiff must show an intentional act by defendant or an act taken, under the circumstances known, in reckless or conscious disregard of probable injurious consequences.

During the trial the court heard testimony that revealed that no special dangers were present during the period between the end of classes until softball practice began. There were no reported problems or hazards between team members or on the softball field. The court remarked that: "Certainly, there is a risk of injury and a danger involved in almost any gathering of teenagers."

It found no evidence of "wilful and wanton" misconduct on the part of the school district and affirmed the judgment of the lower court in granting the defendant summary judgment.

Rules and Regulations

In tort actions an unusually large number of cases involve rules and regulations. Several cases reported in *Physical Education and the Law*[32] illustrate the type of litigation involving the administrator.

Ten students in Indiana, elected to remain inside the classroom to work on an assignment instead of going outside to play during an open recess period.[33] The teacher left the group unsupervised and went outside the immediate area. William Miller opened another student's tackle box in search of a pencil. The box contained a battery and a detonator cap that looked like a Christmas bulb to the boy. He touched the cap to the battery and it exploded, permanently damaging his eye.

The injured student sued the principal for having a rule that permitted a teacher to leave a class unsupervised. The principal admitted that he had formulated a rule that enabled a teacher to have free time during the recess period. The rule allowed a teacher to consider all facets of the situation and, if convinced that the circumstances permitted, to leave the students in the classroom alone. The principal furnished supervision for the open recess on the playground.

The teacher, in the present case, testified that the students were eager to work on their assignment and that no problem children were present in the room. In addition she asked the teacher in the adjoining room to look in on the group from time to time.

Two questions were raised during the trial:

1. Was the principal's rule reasonable?
2. Was the action of the teacher discretionary (a duty requiring the exercise of judgment) or ministerial (a duty which a public officer is required by law to perform)?

The court considered the teacher's act to be discretionary and free from liability and the principal's rule reasonable. It, therefore, dismissed the case against him.

David Flournoy, a student in Colorado, and several classmates in physical education attempted to cross a busy street from the gymnasium to the playground.[34] Flournoy was hit by a speeding car and died from the injuries he sustained.

His parents charged the superintendent and principal with negligent conduct for failing to adopt rules that would provide a safe crossing for the student. They contended that the crossing was dangerous because of the heavy traffic and needed safeguards.

In Colorado, public officials are charged with negligence under the doctrine of *respondeat superior* (imposes liability on an employer for the acts of his employee) when: "they fail to use ordinary care, therein, or where they have been negligent in supervising the acts of their subordinates or have directed or authorized the wrong." [35]

The court stated that public officials are not expected to be held liable for honest mistakes, but on the other hand, they cannot avoid their obligation to the public by failing to fulfill their duties.

The administrators argued that their acts were not the proximate cause of the accident and that they could not have prevented his death by anything they could have done. The district court returned a verdict in favor of the defendants and the plaintiffs appealed. The Supreme Court of Colorado reversed the original decision of the defendants and remanded the case back to a jury for determination of the facts.

One of the judges dissented by pointing out that the administrators did not select the site or control the location of the playground. He felt that they were not guilty of negligence. It is reported that the case was retried and the court ruled in favor of the defendant superintendent and principal.

The courts have considered several cases in which an inherently dangerous condition was not corrected and a student was injured. In a Michigan case,[36] a child was injured on the school playground when her sled hit a steel post. The girl's father sued for $60,000 and argued

210

vehemently that the school authorities had sufficient knowledge of the dangerous situation, but failed to correct it in a reasonable time. He stressed the fact that numerous accidents had resulted from the location of the steel post but that the school officials had continued to ignore it. The court found no breach of duty against the principal and upheld the district's claim of immunity.

The court reacted differently in Washington, D.C., however, when a young boy wandered through a hole in a chain fence on the playground.[37] The boy strayed into a busy street, became confused and was hit by a car and killed as he tried to get back to the playground. The boy's parents sued the school charging the principal with negligence for failing to have the fence repaired. The court ruled that the duty to repair the fence was ministerial and not protected by governmental immunity. The question was asked: "How far does a school have to go to insure the safety of its students"? The court answered that while the school is not an absolute insurer of its students, it does owe a duty to protect its students from the hazard of the street. It considered the gap in the fence, the school's knowledge of its existence, the age of the deceased, the proximity of the busy intersection to the school and then ruled that the defendant was guilty of negligence for failing to correct the dangerous condition that existed.

In another case a New York court ruled that a warning of danger is all that is necessary on the part of a principal.[38] No one was supervising the playground when a boy slipped on a fence on the school grounds. The principal provided supervision in the lunch room, but not on the playground, at noontime. On the day in question, the boy was given permission by his teacher to play outside after lunch.

The principal reminded the court that he had made periodic warnings to all his pupils about the fence from

211

which the boy fell. The boy admitted that he had received several warnings about the fence but that he had deliberately ignored them. The Education Code stated that a warning about the fence was sufficient to provide adequate supervision for the pupils in the school. The court, therefore, concluded that the boy was guilty of contributory negligence and dismissed the case against the principal.

The father of Gordon McDonald sued a Louisiana School Board, the teacher, the principal and a ten-year-old boy, Larry, who injured his son Gordon in school.[39] Bad weather forced the students to go on a "rainy day" schedule which meant that the students could not go outside during the lunch recess but were required to play in their classrooms. Gordon and a boy named Larry were in a special education class. Both boys were considered to be retarded but educable. Gordon was eight months older than Larry.

The boys' teacher went to the lounge for coffee and when she did Gordon began chasing Larry and a fight erupted. Gordon chased Larry out of the classroom and Larry threatened to throw a broom at him if he did not stop coming after him. When Gordon continued to pursue Larry, the latter turned and threw a broom that struck Gordon in the eye. The injury caused Gordon to lose the sight in his eye.

The issue in the case centered around the principal's alleged failure to take precautionary measures with the students to avoid such incidents.

The Louisiana court found no fault with Larry for throwing the broom at the larger boy in self-defense. The court did not consider a common household broom to be inherently dangerous nor did it think throwing the broom constituted excessive force.

Since the teacher had requested another teacher next door to check on her class, the court did not feel the teacher was negligent just because she left her class unsupervised.

It stated: "The fact that each student is not personally supervised every moment of each school day does not constitute fault on the part of the School Board or its employees."

Evidence at the trial indicated that Larry had a record of previous incidents in which fighting took place. The school principal testified, however, that Larry was by no means the worst boy in school. He added that "this is a special education situation involving handicapped children" and to find a record of perfect conduct would be most unusual.

The Louisiana court dismissed the charge of negligence against the principal by ruling that he had not handled the situation in a negligent manner.

Court Cases Involving the School District

School districts still rely heavily on the protection of the doctrine of sovereign and governmental immunity; private schools cling to the doctrine of charitable immunity. These districts argue that funds are not available to meet the awards of lawsuits that would be brought against them.

The common-law principle has protected school districts with immunity in the past without regard to the circumstances of the case in question. Unless a statute existed to the contrary, the doctrine protected the school from liability suits and subsequent damages.

John Weistart and Cym Lowell, writing in *The Law of Sports,* comment on the immunity doctrines by declaring:

> In recent years, however, the courts and legislature have begun to make wholesale inroads into the doctrines, with the result that in many states both public and charitable institutions are accorded the same status as most tort-feasors — that is, they must compensate those who are injured by their wrongful acts.[40]

213

Dr. Betty Van der Smissen, a legal scholar, in a presentation at the Indiana Law and Sports Conference in August, 1981, noted that the immunity doctrines in all fifty states had been modified, abrogated or subjected to exceptions.[41]

Weistart and Lowell note that the doctrine has been under criticism and is declining on the state and local levels. They suggest that the following procedure is in order in the event of a sports-related lawsuit when they comment:

> Since it may, however, protect a governmental entity which is made a defendant in a sports-related injury suit, it will be imperative for an attorney litigating in this area to ascertain the extent of protection that the doctrine provides in the jurisdiction in question.[42]

Today students have more equipment and facilities in physical education and sports than ever before and many spend countless hours in gymnasiums and on athletic fields. When the equipment is used and maintained in a proper manner it is an asset to all who use it. When equipment is defective, however, it can lead to lawsuits when participants are injured. In like manner, unsafe facilities are a common cause for litigation.

George Peters, a California attorney, speaking at the National Conference on Sports Safety, cautioned people who provide equipment and facilities for recreational activities and sporting events that "legal obligations vary from state to state, the attitudes of jurors vary from locality to locality, and the facts of each case are always different."[43]

Peters suggested a possible guideline when considering standards for equipment when he concluded: "Thus, clear statements as to what the specific law is . . . can only

214

mislead. Instead what is desirable is a general under-standing of the relevant legal obligations and trends in the law." [44]

The following judicial decisions are a sampling of recent court cases that help reveal the attitude of the courts toward litigation involving school boards and school districts.

Kervin Merrill was thrown to the floor during a wrestling match in a required physical education class and sustained a broken ankle.[45] The match was supervised by an instructor at the time, and a teacher was near the area where the injury occurred.

The Sixth Judicial Circuit Court entered summary judgment for the school district on the basis of sovereign immunity and the plaintiff appealed. The boy and his guardian contended that the school district purchased liability insurance and could not claim sovereign immunity as a defense.

The Supreme Court of South Dakota responded that the legislature had not granted permission to sue defendants in this type of tort action. "The purchase of liability insurance," it commented, "does not provide that permission."

The court then concluded: "The county is authorized to carry insurance to idemnify itself against its statutory liability, but the fact of insurance does not create a cause of action where none existed in the absence of insurance."

David Ardoin rounded second base and headed for third base when he suddenly fell on a concrete slab and injured himself.[46] His father sued the school board because a slab of concrete 12' by 12" and 30" thick was embedded between second and third base on the softball field. The trial court concluded that the school board was negligent because it failed to provide a safe place for students to play. The school board disagreed and appealed the judgment to the Court of Appeals of Louisiana.

The appeals court questioned the actual location of the concrete slab and whether it violated the standard of care necessary to provide a safe place for participants on the playground. The court stated that:

> The law is settled that a school board is liable if it has actual knowledge or constructive knowledge of a condition unreasonably hazardous to the children under its supervision. It commented that it heard no evidence to prove that the school board knew that the concrete existed on the basepaths but reasoned that: Constructive knowledge of a defect exists if it is so inherently dangerous that the school authorities should have known of it.

The court concluded that any reasonable inspection of the area would have immediately revealed the hazard posed by the concrete to the participants on the school grounds. It therefore upheld the verdict of the lower court and ruled that the awards of $12,000 in general damages and $1,895.60 in medical expenses were valid.

The parents of a retarded student in Louisiana sought damages for the tragic drowning of their son.[47] The boy attended a school located on a fifty acre campus with several ponds on it. He had been a student there for three years and worked on the maintenance crew as part of his training. The school offered experiences in carpentry, masonry, mechanics and other vocations. Each work group had a supervisor who helped the students but did not always stay with them on a continuous basis. While the supervisor was away from the group, the boy fell into the pond and drowned.

The question was raised during the trial whether the school had the duty to provide continuous supervision to its students. The boy's parents insisted that the school did owe such a duty since the students at the school were retarded.

216

The school officials explained that the school intentionally planned a policy of freedom for the students based on their individual mental and physical abilities. They pointed out that the boy was very familiar with the ponds on campus since he passed them often. They also declared that he was not dangerous to himself and did not require special attention. The school authorities indicated that:

> the educational advantages of providing the students some freedom and opportunity to learn self-reliance, and the quality of life advantages of the open space in which students lived and worked, far outweigh the risks of harm attendant, thereto. The risks were minimal and were not unreasonable under the circumstances.

On the other hand, the parents claimed that the unsupervised pond represented an attractive nuisance and contributed to the death of their son. The Court of Appeal of Louisiana responded that:

> Application of the attractive nuisance doctrine is nothing more than nomenclature given to a determination that a defendant has breached its duty of reasonable care for the safety of others by maintaining on its premises an unreasonable and foreseeable hazard to children or others with childlike judgment.

It concluded that the pond existed for years and the boy was aware of it. As such, the court felt that the pond did not present a risk or hazard that was either unreasonable or foreseeable to the students. While it found the drowning of the retarded boy deplorable and tragic, the court ruled that the school and its employees were not liable for the boy's unexpected death.

Sasha Gibbons, a six-year-old first grader, arrived at school at 8:30 a.m. and began swinging on "monkey bars" which were next to a "tether ball pole." [48] She attempted to

217

slide down the pole after she had climbed to the top of the "monkey bars." She injured her thigh on a protruded screw.

At the time she was injured, over 150 students were on the playground under the supervision of one teacher. This teacher was expected to supervise the playground, assist in bus duty and look after students in the basement of the school. The court observed that while adequate supervisory personnel might not have prevented the accident, one teacher responsible for so many duties to so large a group was "totally inadequate and virtually impossible."

The court could not understand why the bars and pole were so close in proximity since most children would be tempted to go from the bars to the pole. The protruding screw became a hazard because of its proximity to the bars. It was foreseeable that children would be inclined to switch from the bars to the pole.

The court concluded that the lack of adequate supervision on the playground, the location of the bars to the pole and the "protruding screw" resulted in negligence on the part of the defendant school board. It therefore awarded the girl $7,500 "for pain, disfigurement, and future cosmetic surgery expenses."

Christine Besette, a six-year-old first grader, fell off a slide on the school playground and injured her arm on a rock that was buried beneath grass and top soil.[49] A teacher's aide who was supervising the playground at the time the injury took place watched Christine climb to the top of the slide but did not see her at the moment she fell off the slide.

Christine's father sued the school district for allegedly failing to properly maintain the playground and provide proper supervision for the students who used the playground.

The trial court favored the defendant school district and the plaintiffs appealed to the Supreme Court of North Dakota. Many questions were raised during the trial that included: (1) whether evidence of the various types of surfaces at other playgrounds was admissible; (2) whether the trial court properly instructed the jury regarding the school district's duty of maintenance and supervision; and (3) whether the trial court properly refused to permit one of plaintiff's attorneys from testifying in behalf of plaintiff.

The court ruled that the evidence supported the trial court's verdict and it affirmed the judgment for the defendant school district.

The trial court issued general instructions regarding negligence to the jury that may be of interest to all who supervise and maintain playgrounds. The trial court stated:

(1) A school must exercise ordinary care to keep its premises and facilities in reasonably safe condition for use of minors who foreseeably will make use of the premises and facilities.

(2) Schools are under a duty to insure the safety of their students during playground activities as well as a duty to properly maintain the premises.

(3) The school owes to its children to exercise such care of them as a parent of ordinary prudence would observe in a comparable circumstance.

(4) The duty of care owed a child is greater than that owed an adult against unreasonable risk of injury. The standard of care used in dealing with adults, however, is not considered adequate for those entrusted with the care of children. The degree of due care increases with the immaturity of the child. . . .

219

(5) Negligence, as applied to a minor child, is the doing of that which an ordinary prudent person of the age, intelligence, experience and capacity of such child would do under the same or similar circumstances, or the failure to do that which such a person would do under the same or similar circumstances.

Robert Foster, a seventeen-year-old mentally retarded student, was selected for the school's Special Olympics basketball team.[50] Foster had been tested and found to have an I.Q. of fifty-two and a mental age of seven years. In addition he was unable to follow simple directions and had a short attention span.

The physical education teacher was the coach of the team and a mathematics teacher assisted her. The school did not have a gymnasium and the team usually practiced outdoors on a dirt court. The coaches decided to prepare for the upcoming Special Olympics by practicing at a nearby gymnasium so the team could get used to playing on a wooden floor.

On the day the team was scheduled to practice at the gymnasium which was located three blocks from the school for the mentally retarded, the coaches decided not to go by bus, but to walk the short distance. The head coach was still in class when the team was ready to leave and, because the students were getting "fidgety," the assistant coach sent her word that he would take the students to the gymnasium. The head coach agreed and said that she would follow in her automobile as soon as class was over.

On the way to the gymnasium, five or six of the eleven mentally retarded students ignored the assistant coach's warning to stay together and ran ahead. When the assistant coach finally got them back together he lined them up in preparation for crossing the busy street. Suddenly Foster ran between two parked cars into the street. He saw an approaching car and tried to stop, but fell when his feet slipped out from under him. He was struck by the car and died three days later from the injuries he received.

Foster's mother sued the driver of the automobile, the coaches, the school district and their insurance companies for the death of her son. She claimed that her son had lived his entire life in a rural setting and was not accustomed to heavy vehicular traffic. She contended that the defendants had failed to select the safest route to travel and had failed to provide an adequate number of supervisors to protect the students.

The trial court found all the defendants except the driver of the automobile guilty of negligence and awarded the boy's mother $10,000 for his pain and suffering and $40,000 for the "loss of her son's love and affection." Both parties appealed the verdict; the defendants arguing that the boy had been guilty of contributory negligence, and the mother seeking additional money for her son's death.

The court of appeal noted that the physical education teacher always went to the room of each student to collect them and take them to and from practice. The court reasoned that this was not the normal custom for adolescents in the average school. It felt that closer supervision was needed with a group of mentally retarded students who were excited over the trip away from school. The court remarked that:

> In this situation there would have been difficulty in controlling a group of normal adolescents, much less one composed of those whose physical energies matched their chronological ages but who have the self-control and judgment of much younger children.

The court believed that if more supervisors had been present, the accident could have been avoided. It felt that the coaches should have foreseen the possibility of injury to

221

their group and ruled that the failure to select a safe route and provide adequate supervision was the proximate cause of the accident and subsequent death to Robert Foster.

The court, therefore, affirmed the judgment of the lower court.

Laura Wilson was struck by a metal soccer goal which fell and hit her as she was kneeling down to tie her shoe during a physical education class.[51] Laura's parents sued fifteen defendants that included the school's superintendent, principal and physical education teacher. The girl's parents insisted that the soccer goal was a nuisance and "sought recovery for wrongful death as well as punitive damages and damages for maintenance of a nuisance." The trial court granted summary judgment to the defendants as to the "nuisance and punitive damages claims" but denied all remaining motions for summary judgment.

The Court of Appeals of Georgia considered the plaintiff's contention that the principal failed to seek and receive approval for the purchase of the soccer goal from the school district. It found, however, that the soccer goal was paid for by groups in the community for joint use of the school and various community organizations. As such, approval for such a purchase was not needed by the principal.

The Court ruled that the defendants were protected by the doctrine of sovereign immunity since they were acting within the scope of their respective authorities. It made an interesting comment when it declared:

> In summary, it appears that the doctrine of sovereign immunity effectively shields all the defendants in this case from liability for the tragic death of plaintiff's daughter. Whatever our personal feelings concerning the justness of that doctrine, we are bound by our oaths to apply the law. Sovereign immunity is the law applicable to this case.

222

Barbara Woodring sued the Board of Education of Manhasset Union Free School District for the wrongful death of her husband.[52] He was a workman in the gymnasium trying to get onto a platform from a step ladder. He grabbed the railing around the platform and it gave way, causing him to fall to his death.

The jury awarded more than $1,400,000 and the Supreme Court, Appellate Division, Second Department upheld the award. It was discovered that a nut and a bolt which should have secured the railing were not in place, that the school had no program of preventive maintenance or inspection, and that the installation of the railing was not in accordance with the proper construction practice.

The court stated that since the platform was used extensively for various school functions and that students were known to hang from the railing and do somersaults, that it was foreseeable that injury would occur if the railings were not properly constructed or maintained.

Thomas Eddy was with a group of students from Harpur College who played a game of "ultimate frisbee" against a group of Syracuse University students in the gymnasium at Syracuse.[53] A janitor reportedly let the group in to play and from all reports the game was not sanctioned by University officials.

"Ultimate frisbee" is played much like soccer with players running toward an opponent's goal line while passing the frisbee and attempting to cross the goal line. This group used the ends of the basketball court as goal lines although glass doors were located at the west end of the gymnasium.

The plaintiff ran into the glass doors and his body went through the unlocked door causing severe lacerations to his arm. He admitted that he knew the glass doors were located at the end of the gymansium and that University officials, in all probability, were unaware of the informal game.

223

The University, as might be expected, argued that the gymnasium was safe for the purposes for which it was constructed. It contended that it could not be expected to foresee the manner for which some people would use it. When the lower court awarded the plaintiff damages, the defendant University appealed the decision.

The Supreme Court, Appellate Division, Fourth Department, decided that the University should have foreseen that, on such a large campus, many students and others would use the gymnasium for unique and novel games. The court also reasoned that the close proximity of the glass doors at the end of the court posed a danger to basketball players and it declared that the University had a duty to protect the users of the gymnasium from harm. In this instance, the court concluded that the University breached its duty by the location of the glass doors which were the proximate cause of the accident. It therefore affirmed the lower court's decision.

The Need To Inform

In 1947 two students were ordered to box for several rounds although neither had previous experience in boxing.[54] One of the students received a hard blow to the temple causing a serious injury that resulted in a delicate brain and spinal operation. A New York court found the physical education teacher guilty of negligence for failing to warn the students of the risks inherent in boxing.

From 1947 until the seventies little attention was given to the importance of issuing warnings to students regarding the risks in various sports activities. In 1978 James Sunday's ski became entangled on a bush or brush on a ski trail in Stratton, Vermont.[55] Sunday was awarded $1.5 million for the injury that caused him to become a permanent quadriplegic. The amount of the award

224

drastically changed the type of advertisement used by ski resorts, from those promoting safe trails and quality maintained slopes, to signs that warned that skiing may be hazardous to your health.

Extreme financial pressure has been placed recently on the manufacturers of football helmets as multi-million lawsuits threaten their existence. A Texas court awarded Mark Daniels, a high school athlete, $1.5 million for a crippling injury he sustained when his football helmet caved in.[56] The court emphasized the importance of warning participants of dangers in sports activities when it declared "here the failure to warn was negligence. A product that does not include a warning is dangerously defective." The most recent case to attract nationwide attention has been referred to as the "Seattle Case" in which a jury awarded Christopher Thompson, a high school athlete who was injured in football, a landmark $6.4 million.[57] A Washington jury based its decision on the fact that Thompson was not warned or informed of the risks inherent in football.

Administrators, coaches, physical education teachers and school boards are cautioned that the failure to warn students of risks in sports activities can lead to liability. Samuel H. Adams and Mary Ann Bayless writing on the implications of the "Seattle Case" suggest ways to communicate to students involved in sports activities:

- •Inform students in very specific terms the dangers involved in each activity

- •All foreseeable dangers should be demonstrated and specifically emphasized. Methods of avoidance and safety techniques should be taught concerning each danger.[58]

They conclude by pointing out the importance of keeping records of material, films, photographs, guest speakers or

225

any resource used to communicate the risks of activities to students.[59]

Ray Perkins, the University of Alabama's football coach, reported that he tape-records his talks on sport safety to his teams so he can have a permanent record for future reference if challenged in court.[60] Perkins realizes the need to issue warnings and to inform his athletes of the risks involved in football. His technique is sound procedure in a day of unprecedented litigation.

In 1947 the importance of communicating warnings was evident in *La Valley*, but it took million dollar awards in the seventies to mandate its importance.

Educational Malpractice

A new area of tort law, educational malpractice, has become a factor in the law as it relates to physical education and sports. Elizabeth Kurker-Stewart and David Carter, Sr., note that it was not until the 1950's that it became an issue.[61] While they comment that the difficulty in winning a law suit has been the plaintiff's inability to prove proximate cause, they predict that:

> the enactment of directive, prescriptive legislation in the form of the Education For All Handicapped Children Act (1975), P.L. 94-142, has powerfully clarified the specific responsibilities of educators toward handicapped children. This clear delineation of responsibilities in special education turned the trend toward increased educational accountability and heightened the possibility that the first educational malpractice suit would be won.

The question of whether damages can be awarded for the "negligent classification, placement or teaching of a student" against a school district was tested in the Supreme Court of Alaska.[62] The case is important for its conclusions.

L.A.H., a seventeen-year-old student at the Borough School District schools suffered from dyslexia. L.A.H. contended that he attended the district's schools from kindergarten through the sixth grade and until the last day of his second year in the sixth grade. School officials failed to diagnose his condition as dyslexia. For a short time he was given special courses to help him overcome his problem but despite the district's knowledge of his disability, it terminated his special courses. L.A.H. complained that this action constituted negligence and caused him to suffer the following: "loss of education, loss of opportunity for employment, loss of opportunity to attend college or post high school studies, past and future mental anguish and loss of income and income earning ability."

D.W.S. had a similar claim. His dyslexic condition was not diagnosed until the fifth grade, but the special services provided were terminated beginning with the seventh grade. D.W.S. sought money damages against the school district citing the same reasons as given by L.A.H.

The Alaska Supreme Court noted that while the claim represented "a claim for first impression in Alaska," two other jurisdictions addressed the question of: "whether a claim may be maintained against a school for failing to discover learning disabilities or failing to provide an appropriate educational program once learning disabilities are discovered."

It referred to *Peter W. v. San Francisco Unified School District*,[63] the earliest case of this type, in which the plaintiff charged that the school district failed to detect his reading disability and place him in an appropriate class. The California court considered the question of whether "an actionable duty of care existed" by stating that:

> The foreseeability of harm to the plaintiff, the degree of certainty that the plaintiff suffered

injury, the closeness of the connection between the defendant's conduct and the injury suffered, the moral blame attached to the defendant's conduct, the policy of preventing future harm, the extent of the burden to the defendant and consequences to the community of imposing a duty to exercise care with resulting liability for breach, and the availability, cost and prevalence of insurance for the risk involved.

The court declared that the issue raised questions that were "highly problematical in educational malpractice claims." It then made several comments that may be reviewed by many courts in future educational malpractice claims when it declared:

Unlike the activity of the highway or the marketplace, classroom methodology affords no readily acceptable standards of care, or cause, or injury. The science of Pedagogy itself is fraught with different and conflicting theories of how or what a child should be taught, and any layman might and commonly does — have his own emphatic views on the subject. The "injury" claimed here is plaintiff's inability to read and write. Substantial professional authority attests that the achievement of literacy in the schools, or its failure, is influenced by a host of factors which affect the pupil subjectively, from outside the formal teaching process, and beyond the control of its ministers. They may be physical, neurological, emotional, cultural, environmental; *they may be present but not perceived, recognized but not identified.* (Emphasis added.)

The court found no rule of care against "which defendants" alleged conduct may be measured — within the law of negligence. It also reasoned that if such lawsuits were permitted, a flood of expensive litigation would result. It commented on the problems that would be added to the burdens of already beleagured school systems when it said:

> Few of our institutions, if any, have aroused the
> controversies, or incurred the public dissatis-
> faction, which have attended the operation of the
> public schools during the last few decades.
> Rightly or wrongly, but widely, they are charged
> with outright failure in the achievement of their
> educational objectives; according to some critics,
> they bear responsibility for many of the social
> and moral problems of our society at large. Their
> public plight in these respects is attested in the
> daily media, in bitter governing board elections,
> in wholesale rejections of school bond proposals,
> and in survey upon survey. To hold them to an
> actionable "duty of care," in the discharge of
> their academic functions, would expose them to
> the tort claims — real or imagined — of
> disaffected students and parents in countless
> numbers. They are already beset by social and
> financial problems which have gone to major
> litigation, but for which no permanent solution
> has yet appeared. The ultimate consequences, in
> terms of public time and money, would burden
> them — and society — beyond calculation.

The Alaska Supreme Court then referred to *Donahue v.
Copiague Union Free School District* [64] in which the facts of
the case were similar to those in *Peter W.* The New York
Court of Appeals was of the firm opinion that judicial
interference would disrupt the administration of the
schools. It declared: "Recognition in the courts of this cause
of action would constitute blatant interference with the
responsibility for the administration of the public school
system lodged by Constitution and statute in school
administrative agencies."

The Alaska Supreme Court reviewed the highly
publicized case of *Hoffman v. Board of Education of the City
of New York* [65] which presented a different problem.

Hoffman was of normal intelligence but due to a faulty diagnosis was placed in classes for the mentally retarded for the majority of his schooling. A New York jury awarded him $750,000 in damages and the appellate division affirmed the decision. The court of appeals using *Donahue* as its guide reversed the decision, denying any award.

After reviewing the previous cases involving claims of educational malpractice, the Alaska Supreme Court agreed with the decisions by making a timely observation that declared:

> In particular we think that the remedy of money damages is inappropriate as a remedy for one who has been a victim of errors made during his or her education. The level of success which might have been achieved had the mistake not been made will, we believe, be necessarily incapable of assessment, rendering legal cause an imponderable which is beyond the ability of courts to deal with in a reasoned way.

The court made it clear that while it did not favor damage suits for educational malpractice cases, it felt that parents who feel that their children have been placed or classified inappropriately do have recourse. It believes that a parent in such a situation can request:

> an independent examination and evaluation of the child, and for a hearing before a hearing officer in the event of a substantial discrepancy. Further, that section (AS 14.30.191 (c)) provides that the proceedings so conducted are subject to the Administrative Procedure Act, which in turn expressly provides for judicial review. (AS 44.62.560.)

The Alaska Supreme Court commented that such procedures for solving classification and placement disputes are best settled through provisions stated above rather than tort action for damages. It felt that administrative and judicial review handled promptly could correct previous errors in time to enable a student to attain an appropriate education. The court concluded that "[m]oncy damages, on the other hand, are a poor, and only tenuously related, substitute for a proper education."

From the cases reviewed in this chapter, we can reasonably conclude that the probability that a lawsuit will result does not vary because the participant was nonhandicapped or an individual with handicapping conditions. It does not vary because the acitivities are carried on during the classes, at recess, between classes, during the noon hour or after school during practice sessions. It does not matter whether the injuries occurred in the gymnasium, on the playground or on the athletic field. Negligence is the basic factor regardless of the time or place.

Summary

Litigation in the area of physical education and sports is at an all-time high and federal legislation will, in all probability, increase participation in these activities with an accompanying rise in lawsuits.

There is no sure criteria for determining what is negligent action and what is not since each case stands individually on its own merit. The key to liability is the presence of negligence since a school and its staff owe their students the duty of care that is required to save them from foreseeable harm.

The elements of negligence are a duty, a breach of duty, proximate cause and damage. To counteract a claim of negligence, the defendant should prove that one of these elements is not present. Other defenses that can result in a verdict of nonliability are contributory negligence, comparative negligence and assumption of risk.

231

The courts make little, if any, distinction between the nonhandicapped and individuals with handicapping conditions in litigation dealing with injuries in physical education and sports programs.

A new trend has emerged that is gaining momentum in the courts. Administrators are being held liable for injuries that occur in the classrooms, playgrounds, gymnasiums and on the athletic fields. The courts are ruling that administrators have an obligation to the student because they have the responsibility for the overall operation of the school.

School administrators are encouraged to follow several guidelines:

1. Assign adequate supervision to physical education and sports activities. The number of supervisors should be determined by the activity, size and age of the group.
2. Supervise physical education classes and sports practices just as an academic class.
3. Work closely with inexperienced or less qualified personnel.
4. Employ qualified personnel in high risk activities or eliminate the activities.
5. Conduct in-service training programs in emergency first aid, CPR, and sports activities.
6. Set policies and develop a policy handbook for all teachers and coaches.
7. Place physical education teachers and coaches under direct supervision of directors of physical education and athletic directors.

School districts are sued along with the teacher, coach and administrator. While many still cling to the doctrine of governmental immunity, all fifty states have modified the immunity doctrine to some extent.

Public Law 94-142 has greatly increased the potential for litigation and heightened the possibility of the first successful educational malpractice award. To date, no plaintiff has won such a lawsuit but this has not stopped the number of suits in the courts. The courts have noted that such issues raise questions that are "highly problematic." The court comments that: "Unlike the activity of the highway or marketplace, classroom methodology affords no readily acceptable standards of care, or cause, or injury."

As yet the court has failed to find any rule of care against which defendants' conduct may be measured within the law of negligence in educational malpractice suits. Other courts reason that such lawsuits are permitted and are successful, a flood of expensive litigation will result. Schools are already beset by social and financial problems and the ultimate consequence of such action in terms of public time and money would burden them and society beyond calculation.

FOOTNOTES

1. New York Times, July 5, 1981.
2. *Id.*
3. WILLIAM L. PROSSER, JOHN W. WADE & VICTOR E. SCHWARTZ, TORTS, CASES AND MATERIALS, 6th Edition, Foundation Press, 1976.
4. HERB APPENZELLER, FROM THE GYM TO THE JURY, The Michie Company, Charlottesville, Virginia, 1970.
5. *Id.*
6. Bolmeier, *Tort Liability and the Schools,* 76 AMERICAN SCHOOL BOARD JOURNAL, March 1958, at 31.
7. Clary v. Alexander County Board of Education, 199 S.E.2d 738 (N.C. App. 1973).
8. Meharey v. United States of America, Civil No. A4-80-54, U.S. District Court (N.W. Div. No. Dakota 1981).
9. JOHN C. WEISTART & CYM H. LOWELL, THE LAW OF SPORTS, The Bobbs-Merrill Company, 1979 at 935.
10. Rutter v. Northeastern Beaver County School District, 437 A.2d 1198 (Pa. 1981).
11. *Id.*
12. Passantino v. Board of Education of City of New York, 383 N.Y.S.2d 639 (N.Y. Sup. Ct. 1976), *rev'd,* 395 N.Y.S.2d 628 (N.Y. App. Div. 1976).
13. Kenneth S. Clarke, *Sports Liability Control,* a presentation at the American Alliance of Health, Physical Education, Recreation and Dance Convention, New Orleans, La., March 17, 1979.
14. Id.
15. *Supra* note 4.
16. Schumate v. Thompson, 580 S.W.2d 47 (Tex. 1979).
17. Landers v. School District No. 203, 383 N.E.2d 645 (Ill. 1978).
18. Montague v. School Board of the Thornton Fractional Township North High School District, 373 N.W.2d 719 (Ill. 1978).
19. Stineman v. Fontbonne College, 664 F.2d 1082 (8th Cir. 1981).
20. Brahatcek v. Millard School District, School District No. 17, 273 N.W.2d 680 (Neb. 1979).
21. Fantini v. Alexander, 410 A.2d 1190 (N.J. 1980).
22. De Mauro v. Tusculum College, 603 S.W.2d 115 (Tenn. 1980).
23. Stehn v. Benarr MacFadden Foundations, Inc., 434 F.2d 811 (6th Cir. 1970).

24. *Supra* note 4.

25. Green v. Orleans Parish School Board, 365 So. 2d 834 (La. App. 1979), *cert. denied,* 367 So. 2d 393.

26. Cook v. Bennett, 288 N.W.2d 609 (Mich. App. 1980).

27. Larson v. Independent School District No. 314, Braham, 289 N.W.2d 112 (Minn. 1980).

28. Vargo v. Svitchan, 301 N.W.2d 1 (Mich. App. 1981).

29. *Supra* note 26.

30. *Id.*

31. Pomrehn v. Crete-Monee High School District, 437 N.E.2d 1387 (Ill. App. 1981).

32. Herb Appenzeller, PHYSICAL EDUCATION AND THE LAW, The Michie Company, Charlottesville, Virginia, 1978.

33. Miller v. Griesel, 297 N.E.2d 463 (Ind. App. 1973).

34. Flournoy v. McComas, 488 P.2d 1104 (Colo. 1971).

35. Liber v. Flor, 415 P.2d 332 (Colo. 1966).

36. Stevens v. City of St. Clair Shores, 115 N.W.2d 69 (Mich. 1962).

37. Ballard v. Polly, 387 F. Supp. 895 (D.C. Cir. 1975).

38. Schuyler v. Board of Educ. of Union Free School Dist. No. 7, 239 N.Y.S.2d 769 (N.Y. App. Div. 1963).

39. McDonald v. Terrebonne Parish School Bd., 253 So. 2d 558 (La. App. 1971).

40. *Supra* note 9.

41. Betty Van der Smissen, presentation at Law and Amateur Sports Conference, Indianapolis, Indiana, August 20, 1981.

42. *Supra* note 9.

43. George Peters, Liability In Informal Sports and Recreational Programs, Proceeding at the Second National Conference on Sports Safety, Chicago, Illinois, 1979.

44. *Id.*

45. Merrill v. Birhanzel, 310 N.W.2d 522 (S.D. 1981).

46. Ardoin v. Evangeline Parish School Board, 376 So. 2d 372 (La. 1979).

47. Hunter v. Evergreen Presbyterian Vocational School, 338 So. 2d 164 (La. App. 1976).

48. Gibbons v. Orleans Parish School Board, 391 So. 2d 976 (La. 1980).

49. Besette v. Enderlin School Dist. No. 22, 310 N.W.2d 759 (N.D. 1981).

50. Foster v. Houston General Insurance Company, 407 So. 2d 759 (La. App. 1981).

51. Truelove v. Wilson, 285 S.E.2d 556 (Ga. 1981).

52. Woodring v. Board of Education of Manhasset Union Free School District, 435 N.Y.S.2d 52 (1981).

53. Eddy v. Syracuse University, 433 N.Y.S.2d 923 (App. Div. 1980).

54. LaVelly v. Stanford, 70 N.Y.S.2d 460 (1947).

55. Sunday v. Stratton Corp., 390 A.2d 398 (Vt. 1978).

56. Rawlings Sporting Goods v. Daniels, No. 6257, Civil Court of Appeals, Tenth Judicial District, Waco, Texas, 1981.

57. Samuel H. Adams and Mary Ann Bayless, How the Seattle Decision Affects Liability and You, ATHLETIC PURCHASING & FACILITIES, Vol. 6, No. 7, July, 1982.

58. Id.

59. Samuel H. Adams and Mary Ann Bayless, *Clear Specific Instruction Is Your Best Position,* ATHLETIC PURCHASING AND FACILITIES, Vol. 8, No. 8, Aug. 1982.

60. Ray Perkins in a speech at the Fifth Annual Sports Medicine Symposium, Pensacola, Florida, February 18, 1982.

61. Elizabeth A. Kurker-Stewart & David G. Carter, Sr., *Educational Malpractice and P.L. 94-142: A New Dilemma for Educators,* NOLPE SCHOOL LAW JOURNAL, Vol. 10, No. 1, 1981.

62. D.S.W. v. Fairbanks North Star Borough School District, 628 P.2d 554 (Alaska 1981).

63. Peter W. v. San Francisco Unified School District, 131 Cal. Rptr. 854 (1976).

64. Donahue v. Copiague Union Free School District, 418 N.Y.S.2d 375 (1979).

65. Hoffman v. Board of Education of the City of New York, 418 N.Y.S.2d 378 (1978).

CHAPTER 8

Conclusions and Recommendations

A new era has arrived for individuals with handicapping conditions, and new opportunities in physical education and sports will play a major role in it. The new era began with the efforts of many individuals as early as 1817 when the first residential school for the deaf was established in Hartford, Connecticut. It was given impetus through the media, the Congress and the courts.

The media have created a public awareness both of problems and potential solutions by highlighting the accomplishments of exceptional individuals. Congress has created a new political and administrative climate by enacting statutes mandating new opportunities for those who can benefit from them. Much of the legislation began in the 1950's and the series of legislative acts culminated in the passage of the Rehabilitation Act of 1973 and the Education For All Handicapped Children Act (1975). These two laws are recognized as the most important laws for individuals with handicapping conditions.

The importance of physical education is stressed in Public Law 94-142 and section 504 of the Rehabilitation Act as it is the only curricular area identified in the legislation. Both Public Law 94-142 and section 504 of the Rehabilitation Act emphasize the importance of interscholastic and intercollegiate athletics as extracurricular activities. The courts are increasingly positive concerning the benefits of sports participation and the right of individuals to obtain them. It has been said that participation in physical education and sports can change society's stereotyped view of the disabled and serve as an invaluable therapeutic tool. It is important for the sense of dignity, physical strength, coordination and endurance it offers the person.

237

With the passage of the Rehabilitation Act and Public Law 94-142, students from elementary school through post-university levels will have the right to participate in physical education and sports programs as never before. While the increased emphasis on physical education and sports will present students with new opportunities, it will also create additional hazards for them. School officials will be required to understand two areas regarding individuals with handicapping conditions, the legal mandates of the federal legislation and the legal aspects of tort liability.

Public Law 94-142 has four key mandates that require understanding. They include: a free appropriate education, least restrictive placement, due process and individualized education programs. It is important that judicial decisions be reviewed so that compliance can be achieved in a manner that is educationally and legally sound.

Teachers, coaches, administrators and school boards will become involved in numerous cases involving tort liability. The very nature of their work places their students in situations that can result in injuries and subsequent lawsuits. The courts do not distinguish between injuries to individuals with handicapping conditions and the nonhandicapped. The key to liability is the presence of negligence.

There are no hard and fast criteria for determining negligent action since each case is determined on its own merit. The probability that a lawsuit will result does not vary because the activities are carried on during the classes, at recess, between classes, during the noon hour or after school during practice sessions. It does not matter whether the injuries occurred in the gymnasium, on the playground or on the athletic field. Negligence is the basic factor regardless of the time or place.

CONCLUSIONS AND RECOMMENDATIONS

A new era of tort law that may become highly litigated is educational malpractice. Public Law 94-142 encourages lawsuits for alleged negligent placement, classification and teaching. To date no case has reportedly been won by a plaintiff, but the possibility exists that proximate cause may be established in a future case and the way will be open to a flood of educational malpractice cases. If a plaintiff is successful in such a case, educational accountability will be increased along with a burden in terms of public time and money beyond calculation.

Although recent legislation prohibits discrimination in physical education and sports participation, many athletic governing organizations have rules that deny these individuals the opportunity to participate because of age restrictions or conditions such as mental retardation. Many students with handicapping conditions are no longer willing to accept exclusion from such programs and are seeking redress in court in ever-increasing numbers. The courts are consistent in ruling that rules based on safety and fairness are not discriminatory and do not violate equal protection safeguards. Federal legislation has not liberalized the rules regarding participation in sports by mentally retarded students. The number of states allowing participation has not changed dramatically in their favor and some states that permitted participation have actually reversed their policy and now deny participation.

It is essential that teachers, coaches, administrators and school boards become familiar with the statutes and judicial decisions in their profession. There is a presumption that most educators are familiar with the basic processes of law, recent legislation and judicial decisions affecting their profession. This appears to be the exception, however, rather than the rule.

239

A knowledge of the law can prevent litigation, build confidence and help set parameters necessary to comply with the law and develop programs that are educationally and legally sound.

Recommendations

I. *General*

- Administrators, coaches, parents, physical education teachers and school board members should understand the mandates of the federal laws regarding individuals with handicapping conditions.
- Since laws and judicial decisions are often in a state of flux, periodic review is essential to know their current status at all times.
- School officials should voluntarily initiate programs that are in compliance with the law rather than by judicial fiat.
- Physical education teachers should meet with planning teams to assist in the development of their student's IEP.
- Research should be conducted in motor development to assist physical education teachers and coaches in their programs.
- Pre-service programs should be instituted with an emphasis on training specialists.
- In-service workshops should be conducted to provide information on recent legislation and legal liability.
- School officials should work as partners with parents in decision-making rather than as adversaries.

- Parents should exhaust administrative remedies as defined by the school system before instituting a lawsuit.
- Sport governing organizations should review their rules and regulations periodically to make certain they comply with the law and are effective.
- Sport governing organizations should experiment with a "model" that liberalizes traditional rules to enable more students to participate in sports.
- Administrators, coaches and physical education teachers should permit impaired students to participate in physical education and sports according to Public Law 94-142 and section 504 of the Rehabilitation Act.
- Local communities should become involved in the education and development of programs and serve as resources.
- The media should be informed of achievements, problems and solutions to keep the public informed in an attempt to eliminate negative attitudes and promote beneficial programs and legislation.
- Terminology should concentrate on the handicapping condition rather than the individual, on ability rather than disability.
- The provisions of Public Law 94-142 should be extended to the nonhandicapped as well as to individuals with handicapping conditions.
- The welfare of the individual should be the basis of all decisions and the paramount goal in the operation of the educational program.

II. *Legal Liability*

Supervision

- School boards should adopt policies prohibiting unsupervised physical education classes and athletic practice sessions for any reason.
- Administrators should assign adequate supervisory personnel for groups engaged in physical activities. The number of supervisors should be determined by the nature and size of the group and the type of activity involved.
- Administrators should supervise the physical education and athletic programs as well as the academic subjects.
- Administrators should work closely with less qualified physical education teachers and athletic coaches. Special supervision should be provided until the teachers and coaches become qualified.
- Administrators should provide supervision on playgrounds and in gymnasiums before school begins in the morning especially if rough, rowdy, or dangerous activities are involved.
- High risk activities should be eliminated from programs when qualified instructors and coaches are not available.
- All athletic contests involving physical contact should be scheduled on the basis of equitable competition in regard to size, skill, and other controlling factors.

Instruction

- School boards should employ competent, qualified personnel for the physical education and athletic programs. The standards for these important positions should be high.

- School boards should conduct in-service training in tort liability and first aid for all physical education teachers and coaches.
- Physical education teachers and coaches should warn the participants of all possible dangers inherent in the activities in which they are involved.
- Physical education teachers should follow adopted syllabi whenever possible. If the teacher deviates from an adopted program it should be based on sound reasons. Extra precautions for safety should be taken.
- Physical education teachers and athletic coaches should not assign pupils activities that are beyond their ability and capacity. Pupils should be assigned activities commensurate with their size, skill, and physical condition.
- Special care and training should be provided in gymnastics, tumbling, and activities in which dangerous equipment is in use.

Equipment and Facilities

- School boards and school administrators should set policies concerning the inspection of equipment and facilities. The line of responsibility must be clearly delegated and defined so that a specific person or department is responsible for the duty of periodic inspection.
- Accurate records should be kept of all equipment and facility inspection. The records should include the inspector's name, the date of the inspection, the condition of the equipment and facilities, and the necessary recommendations for repair.

243

- All activities that involve the use of defective equipment or unsafe facilities should be curtailed or eliminated until the defects are corrected.
- Special attention should be given ropes, ladders, lockers, and bleachers in the periodic inspection.
- Safety rules should be adopted regulating the use of swimming pools, trampolines, springboards, and all other potentially dangerous equipment.
- Physical education and athletic facilities should be maintained so that they are as safe as the academic classroom.
- School officials should adopt safety rules regulating vehicular traffic on all playgrounds and other areas which pupils and spectators use. Periodic warnings should be made regarding any dangerous situation that exists.

APPENDIX A

Legislative Digest

Part 1

Public Laws Relating to Handicapped Students*

Legislation that led to the passage of Public Law 94-142
and
the Rehabilitation Act

Public Law 815 (H.R. 2317, September 23, 1950) [1]

The purpose of this law was to allocate monies for the construction of school facilities on properties owned or operated by the federal government. Such properties included federal possessions controlled by the Atomic Energy Commission and all Indian reservations and facilities under the direction of the Alaska Public Works Act, 1949.

The law made a special point when it excluded the building of any athletic stadia, or structure of facilities whereby an admission would be charged the general public. This law also noted that all children within those age limits set by their specific states would receive federal monies for their education.

Congress appropriated three million dollars for this project.

---

*Portions of this Appendix are taken from the Library of Congress, Congressional Research Service by Angela Giordano-Evans, HV 750 A, January 12, 1976, Education of the Handicapped: *Legislative Histories From the 83rd Through the 94th Congress, 1st Session.*

Public Law 874 (H.R. 7940, September 30, 1950)[2]

The primary purposes of this law were: to provide money for local educational agencies in areas affected by federal activities; to provide an education for children residing on federal property; to provide an education for children whose parents are employed on federal property; and to provide financial assistance for agencies upon which a burden rests due to the acquisition of real property by the United States government.

The law excluded all children of Indian descendants and no local agency could use these funds to construct any facilities or to buy any land for present or future use. Total amount of dollars allotted for this law is not mentioned in the statutes.

Public Law 89-10 (H.R. 2362, April 11, 1965): Elementary and Secondary Act of 1965[3]

This law was designed to help establish a better education for low-income families and to better meet the special needs of those children with varying talents. Monies were made available for the following: construction, remodeling, and acquiring special equipment and instructors for the handicapped and for the preschool age child. All phases of the child's educational program were to benefit, including comprehensive guidance and counseling, school health, physical education and recreation.

Congress set the age range for all children eligible to receive these funds. That range was five to seventeen years of age. One hundred million dollars was appropriated to fund this law.

Public Law 89-313 (H.R. 9022, November 1, 1965): Elementary and Secondary Education Act Amendments[4]

One of the provisions of this law provided for grants to

246

state educational agencies for the education of handicapped children in state-supported institutions beginning in FY 1966. The maximum basic grant to which a state would be eligible was determined by multiplying the number of children in average daily attendance at state-supported schools for the handicapped by the average per pupil expenditure in the state. "Handicapped" included mentally retarded, hard of hearing, deaf, speech impaired, visually handicapped, seriously emotionally disturbed, crippled and other health impaired children.

Public Law 89-750 (H.R. 13161, November 3, 1966): Elementary and Secondary Education Amendments of 1966 [5]

These amendments added a new Title VI (Education of Handicapped Children) to the Elementary and Secondary Education Act. The new title authorized $50 million for the fiscal year 1967 and increased to $150 million by the fiscal year 1968 to those states that would initiate, expand and improve programs and projects for the education of the handicapped.

These amendments also established a National Advisory Council on Handicapped Children consisting of representatives of government, research, teaching and training professions. A Bureau for the Education and Training of the Handicapped was also mandated through this legislation.

Public Law 90-247 (H.R. 7819, January 2, 1968): Elementary and Secondary Education Amendments of 1967 [6]

This legislation amended Title VI of the Elementary Secondary Education Act by adding new Parts B, C, and D.

Part B, Regional Resource Centers for Improvement of the Education of Handicapped Children, authorized grants or contracts with institutions of higher education, state educational agencies or other non-profit private institutions or agencies to pay the cost of establishing or operating the regional resource centers for the improvement of education of the handicapped in those regions.

Part C, Centers and Services for Deaf-Blind Children, authorized grants and contracts to public and non-profit private agencies to establish and operate centers for deaf-blind children.

Part D, Recruitment of Personnel and Information on Education of the Handicapped, authorized grants or contracts with public or non-profit private agencies to improve recruiting of education personnel and to improve dissemination of information concerning educational opportunities for the handicapped.

The basic authorization for the grant to state programs was extended from $162 million in 1969 to $200 million by 1970.

Public Law 91-230 (H.R. 514, April 13, 1970): Elementary and Secondary Education Amendments of 1969 [7]

The primary purpose of these amendments was to extend the basic federal assistance program for elementary and secondary school systems through the fiscal year 1973. These amendments also authorized a new program under Part G of Title VI aimed at improving the education of children with specific learning disabilities. The term "children with specific learning disabilities" is defined. The authorizations for Part G were twelve million dollars in 1970. This was to be increased to thirty-one million dollars for the fiscal year 1973.

Public Law 92-318 (S. 659, June 23, 1972): Education Amendments of 1972 [8]

This law extends and amends various programs authorized under the Higher Education Act of 1965, the Vocational Education Act of 1963 and other federal education statutes and creates a National Institute of Education to uncover new knowledge and stimulate reform in the American educational system.

Section 465, Cancellation of Loans to Certain Public Services, reduces the period for forgiveness of federal direct loans to teachers of the handicapped from seven to five years.

Public Law 93-112 (H.R. 8070, September 26, 1973): Rehabilitation Act of 1973 [9]

This legislation provided a statutory basis for the Rehabilitation Services Administration. The law also provided the following programs: to develop and implement comprehensive services to meet the needs of the handicapped, to assist in the construction and improvement of rehabilitation centers, to promote and expand employment opportunities in both the public and private sectors of business, and to evaluate existing approaches to architectural and transportation barriers confronting handicapped persons. Established within the law is the National Center for Deaf-Blind Youths and Adults.

No money was appropriated with this legislation.

Public Law 93-380 (H.R. 69, August 21, 1974): Education Amendments of 1974 [10]

This education law amended and expanded the Education of the Handicapped Act, Public Law 90-247. Some changes were as follows:

249

1. Payment rate per child was to be based on the State's number of children ages three through twenty-one times eight dollars and seventy-five cents.
2. Additional provisions for State plans would provide (1) assurances that all children residing in the State who are handicapped be given special educational services; (2) that confidentiality of data and information regarding these handicapped youths be guarded; (3) and a goal of providing full educational opportunities to all handicapped be established.
3. This law adds new provisions for procedural safeguards in decisions regarding the identification, evaluation and educational placement of handicapped children.
4. Passage established a new authorization for regional education programs. Grants to and contracts with institutions of higher education including junior and community colleges, vocational and technical institutions and other nonprofit educational agencies to develop specially designed modified programs of vocational, technical, post-secondary or adult education for the handicapped.
5. Updated by this amendment were current laws regarding captioned films and educational media for handicapped persons by providing for grants and contracts to provide for: the captioning of film; distribution of films and other educational media and equipment through state schools for the handicapped.

Public Law 93-516 (H.R. 17503, December 7, 1974): Rehabilitation Act Amendments of 1974 [11]

Passage of these Amendments was to extend the

appropriations in the Rehabilitation Act of 1973 for one year. Transferred in this passage was the Rehabilitation Services Administration to the Office of the Secretary of Health, Education, and Welfare. The law also wanted to improve operating programs, where appropriate, to demonstrate methods of making recreational activities fully accessible to handicapped individuals.

Public Law 94-142 (S. 6, November 29, 1975): Education for All Handicapped Children Act of 1975 [12]

This law amended and extended the Part B provisions of the Education of the Handicapped Act, Public Law 90-247, as amended, by increasing federal financing of education programs on the elementary and secondary education level for all handicapped children.

This legislation changed the state grant program under Part B of the Education of the Handicapped Act into a state entitlement program. The entitlement formula commonly referred to as the "Mathias Amendment" was incorporated in the 1974 Education Amendments. That entitlement is based on the number of all children in a state aged three to twenty-one, inclusive, times eight dollars and seventy-five cents. The new formula would be based on the number of handicapped children between the ages of three and twenty-one years in a state receiving a free appropriate education times forty percent of the national average per pupil expenditure.

An emphasis was placed on the development of a custom-tailored program for each handicapped child with inputs from all principals in the child's educational environment. This plan was to be maintained and revised at the beginning of each school year and reviewed, if appropriate, periodically at least annually during the school year.

251

This law provides for an impartial due process hearing to be held by the state or local educational agency in which the individuals initiating the complaints may be accompanied by counsel, present evidence, cross-examine witnesses and obtain written findings of facts and decisions. The decision of the local educational agency hearing can be appealed to the state level and the decision on the state level can be appealed to a state or district court.

These federal mandates authorized such sums as may be necessary for grants to state, local or intermediate educational agencies for the removal or alteration of architectural barriers to the handicapped.

Congress authorized the sum of $100 million for the fiscal year 1976 and authorized $200 million for the fiscal year 1977. By 1980, Congress said that authorizations would equal sums that equal twenty percent of the national average per pupil expenditure times the number of handicapped children and by 1982, the authorizations would equal an amount equal to forty percent of the national average per pupil expenditure times the number of handicapped children.

FOOTNOTES

1. Public Law 815, Statutes at Large 64 (1952).

2. Public Law 874, Statutes at Large 64 (1952).

3. Public Law 89-10, Elementary and Secondary Act of 1965, Statutes at Large 79 (1966).

4. Public Law 89-313, Elementary and Secondary Education Act Amendments, Statutes at Large 79 (1966).

5. Public Law 89-750, Elementary and Secondary Education Amendments of 1966, Statutes at Large 80 (1967).

6. Public Law 90-247, Elementary and Secondary Education Amendments of 1967, Statutes at Large 81 (1967).

7. Public Law 91-230, Elementary and Secondary Education Amendments of 1969, Statutes at Large 84 (1970).

8. Public Law 92-218, Education Amendments of 1972, Statutes at Large 86 (1972).

9. Public Law 93-112 (H.R. 8070, September 26, 1973): Rehabilitation Act of 1973.

10. Public Law 93-380, Education Amendments of 1974, Statutes at Large 88 (1974).

11. Public Law 93-516, Rehabilitation Act Amendments of 1974, Statutes at Large 88 (1976).

12. Public Law 94-142, Education for All Handicapped Children Act of 1972, Statutes at Large 89 (1975).

PART 2

Public Laws Relating to Students With Handicapping Conditions

Public Law 83-531 (H.R. 9040, July 26, 1954): Cooperative Research Act

This law made provision for educational research to be conducted by the Office of Education in cooperation with universities, colleges and state educational agencies.

Authority for appropriations included sums that may be necessary to carry out the program. For the fiscal year 1955, one million dollars was appropriated for this Act; two-thirds of this sum was earmarked for the retarded.[1]

Public Law 85-905 (H.R. 13678, September 2, 1958): Captioned Films for The Deaf

This law established within the Department of Health, Education and Welfare a loan service of captioned films for the deaf and severely hard of hearing. The primary purposes of this law were to bring to deaf persons understanding and appreciation of those films which played such an important part in the general and cultural advancement of hearing persons; to provide through these films enriched educational and cultural experiences through which deaf persons could be brought into better touch with the realities of their environment; and to provide a wholesome and rewarding experience which deaf persons could share together. The law authorized the Secretary of Health, Education and Welfare to acquire films and provide for their captioning. Such captioned films would then be distributed through state schools for the deaf and such other agencies which the Secretary deemed appropriate to serve as regional centers for the distribution of the captioned films.

This law authorized $250,000 annually to carry out the purposes of this law.[2]

Public Law 85-926 (H.R. 13840, September 6, 1958): Grants for Teaching in the Education of Handicapped Children

This law authorized the Commissioner of Education to make grants to public or other nonprofit institutions of higher education to assist them in providing training of professional personnel to train teachers in fields related to the education of mentally retarded children. It also authorized grants to state educational agencies to assist them in establishing and maintaining fellowships and/or traineeships for persons preparing as teachers of mentally retarded children. Authorizations for this law were made at one million dollars annually for ten fiscal years.[3]

Public Law 86-158 (H.R. 6769, August 14, 1959): Fiscal Year 1960 Act for Health, Education, Welfare, and Labor

This appropriation act specifically amended section 2 of Public Law 85-926 by adding the following provision, "Provided that section 2 of such act is amended by adding at the end thereof the following: such grants shall be available to assist such institutions in meeting the costs of training such personnel." This law added authorization for support grants to institutions of higher learning to help those institutions meet the costs of training personnel to teach the handicapped.[4]

Public Law 87-276 (S. 336, September 22, 1961): Teachers for the Deaf

This law provided for grants-in-aid to accredited public

and nonprofit institutions of higher education which were approved training centers for teachers of the deaf to assist these institutions in providing teacher training for teachers of the deaf. These grants could be used for establishing and maintaining scholarships for qualified persons.

This law also provided for the establishment of an Advisory Committee on the Training of Teachers of the Deaf. The Committee, consisting of twelve members, was charged with periodic review of the grants-in-aid program and submitting recommendations for legislation and review of all applications. Authorization of appropriations included $1,500,000 for the fiscal year 1962, and $1,500,000 for the following year.[5]

Public Law 87-715 (S. 2511, September 28, 1962): Loan Service of Captioned Films for the Deaf

The law amended Public Law 85-905 by expanding the objectives of that Act to include educational advancement of deaf persons by carrying on research in the use of educational and training films for the deaf, the distribution of these films to the deaf, and the training of persons in the use of films for the deaf.[6]

Public Law 88-164 (S. 1576, October 31, 1963): Mental Retardation Facilities and Community Mental Health Centers Construction Act

This law authorized financial assistance for the handicapped in three different areas; the construction of facilities, community mental health centers and training personnel in the education of handicapped.

Title I of this law provided for project grants for the construction of centers for research on mental retardation and related aspects of human development. Six million dollars for the fiscal year 1965 and six million dollars for the fiscal years 1966 and 1967 were authorized. The federal share was set at seventy-five percent. In addition, it provided five million dollars in 1964, $7,500,000 for 1965, and finally ten million dollars for 1966 and 1967 for project grants for the construction of university affiliated facilities to provide a full range of in-patient and out-patient services for the mentally retarded. To be included were facilities which would aid in demonstrating specialized services for the diagnosis and treatment of the mentally retarded. The government was to pick up seventy-five percent of this cost.

Title II of this law authorized thirty-five million dollars in 1965, fifty million dollars for 1966 and sixty-five million dollars in 1967 for the construction of community mental health centers.

Title III authorized $11,500,000 for 1964 and up to $19,500,000 for 1966 to be used in the training of teachers of mentally retarded and other handicapped children. This law amended Public Law 85-926 to provide training of personnel in all areas of education for the handicapped at all levels of preparation from teacher training to the training of college instructors, research personnel and the administration and supervisors of teachers of the handicapped. This title also expanded the areas of teacher training to include the hard of hearing, deaf, speech impaired, visually handicapped, seriously emotionally disturbed, crippled and other health-impaired children.[7]

Public Law 89-36 (H.R. 7031, June 8, 1965): National Institute for the Deaf Act

This legislation provided for a residential facility to give postsecondary technical training for the deaf to prepare them for successful employment. A twelve member Ad Hoc Advisory Board on Establishment of the National Technical

Institute for the Deaf was appointed by the Secretary of Health, Education and Welfare to review proposals from institutions of higher education which offered to enter into an agreement with the Secretary for the construction and operation of a National Technical Institute of the Deaf, to make recommendations with respect to such proposals and with respect to the establishment and operation of the Institute. The Institute was to provide a broad, flexible curriculum suited to the individual needs of young deaf adults with potential for further training and education. The Institute would serve as a practice teaching center for training teachers, instructors and rehabilitation counselors for the deaf and would serve as a research facility for the study of educational problems of the deaf.[8]

Public Law 89-105 (H.R. 2985, August 4, 1965): Mental Retardation Facilities and Community Mental Health Centers Construction Act of 1965

This legislation amended Public Law 88-164. Public Law 89-105 authorized $19,500,000 for the year 1966, twenty-four million dollars for the year 1967, and thirty million dollars for 1968 to cover grants for staffing community mental health centers with technical and professional personnel during the first fifty-one months of their operations. In addition, the 1965 amendments extended and expanded the existing grants program for training teachers of handicapped children. It provided for grants to institutions of higher learning for the construction, equipping and operation of a research facility for studying the education of the handicapped.[9]

Public Law 89-258 (S. 2232, October 19, 1965): Captioned Film for the Deaf Act

This law amended Public Law 85-905 by extending the

availability of captioned films to include films of a cultural nature. It also provided for research in the use of educational media for the deaf. Educational media were also made available to persons directly involved in assisting the deaf as well as to the deaf themselves.

This law authorized three million dollars for the fiscal year 1966 and up to seven million dollars in 1970 to carry out the program. It also provided for the establishment of a National Advisory Committee on the Deaf.[10]

Public Law 89-511 (H.R. 14050, July 19, 1966): Library Services and Construction Act Amendments of 1966

Part A of Title IV authorized a program to assist the states in providing library services to state institutions for inmates, patients, residents, as well as physically and mentally handicapped students who are in residential schools for the handicapped operated or substantially supported by the state.

Federal funds were also authorized to be used by the state library agency to plan and initiate programs, to provide books, other library materials and library services for the handicapped. Authorization of appropriations for this program ranged from five million dollars in 1967 to fifteen million dollars in 1971.

Part B of Title IV (Library Services to the Physically Handicapped) provided funds to state agencies for the establishment and improvement of library services for individuals who were certified by competent authority as unable to read or to use conventional printed materials as a result of physical limitations. Such services were to be provided through public or nonprofit library agencies or organizations.[11]

Public Law 89-694 (H.R. 17190, October 15, 1966): Gallaudet College — Model Secondary School for the Deaf to Serve the National Capital Area

This law authorized the Secretary of Health, Education and Welfare, after consultation with the National Advisory Committee on the Education of the Deaf, to enter into an agreement with Gallaudet College to establish a model secondary school for the deaf, to serve primarily residents of the District of Columbia and nearby states.

This high school while serving primarily the needs of the National Capital area and nearby states, would also provide a model for the develoment of similar programs across the country. In addition, the formulation of new educational methods and educational technology and specific curriculum offerings would contribute to the nation's total educational program for the deaf.[12]

Public Law 89-752 (H.R. 14644, November 3, 1966): Higher Education Amendments of 1966

This act amended the National Defense Education Act of 1958 by providing for cancellation of loans made under this Act to students who later taught handicapped students. The rate of cancellation provided was fifteen percent of the loan for each year spent teaching the handicapped.[13]

Public Law 90-170 (H.R. 6430, December 4, 1967): Mental Retardation Facilities and Mental Health Centers Construction Act

This Act: (1) extended through June 30, 1970, the programs under which matching grants were made for the construction of university-affiliated mental retardation facilities and community mental retardation facilities; (2) established a new grant program to pay a portion of the costs for compensation of professional and technical personnel in community facilities for the mentally retarded, for initial operation of new facilities, or of new services in a facility; (3) extended until June 30, 1970, the existing program of training in the education of handicapped children; and (4) established a new program for training and research in physical education and recreation for the mentally retarded and other handicapped children.

With regard to staffing community mental retardation facilities, grants were authorized to meet a portion of the costs of professional and technical personnel for initial operation of new facilities or for new services in existing facilities for the mentally retarded.

Staffing grants could also be made for the initial operation of new facilities and new services in existing facilities. Federal funds could be used to supplement and increase to the extent practical, the level of state, local and other non-federal funds for mental retardation purposes.

The law authorized fifty-five million dollars to carry out this program. Four million dollars of the appropriated money was available under Title V which enabled the Secretary to make grants to state or local educational agencies, public or private educational or research agencies and organizations for research and demonstration projects relating to physical education or recreation for mentally retarded and other handicapped children.[14]

Public Law 90-415 (H.R. 18203, July 23, 1968): Increase the Size of the Board of Directors of Gallaudet College and for Other Purposes

This Act added eight new members to the Board of Directors of Gallaudet College (increasing the size from thirteen to twenty-one members), in order to involve persons from the fields of medicine, communications, technology, special education and higher education.[15]

261

Public Law 90-538 (H.R. 18763, September 30, 1968): Handicapped Children's Early Education Assistance Act

This Act enabled the Commissioner of Education to make grants and contracts to public and private non-profit agencies for the development and implementation of experimental programs in early education for the handicapped. These grants were to be distributed on a broad geographical basis throughout the nation.

The model preschool program had objectives of stimulating all areas of the handicapped child's development including his emotional, physical, intellectual, and social needs. In fact, the report of the House Committee on Education and Labor urged that programs encompass not only all disabilities, but all age groups from birth to six years of age.

This Act also provided for the participation of parents in the development and operation of the program. Another aim of the Act was to acquaint the community with the problems and potentials of handicapped children.

Handicapped children were defined as mentally retarded, hard of hearing, deaf, speech impaired, visually handicapped, seriously emotionally disturbed, crippled, or other health impaired children who need special education services. The Act authorized one million dollars in 1969 but raised the figure to ten million dollars in 1970 and twelve million dollars in 1971. The sums appropriated for the first year were to be used for the planning of centers.[16]

Public Law 90-570 (H.R. 18366, October 16, 1968): Vocational Education Act, Amendments of 1968

This law amended the Act of 1963, retained the comprehensive State grant program on a continuing basis and authorized a new program for five years. The law appropriated monies starting at $355,000,000 in 1969 to $565,000,000 in 1973. These authorizations were for State Vocational Education Programs and Research and Training in Vocational Education. There were also special authorizations for certain categorical programs.

This legislation provided that at least ten percent of each State's allotment for funds appropriated for any fiscal year beginning after June 30, 1969, were to be used only for vocational education for handicapped persons who, because of their handicapping condition, could not succeed in the regular vocational education program without special educational assistance or who would require a modified vocational education program.[17]

Public Law 90-575 (S. 3769, October 16, 1968): Higher Education Amendments of 1968

Under these amendments the Commissioner of Education was authorized to make grants or contracts with institutions of higher learning to help them carry out a program of Special Services for Disadvantaged Students. These programs of special services were for students enrolled or accepted by an institution receiving the grant and who, by reason of deprived educational, cultural or economic background, or physical handicap were in need of such services to help them initiate or continue their post-secondary education.

This law extended the cancellation of loans made to students who later taught handicapped children for two additional years. These forgiveness provisions were to apply only to loans made prior to July 1, 1970.[18]

Public Law 91-517 (S. 2846, October 30, 1970): Developmental Disabilities Services and Facilities Construction Amendments of 1970

This Act amends Public Law 88-164. The legislation

provided states with broader responsibilities for planning and implementing a comprehensive program of services and offered local communities a strong voice in determining needs, establishing priorities and developing a system for delivering services.

The scope of the existing program was broadened to include not only the mentally retarded but also persons suffering from other serious developmental disabilities originating in childhood. The term developmental disability referred to "a disability attributable to mental retardation, cerebral palsy, epilepsy or another neurological condition found by the Secretary of Health, Education and Welfare to be closely related to mental retardation or to require similar treatment to that required for mentally retarded individuals . . . ." In addition, the disability must be substantial in nature and must have continued or be expected to continue indefinitely.

States were to use formula grant funds authorized under Title I of the Act to support: (1) a full array of services required by developmentally disabled children and adults; (2) the construction of facilities; (3) state and local planning; (4) administration; (5) technical assistance; (6) training of specialized personnel; and (7) the development and demonstration of new service techniques. The Title I allotments to the states were to be calculated on the basis of population, need for services, and financial need of the state. However, each state was to receive a minimum of $100 thousand per year.[19]

Public Law 91-587 (S. 4083, December 24, 1970): Model Elementary School for the Deaf Act

This law authorized Gallaudet College in the District of Columbia to provide day and residential facilities for the elementary education of the deaf. Kendall School was to be maintained for this purpose as a demonstration elementary school for the deaf, providing an educational program which would stimulate the development of similar excellent programs throughout the national.[20]

Public Law 92-424 (H.R. 12350, September 19, 1972): Economic Opportunity Amendments of 1972

Under this Act, the Secretary of Health, Education and Welfare was to provide policies and procedures designed to assure that not less than ten percent of the total number of enrollment opportunities in the nation in the Head Start program were to be available for handicapped children and that services were to be provided to meet their special needs.[21]

Public Law 93-644 (H.R. 14449, January 4, 1975): Community Services Act of 1974

Title V of the Act provided for a Head Start Follow Through Act. This Act extended the Head Start program through the year 1977. Head Start programs within each State were not to receive less funds for any fiscal year than were obligated for use within that State in the fiscal year 1975.

Prior to this legislation, the Head Start legislation required that not less than ten percent of the total enrollment opportunities in Head Start throughout the nation be available for handicapped children. This new Act required that beginning in 1976 at least ten percent of each state's Head Start enrollment would have to be for handicapped children.[22]

Public Law 96-536 (1981)

This law, called the Second Continuing Resolution for 1981, gave the Administration the authority to reduce the funding of programs authorized by the Education for All Handicapped Children Act by twenty-five percent or approximately $270 million.[23]

Public Law 97-12 (June 5, 1981)

This law, referred to as the Supplemental Appropriations and Recissions Act, provided for the reduction of programs under the Education for All Handicapped Children Act by seven percent, or seventy-six million dollars.[24] The budget authority for the States' grant programs, was reduced by five percent, from $922 million to $874.5 million. In addition, individual project grants were cut by sixteen percent representing a decrease from $180.1 million to $150.7 million (Parts C-F).

Public Law 97-35 (August 13, 1981)

Public Law 97-35 is known as the Omnibus Budget Reconciliation Act of 1981. The current programs under the Education for All Handicapped Children Act are not included in this Act.[25] The Act extended and placed a ceiling on the authorizations of appropriations for all programs under the Education for All Handicapped Children Act, provided $969.9 million for 1982 and $1,017 million for 1983 and 1984 for Part B-State grant program. The Act authorized "$25 million for (each of) 1982 and 1983 for the Preschool Incentive Program; and $155 million for each of the 1982 and 1983 project grant programs."

It is especially important because it approved ceilings for the Education for All Handicapped Children Act under the Omnibus Budget Reconciliation Act of 1981 which reflects an increase of twelve percent over the 1981 appropriation figures.

Public Law 97-92 (December 15, 1981)

This law provided temporary funding through March 31, 1982 of all Department of Education programs including the Education for All Handicapped Children Act.[26]

Public Law 97-161 (March 31, 1982)

This law extended "further continuing appropriations" through September 30, 1982 and continued authorized levels of funding under P.L. 97-92 for all Department of Education and Education for All Handicapped Children Act programs.[27]

Public Law 97-257 (1982).

Public Law 97-257 provides $26.5 million in additional funds for programs of education for individuals with handicapping conditions.[28] As such the Act provides a $15.7 million supplement for special education personnel development, $7.2 million for early childhood education and $3.6 million for innovation and development. Under this Act and the provisions of P.L. 97-161, appropriations are available of $1,068,580,000; Part B funding of $931,008,000 which represents eighty-seven percent of the total 1982 budget available to the Education for All Handicapped Children programs.

FOOTNOTES

1. Public Law 83-531, Cooperative Research Act, Statutes at Large 68 (1955).

2. Public Law 85-905, Captioned Films for the Deaf, Statutes at Large 72 (1959).

3. Public Law 85-926, Grants for Teaching in the Education of Handicapped Children 72 (1959).

4. Public Law 86-158, Fiscal Year 1960 Act for Health, Education, Welfare, and Labor, Statutes at Large 73 (1960).

5. Public Law 87-276, Teachers for the Deaf, Statutes at Large 75 (1962).

6. Public Law 87-715, Loan Service of Captioned Films for the Deaf, Statutes at Large 76 (1963).

7. Public Law 88-164, Mental Retardation Facilities and Community Mental Health Centers Construction Act, Statutes at Large 77 (1964).

8. Public Law 89-36, National Institute for the Deaf Act, Statutes at Large 79 (1966).

9. Public Law 89-105, Mental Retardation Facilities and Community Mental Health Centers Construction Act of 1965, Statutes at Large 79 (1966).

10. Public Law 89-258, Captioned Film for the Deaf Act, Statutes at Large 79 (1966).

11. Public Law 89-511, Library Services and Construction Act Amendments of 1966, Statutes at Large 80 (1967).

12. Public Law 89-694, Gallaudet College — Model Secondary School for The Deaf to Serve the National Capital Area, Statutes at Large 80 (1967).

13. Public Law 89-752, Higher Education Amendments of 1966, Statutes at Large 80 (1967).

14. Public Law 90-170, Mental Retardation Facilities and Mental Health Centers Construction Act, Statutes at Large 81 (1968).

15. Public Law 90-415, Increase the Size of the Board of Directors of Gallaudet College and for Other Purposes, Statutes at Large 82 (1969).

16. Public Law 90-538, Handicapped Children's Early Education Assistance Act, Statutes at Large 82 (1969).

17. Public Law 90-570, Vocational Education Act, Amendments of 1968, Statutes at Large 82 (1969).

18. Public Law 90-575, Higher Education Amendments of 1968, Statutes at Large 82 (1969).

19. Public Law 91-517, Developmental Disabilities Services and Facilities, Construction Amendments of 1970, Statutes at Large 84 (1971).

20. Public Law 91-587, Model Elementary School for the Deaf Act, Statutes at Large 84 (1971).

21. Public Law 92-424, Economic Opportunity Amendments of 1972, Statutes at Large 86 (1973).

22. Public Law 93-644, Community Services Act of 1974, Statutes at Large 88 (1975).

23. Public Law 96-536 (1981).

24. Public Law 97-12 (June 5, 1981).

25. Public Law 97-35 (August 13, 1981).

26. Public Law 97-92 (December 15, 1981).

27. Public 97-161 (March 31, 1982).

28. Public Law 97-257 (1982).

APPENDIX B

Funding Formula Public Law 94-142

The Education of All Handicapped Children Act of 1975

(Amends P.L. 91-230 Education of the Handicapped Act)

November 29, 1975

It is the purpose of this Act to assure that all handicapped children have available to them [within the time periods specified in section 612(2)(B)], a free appropriate public education which emphasizes special education and related services designed to meet their unique needs. (Effective 10/1/77.)

The term "free appropriate public education" means special education and related services which (a) have been provided at public expense, under public supervision and direction, and without charge, (b) meet the standards of the state educational agency, (c) include an appropriate preschool, clementary, or secondary school education in the state involved, and (d) are provided in conformity with an individualized education program.

Formula

The Act establishes a formula in which the federal government makes a commitment to pay a gradually-escalating percentage of the national average expenditure per public school child times the number of handicapped children being served in the school districts of each state in the nation ages five to seventeen, inclusive. That percentage will escalate on a yearly basis until 1982 when it will become a permanent forty percent for that year and all subsequent years.

Here is the scale:

Fiscal 1978 — five percent
Fiscal 1979 — ten percent
Fiscal 1980 — twenty percent
Fiscal 1981 — thirty percent
Fiscal 1982 — forty percent

It should be carefully noted that such a formula carries an inflation factor, i.e., the actual money figure fluctuates with inflationary-deflationary adjustments in the national average per pupil expenditure.

Formula "Kick-In"

As obviously indicated in the preceding heading, the new formula will not go into operation until fiscal 1978.

It will be recalled that existing law was already moving toward a permanent, significant increase in the federal commitment. Public Law 93-380, the Education Amendments of 1974 (signed August 21 of 1974), created the first entitlement for handicapped children, based upon factors of the number of *all* children aged three to twenty-one within each state times $8.75. This formula (called the "Mathias formula" after its originator), amounting to a total annual authorization of $680 million, was authorized for fiscal 1975 only — with a view toward permitting an emergency infusion of money into the states while at the same time deferring to final determination of a permanent new funding formula as now contained in the Act. This "Mathias formula" would be retained in both bills until "kick-in" of the new formula.

Ceilings

For the two years of fiscal 1976 and 1977 when the formula remains under the "Mathias entitlement," the

272

conferees set authorization ceilings of $100 million for fiscal 1976 and $200 million for fiscal 1977. On the basis of the current national average per pupil expenditure, the following authorization ceilings are generated for the first years on the new formula:

Fiscal 1978 — $387 million (on the five-percent factor)

Fiscal 1979 — $775 million (on the ten-percent factor)

Fiscal 1980 — $1.2 billion (on the twenty-percent factor)

Fiscal 1981 — $2.32 billion (on the thirty-percent factor)

Fiscal 1982 — $3.16 billion (on the forty-percent factor)

Counting Limitation

The Act addresses the potential threat of "over-counting" children as handicapped in order to generate the largest possible federal allocation. The measure prohibits counting more than twelve percent as handicapped served within the total school-age population of the state between the ages of five and seventeen. (Effective 10/1/77.)

Learning Disabilities

The Act retains, with minor alterations, the existing federal definition of handicapped children (EHA, section 602 (1) and (15) of extant law), and this definition includes children with specific learning disabilities. However, it would appear at this point of interpretation of conference action that the Commissioner may, within one year, provide detailed regulations relative to SLD, including the development of a more precise definition, the prescription of comprehensive diagnostic criteria and procedures, and the prescription of procedures for monitoring of said regulations by the Commissioner. If the authorizing committees of the

273

House and Senate disapprove the Commissioner's regulations, then a ceiling on the number of children with learning disabilities who may be counted by the state for purposes of the formula will be included when the new formula takes effect. The ceiling would provide that not more than one-sixth of the twelve percent of school-age children aged five to seventeen who may be counted as handicapped children served may be children with specific learning disabilities. (Effective 10/1/77.)

Priorities

Existing law (Public Law 93-380), in conformance with the overall goal of ending exclusion, orders a priority in the use of federal funds for children "still unserved." The Act maintains and broadens that priority in the following manner:

- First priority to children "unserved" (Effective FY1975.)
- Second priority to children inadequately served when they are severely handicapped (within each disability) (Effective 10/1/77.)

Beneficiaries

The Act stipulates that all handicapped children, aged three to twenty-one years, may enjoy the special education and related services provided through this measure. There is also provision for the use of federal monies for programs of early identification and screening. (Effective 10/1/77.)

Pass-Through

The Act contains a substantial pass-through to the local school districts. In the first year of the new formula, fifty percent of the monies going to each state would be allocated to the State education agency, and fifty percent would be allocated to the local education agencies. In the following year, fiscal 1979, the LEA entitlement would be enlarged to seventy-five percent of the total allocation to a given state, with the SEA retaining twenty-five percent. This seventy-five to twenty-five arrangement commencing in fiscal 1979 becomes the permanent distribution arrangement. The current state-control of all funds is retained for the remainder of fiscal 1976 and fiscal 1977.

Constraints Upon Localities

Though the Act authorizes a substantial local entitlement, there are numerous "strings attached." Initially, the state education agency will act as the clearinghouse of all data from the localities gathered in order to determine local entitlement, and the state will transmit that information to the Commissioner. Furthermore, the state education agency may refuse to pass through federal monies generated when:

- the school district does not conform to the overall state-plan requirements contained in this Act and in existing law (such as "full service" goal, confidentiality, etc.);
- the school district fails to meet the local application requirements;
- the state deems the local district unable to make effective use of its entitlement unless it consolidates its entitlement with the entitlement of one or more other school districts (this apparently allows grant flexibility in funding arrangements — intermediate districts, special districts, etc.);
- when the program for handicapped children within the school district is of insufficient size and scope;

- when the school district is maintaining "full service" for all its handicapped children with state and local funds. (This provision will end when all districts within the state have reached "full service," at which time a degree of supplanting will in effect be permitted.)

Most significantly, the Act sets a flat monetary minimum. If a school district, after counting all of its handicapped children served, cannot generate an allocation for itself of at least $7,500, a pass-through to that school district does not occur. This provision is, of course, also aimed at encouraging various sorts of special education consortia in order to make a meaningful use of the federal dollars. (Effective 10/1/77.)

State and Local Requirements

The Act makes a number of critical stipulations which must be adhered to by both the state and its localities. These stipulations include:

- assurance of extensive child identification procedures;
- assurance of "full service" goal and detailed timetable;
- a guarantee of complete due process procedures;
- the assurance of regular parent or guardian consultation;
- maintenance of programs and procedures for comprehensive personnel development;
- assurance of special education being provided to all handicapped children in the "least restrictive" environment;
- assurance of nondiscriminatory testing and evaluation;
- a guarantee of policies and procedures to protect the confidentiality of data and information;

276

- assurance of the maintenance of an individualized program for all handicapped children;
- assurance of an effective policy guaranteeing the right of all handicapped children to a free, appropriate public education, *at no cost* to parents or guardian. (Effective FY1975 — 1977.)

It is most important to observe that an official, written document containing all of these assurances is now required (in the form of an application) of *every* school district receiving its federal entitlement under this Act.

Hold Harmless

The Act stipulates that every state will be "held harmless" at its actual allocation for fiscal 1977 (the last year of appropriations under the "Mathias formula").

Excess Cost Requirement

The Act provides that federal monies must be spent only for those "excess cost" factors attendant to the higher costs of educating handicapped children. A given school district must determine its average annual per pupil expenditure for all children being served, and then apply the federal dollars only to those additional cost factors for handicapped children beyond the average annual per pupil expenditure. Such a requirement does not obtain for the state education agency in the utilization of its allocation under this Act. (Effective 10/1/77.)

Individualized Instruction

The Act requires the development of an individualized written education program for each and every handicapped child served, to be designed initially in consultation with parents or guardian, and to be reviewed and revised as necessary at least annually. This provision takes effect in the first year under the new formula, fiscal 1978.

The term "individualized education program" means a written statement for each handicapped child developed in any meeting by a representative of the local educational agency or an intermediate educational unit who shall be qualified to provide, or supervise the provision of, specially designed instruction to meet the unique needs of handicapped children, the teacher, the parents or guardian of such child, and, whenever appropriate, such child, which statement shall include (a) a statement of the present levels of educational performance of such child, (b) a statement of annual goals, including short-term instructional objectives, (c) a statement of the specific educational services to be provided to such child, and the extent to which such child will be able to participate in regular educational programs, (d) the projected date for initiation and anticipated duration of such services, and (e) appropriate objective criteria and evaluation procedures and schedules for determining on at least an annual basis, whether instructional objectives are being achieved. (Effective 10/1/77.)

Full Service Date

It is generally agreed that the Congress ought to fix a chronological date, however innately arbitrary, beyond which no state or locality may without penalty fail to guarantee the handicapped will not be excluded outright from the public educational systems. Also, it is felt that the states ought to be given a reasonable, but not lengthy, time period in which to reach "full service."

The Act requires that every state and its localities, if they are to continue to receive funds under this Act, must be affording a free public education for all handicapped children aged three to eighteen by the beginning of the school year (September 1) in 1978, and further orders the availability of such education to all children aged three to twenty-one by September 1, 1980. However, these mandates carry a "big 'if'" in the area of preschool, apparently in the age range of three to five. Under the Act, such mandate for children in that group would apply only when there is a similar mandate in state law or practice.

Due Process

The vital provisions of existing law (Public Law 93-380, the "Stafford guarantees") toward the guarantee of due process rights with respect to the identification, evaluation, and educational placement of handicapped children are constructively refined in the Act toward at least the following objectives:

- to strengthen the rights of all involved;
- to conform more precisely to court decrees;
- to clarify certain aspects of existing law;
- to guarantee the rights of all parties relative to potential court review;
- to insure maximum flexibility in order to conform to the varying due process procedures among the states.

Federal Sanction

If the Commissioner finds substantial noncompliance with the various provisions of this Act, with emphasis upon the guarantees for children and their parents, he shall terminate the funding to a given locality or state under this Act, as well as the funding of those programs specifically designed for handicapped children under the following titles:

279

- Part A of Title I of the Elementary and Secondary Education Act.
- Title III of the Elementary and Secondary Education Act (innovative programs) and its successor, Part C. Educational Innovation and Support, section 431 of Public Law 93-380.
- The Vocational Education Act (Effective 10/1/77.)

SEA Authority

The Act requires that the state educational agency be responsible for ensuring that all requirements of the Act are carried out, and that all education programs within the state for all handicapped children, including all such programs administered by any other state or local agency, must meet state educational agency standards and be under the general supervision of persons responsible for the education of handicapped children. This provision establishes a single line of authority within one state agency for the education of all handicapped children within each state.

This provision is included in the Act for at least the following reasons:

- to centralize accountability, both for the state itself and from the standpoint of the federal government as a participant in the educational mission;
- to encourage the best utilization of education resources;
- to guarantee complete and thoughtful implementation of the comprehensive state plan for the education of all handicapped children within the state as already required in Public Law 93-380, the Education Amendments of 1974, with the further planning provisions of this Act;

280

- to ensure day-by-day coordination of efforts among involved agencies;
- to terminate the all too frequent practice of the bureaucratic "bumping" of children from agency to agency with the net result of no one taking substantive charge of the child's educational well-being;
- to squarely direct public responsibility where the child is totally excluded from an educational opportunity;
- to guarantee that the state agency which typically houses the greatest educational expertise has the responsibility for at least supervising the educational mission of all handicapped children;
- to insure a responsible public agency to which parents and guardians may turn when their children are not receiving the educational services to which they are entitled.

Special Evaluations

The Act orders a statistically valid survey of the effectiveness of individualized instruction as mandated in the legislation. The Act also orders the U.S. Commissioner to conduct an evaluation of the effectiveness of educating handicapped children in the least restrictive environment and orders the Commissioner to evaluate the effectiveness of procedures to prevent erroneous classification of children.

Supplanting

The Act carries a stipulation which permits the U.S. Commissioner to waive the provision against supplanting of state and local funds with federal dollars when a state presents clear and convincing evidence that all handicapped children within said state do in fact have available to them a free, appropriate public education.

Employment

The Act stipulates that recipients of federal assistance under this Act shall make positive efforts to employ and advance in employment qualified handicapped individuals.

Architectural Barriers

The Act authorizes such sums as may be necessary for the U.S. Commissioner to award grants to pay all or part of the cost of altering existing buildings and equipment to eliminate architectural barriers in educational facilities. Such provision is aimed at assuring certain handicapped children an appropriate public education in the least restrictive environment.

Lifetime

The Act establishes a permanent authorization with no expiration date.

Preschool Incentive

The Act carries a special incentive grant aimed at encouraging the states to provide special education and related services to its preschool handicapped children. Each handicapped child in the state aged three to five who is counted as served will generate a special $300 entitlement. It should be noted that this incentive entitlement goes to the state education agency and must be used by the SEA to provide preschool services. Additionally, this entitlement is a separate "line item" appropriation, independent of the larger Act entitlement. (Effective 10/1/77.)

Advisory

The Act provides that each state shall have a planning and advisory panel with the following duties:

- advise the state education agency on unmet needs and prescribe general policies for educating handicapped children;
- comment publicly on rules and regulations issued by the state and procedures proposed by the state for distribution of funds;
- assist the state in developing and reporting such data and evaluations as may assist the U.S. Commissioner. (Effective 10/1/77.)

Legislative Format

The Act amends the existing Education of the Handicapped Act and rewrites Part B of the Act. In that context, it is important to observe that all of the important advances made in Part B through Public Law 93-380 (Education Amendments of 1974) are retained in the Act, and, in many instances, are considerably improved upon.

Impact

The Act provides for an annual evaluation of the effectiveness of this legislation toward assistance in the achievement of a free, appropriate public education for all of the Nation's handicapped children.

Supervision of State Programs for the Handicapped

The state educational agency shall be responsible for assuring that the requirements of this part are carried out and that all educational programs for handicapped children within the state, including all such programs administered by any other state or local agency, will be under the general supervision of the persons responsible for educational programs for handicapped children in the state educational agency and shall meet education standards of the state educational agency. (Effective 10/1/77.)

APPENDIX C

Individualized Educational Plans

South Carolina School for the Deaf and the Blind

South Carolina School for the Deaf and the Blind

I.E.P. Committee: Date:_____

Name   Position

_____

_____

_____   _____
                                          (Parent's signature)

_____

_____

Name:_____Educational Department_____
       (Last)   (First)   (Middle)

Address:_____Date of Birth:_____

        _____Age:_____

Educational Services Recommended:
   (Indicate the service, the provider of service, and initiation/termination dates)

_____

_____

_____

_____

_____

Special Support Services Recommended:

   (Indicate the service, the provider of service, and initiation/termination dates)

_____

_____

_____

_____

Special Medical Conditions and Precautions:

_____

_____

THE RIGHT TO PARTICIPATE

Name of Student _____
Date _____
Assessed by _____

General Learning Style (specify source(s) of information):

____Student is able to be
   absorbed by tasks.
____Student has normal activity
   level within classroom
____Student is ready to respond
   to task demands
____Student is socially confident
   with classroom dynamics
____Student is realistically self-
   confident about ability in
   classroom activities.
____Student is comfortable in
   adult company.
____Student shows persistence
   during task engagement.
____Student reacts to failure
   realistically.

____Student is challenged by
   hard tasks.
____Student needs minimal teacher
   support for continuous task
   engagement.

____Student is easily distracted
   during task engagement.
____Student is overly active or has
   a depressed activity level
   within the classroom.
____Student usually needs urging to
   respond to task demands.
____Student is socially shy, reserved, or
   reticent within classroom dynamics.
____Student either distructs own ability
   or is over confident about ability
   in classroom activities.
____Student is ill-at-ease in
   adult company.
____Student gives up easily during
   task engagement.
____Student withdraws, shows hostility, or
   denies failure experiences within
   classroom activities.
____Student prefers only easy tasks and
   avoids hard tasks.
____Student needs constant teacher praise
   and encouragement for continuous
   task engagement.

Other Information:

Nature of Sensory Impairment (specify source(s) and date of information):

   Age of Onset:_____
   Cause of Loss:_____

Severity of Loss:_____
_____

Type of Correction:_____

Loss After Correction:_____

Special Considerations:_____
_____

Level of Sensory Acuity in:
   Visual Mode (deaf/hearing impaired students)_____
   Auditory Mode (for blind/visually impaired students)_____

286

INDIVIDUALIZED EDUCATIONAL PLANS

Name of Student_____

Date_____

Assessed By   _____

Profile of Performance in_____

Textbook_____   Stopping Point_____

Level   _____

X= Skills (proficiency level at 70% of mastery or 70% of time)

0= Deficiencies (proficiency level less than 70% of mastery or 70% of time)

Standardized Achievement Date;   Instrument_____

Form_____   Date_____
Sub-test_____   Grade Equivalent_____
Sub-test_____   Grade Equivalent_____
Sub-test_____   Grade Equivalent_____

287

I. E. P. Annual Goal Statement and Short-term Objective Sequence

Name of Student _____

Date _____

Developed by _____

Area of Performance _____

Annual Goal/Short-term Objectives	Nature of assessment procedure to evaluate outcome

INDIVIDUALIZED EDUCATIONAL PLANS

INDIVIDUAL INSTRUCTION RECORD

Subject Area: _____

Grade Level: _____

Student's Name _____

Birth Date: _____

Objectives	Learning Activities and/or Strategies	Resource Materials	Date

Note:

1. McIver serves 230 moderately, severely and profoundly mentally handicapped boys and girls and autistic children.

2. All students functioning above SPH are divided into four levels of functional ability. *All SPH receive individually written IEP's.*

3. The physical education emphasis for each level is described with appropriate tests, and mimeographed annual goals (are ongoing year to year) activities and objectives. To individualize the IEP, needs and test results for each child are recorded, specific objectives underlined for each child and specific evaluative criteria written in for each child. This process insures individualization though the main body of the IEP is mimeo. This has proved to be an effective procedure for a special school where large numbers are in the physical education program, and IEP's must be written for all.

McIver School of Special Education
Greensboro, North Carolina

Pauline A. Loeffler, Ph.D.
Director of Adapted and Special Physical Education

290

NAME Johnny Miller	AGE 11	ADAPTED PE 1982/83	LEVEL 2	CLASSROOM TEACHER	Smith

Present Level of Educ. Functioning	Annual Educational Goals	Instructional Objectives	Objective Criteria and Evaluation
Schilling/Kiphard Body Coordination Test Date _____ Score _____ Vodola Motor Ability Test Level 2 Date May, 1982 Score 50/80 possible Arnheim Basic Motor Ability Test Date _____ (Items scored individually) Vodola Physical Fitness Test Level 2 Date April 1982 Score Items Individual Toronto Fitness Test Date _____ Score _____ Arnheim Body and Space Perception Level 1 2 x 3 4 Date June 1982 Score 19/21 possible Needs 1. Gross body coordination-jumping ability 2. Abdominal strengthening 3. Recognition of right and left 4. To decrease aggression toward others	1. To develop efficient and effective motor skills 2. To develop and maintain an effective level of physical fitness 3. To develop a positive self-image 4. To develop desirable social behavior 5. To develop interest and skills for recreational participation	1. To improve gross body coordination, balance and posture, eye-hand and eye-foot coordination, eye-hand and eye-foot accuracy, rhythmic coordination and timing, manipulative ability 2. To improve strength, flexibility, endurance, agility, balance, leg power, body mechanics 3. To recognize body parts, improve awareness of laterality and directionality (left, right, front, back, side, forward, backward, sideways); recognize limb movements (bend, straighten, lift, turn) 4. To take turns, to share, play safely, follow directions, serve as leader, demonstrate skills, accept responsibility, be cooperative 5. To participate in activities used in school, family, community recreation for fun	1. Will show 10% improvement in total score of Vodola Mat Level 2 Will jump with both feet leaving floor 100% June 1 2. Will perform 5 continuous body curls unassisted by February 1 3. Will know right hand 100% by June 1 Will not push anyone while on apparatus 100% by February 1 McIver Field Days, swimming, roller skating, putt-putt golf, ice skating, horseback riding, bowling, World-Wide Games, board games, New Games, recreational games

291

THE RIGHT TO PARTICIPATE

Descriptor Term: Position Paper	Descriptor Code:
	P EDB
	Source:
Other Descriptor Terms: Individualizing Instruction	SBE/Aug. 16, 1974 Reaff. Nov. 17, 1976

Fundamental to the existence of a democratic society is a belief in the worth, dignity and uniqueness of the individual. The public schools are looked to as institutions for the perpetuation of the democracy and as laboratories in which democracy may be practiced. Thus, the concept of the student as an individual must be paramount in the operation of a school. School officials must recognize, and their practice must amplify that recognition, that existence of individual differences in personality, personal maturation timetable, temperament, interest, aspiration, self-image, and ability among students is not only a reality but acceptable and desirable.

Individualizing instruction is that educational process which identifies and meets individual student needs. This means that program flexibility must be initiated and maintained to permit and encourage a variety of options. Individualizing instruction must include a consideration of an environment which encourages teachers to adopt an individualized approach to instruction.

Instruction may be individualized for students in a variety of group settings or on a one-to-one basis so long as the learning experiences are appropriate for the individual.

It is the position of the State Board of Education that meeting the needs of each student is the fundamental concern in all curriculum and instruction efforts at all levels of the education system. This position is based on the philosophical premise that the education system exists for the sake of the student, not the student for the system.

The State Board of Education also takes the position that the following elements are essential to success in individualizing instruction:

1. Identification of individual learning potential and status.

2. Adjustment of programs and facilities to the changing needs and interests of students by providing a variety of learning options in content difficulty, teaching style, teacher expectations, rate, method, and evaluation.

3. A system for recording and interpreting student progress and understanding student characteristics which is reasonable in its teacher and student time demands.

4. A climate for healthy development of student self-image.

5. An instructional staff and other available human resources which has competency sufficient to accomplish the things stated and implied in the four elements listed above.

New ☐   Revised ☐   Substitute ☐

INDIVIDUALIZED EDUCATIONAL PLANS

3. Credit Transferred from Other Utah Public Schools

   A school may not reduce nor re-evaluate student credit officially transferred from any other public school in the State of Utah.

4. Provision for Class Discussions and Group Work

   Within the state law attendance requirements shall be established by the local board of education but in all cases (and particularly in schools with provision for earning credit on a performance basis) sufficient attendance shall be required to insure that students receive the educational benefit of extensive class discussion and group work and are prepared for the next step in life.

II. SENIOR HIGH SCHOOL PROGRAM OF STUDIES

A. UNIT OF CREDIT

   A unit of credit or any fraction thereof shall be given upon satisfactory completion of a course of study or learning experience in harmony with the adopted state course of study, with the duration of the course offering being 150 clock hours, unless the course is offered on a performance basis, in which case minimum standards of performance will be established by local boards of education in terms of skills, knowledge, attitudes and values.

   (See Alternate Ways of Earning Credit, p. 9.)

B. AN INDIVIDUAL EDUCATION PLAN FOR EACH STUDENT

   An individual education plan for the projected education program to be pursued by each student during membership in the school will be developed cooperatively by the student, designated school personnel, and parents. This plan will be guided by items C. 1, 2, and 3 below and individual student needs; include a tentative career goal; be viewed as a tentative plan; and be reviewed formally by the parties concerned at least annually. Attention will be given in each plan to an area of concentration (perhaps as much as four to five units) in a career cluster related to the student's career goal.

C. EARNED UNITS OF CREDIT

   Based on adopted state courses of study, each student in grades 10-12 will earn a minimum of 15 units of credit (the district may require more) in the following areas of study:

293

APPENDIX D

Disqualifying Conditions For Sports

(A Guide for Medical Evaluation for Candidates for School Sports, Publication of the American Medical Association, Revised, 1976, pp. 7-8.)

Conditions	Collision [1]	Contact [2]	Noncontact [3]	Other [4]
General				
Acute infections:				
Respiratory, genitourinary, infectious mononucleosis, hepatitis, active rheumatic fever, active tuberculosis	X	X	X	X
Obvious physical immaturity in comparison with other competitors	X	X		
Hemorrhagic disease: Hemophilia, purpura, and other serious bleeding tendencies	X	X	X	
Diabetes, inadequately controlled	X	X	X	X
Diabetes, controlled				
Jaundice	X	X	X	X

295

Conditions	Collision [1]	Contact [2]	Noncontact [3]	Other [4]
Eyes				
Absence or loss of function of one eye	X	X		
Respiratory				
Tuberculosis (active or symptomatic)	X	X	X	X
Severe pulmonary insufficiency	X	X	X	X
Cardiovascular				
Mitral stenosis, aortic stenosis, aortic insufficiency, coarctation of aorta, cyanotic heart disease, recent carditis of any etiology	X	X	X	X
Hypertension on organic basis	X	X	X	X
Previous heart surgery for congenital or acquired heart disease*				
Liver				
Enlarged	X	X		
Skin				
Boils, impetigo, and herpes simplex gladiatorum	X	X		

DISQUALIFYING CONDITIONS FOR SPORTS

Conditions	Collision [1]	Contact [2]	Noncontact [3]	Other [4]
Spleen				
Enlarged spleen	X	X		
Hernia				
Inguinal or femoral hernia	X	X	X	
Musculoskeletal				
Symptomatic abnormalities or inflammations	X	X	X	X
Functional inadequacy of the musculoskeletal system, congenital or acquired, incompatible with the contact or skill demands of the sport	X	X	X	
Neurological				
History or symptoms of previous serious head trauma, or repeated concussions, Controlled convulsive disorder**	X			

Conditions	Collision [1]	Contact [2]	Noncontact [3]	Other [4]
Convulsive disorder not completely controlled by medication	X	X	X	
Previous surgery on head	X	X		
Renal				
Absence of one kidney	X	X		
Renal disease	X	X	X	X
Genitalia*				
Absence of one testicle				
Undescended testicle				

298

FOOTNOTES

1. Football, rugby, hockey, lacrosse, etc.
2. Baseball, soccer, basketball, wrestling, etc.
3. Cross country, track, tennis, crew, swimming, etc.
4. Bowling, golf, archery, field events, etc.

* Each patient should be judged on an individual basis in conjunction with his cardiologist and operating surgeon.

** Each patient should be judged on an individual basis. All things being equal, it is probably better to encourage a young boy or girl to participate in a non-contact sport rather than a contact sport. However, if a particular patient has a great desire to play a contact sport, and this is deemed a major ameliorating factor in his/her adjustment to school, associates, and the seizure disorder, serious consideration should be given to letting him/her participate if the seizures are controlled.

*** The Committee approves the concept of contact sports participation for youths with only one testicle or with an undescended testicle(s), except in specific cases such as an inguinal canal undescended testicle(s), following appropriate medical evaluation to rule out unusual injury risk. However, the athlete, parents and school authorities should be fully informed that participation in contact sports for such youths with only one testicle does carry a slight injury risk to the remaining healthy testicle. Following such an injury, fertility may be adversely affected. But the chances of an injury to a descended testicle are rare, and the injury risk can be further substantially minimized with an athletic supporter and protective device.

APPENDIX E

Nondiscrimination in Federally Assisted Programs

Policy Interpretations

INTRODUCTION

The following four policy interpretations are issued by the Office for Civil Rights under the procedures announced in the FEDERAL REGISTER on May 1, 1978, 43 FR 18630. They interpret the Department's regulation issued under section 504 of the Rehabilitation Act of 1973.

DAVID S. TATEL,
Director,
Office for Civil Rights.

AUGUST 8, 1978.

SECTION 504 OF THE REHABILITATION ACT OF 1973

Policy Interpretation No. 3

Subject: "Program Accessibility" Requirements.

Policy Interpretation: A recipient is not required to make structural modifications to its existing facilities if its services can be made effectively available to mobility impaired persons by other methods. In selecting from among other methods, recipients must give priority to those that offer handicapped and nonhandicapped persons programs and activities in the same setting. Because of the administrative impossibility of continually determining, on an up-to-date basis, whether mobility impaired individuals will be entitled to services by a given recipient, and for other reasons set forth below, the absence of mobility impaired persons residing in an area cannot be used as the

301

test of whether programs and activities must be made accessible.

Discussion: The Department has been asked by recipients conducting modest programs (e.g., libraries in rural areas, small welfare offices, day care centers and senior citizens centers): (1) Whether they must make structural changes to their buildings to accommodate persons who are mobility impaired; and (2) whether they must make their services accessible to mobility impaired persons even if no such persons are known to live in their service area.

The Section 504 regulation was carefully written to require "program accessibility" not "building accessibility," thus allowing recipients flexibility in selecting the means of compliance. For example, they may arrange for the delivery of their services at alternative sites that are accessible or use aides or deliver services to persons at their homes. The regulation does *not* require that all existing facilities or every part of an existing facility be made accessible; structural changes are *not* necessary if other methods are effective in making the recipient's services available to mobility impaired persons. For example, a library building in a rural area with one room and an entrance with several steps can make its services accessible in several ways. It may construct a simple wooden ramp quickly and at relatively low cost. Mobility impaired persons may be provided access to the library's services through a bookmobile or by special messenger service or clerical aid or any other method that makes the resources of the library "readily accessible." However, recipients are required to give priority to methods that offer handicapped and nonhandicapped persons programs and activities in the same setting.

There is an additional option for recipients that have fewer than 15 employees and that provide health, welfare,

302

or other social services. If such a recipient finds, after consulting with a handicapped person seeking services, that only a significant alteration to its existing facilities will make its program accessible, the recipient may refer the handicapped person to another provider of the same services that is accessible. The referring recipient has the obligation to determine that the other provider is accessible and is willing to provide the services.

The section 504 regulation does not condition the requirement of "program accessibility" upon handicapped persons residing in the recipient's service area. Such a condition would be administratively unworkable. It would require the establishment of arbitrary geographic boundaries for each recipient's service area, the identification of all handicapped persons in that area and periodic surveys to determine whether handicapped persons have moved into or out of the service area. It would also ignore the needs of those persons who temporarily become mobility impaired or those mobility impaired persons who visit a service area. Moreover, mobility impaired persons may decide not to settle in a community because its services are not accessible.

The Department concludes, as it did when the section 504 regulation was adopted, that because the "standard (for program accessibility) is flexible" the regulation "does not allow for waivers" (See "Authority" section below).

Coverage: This policy interpretation applies to any public or private institution, person, or other entity that receives or benefits from HEW financial assistance. For further information, see definition of "recipient" at 45 CFR section 84.3(f).

Authority: Regulation issued under section 504 of the Rehabilitation Act of 1973, 45 CFR § 84.22 and appendix A.

Section 84.22:

(a) *Program accessibility.* A recipient shall operate each program or activity to which this part applies so that the program or activity, when viewed in its entirety, is readily accessible to handicapped persons. This paragraph does not require a recipient to make each of its existing facilities or every part of a facility accessible to and usable by handicapped persons.

(b) *Methods.* A recipient may comply with the requirements of paragraph (a) of this section through such means as redesign of equipment, reassignment of classes or other services to accessible buildings, assignment of aides to beneficiaries, home visits, delivery of health, welfare, or other social services at alternate accessible sites, alteration of existing facilities and construction of new facilities in conformance with the requirements of § 84.23, or any other methods that result in making its program or activity accessible to handicapped persons. A recipient is not required to make structural changes in existing facilities where other methods are effective in achieving compliance with paragraph (a) of this section. In choosing among available methods for meeting the requirement of paragraph (a) of this section, a recipient shall give priority to those methods that offer programs and activities to handicapped persons in the most integrated setting appropriate.

(c) *Small health, welfare, or other social service providers.* If a recipient with fewer than 15 employees that provides health, welfare, or other social services finds, after consultation with a handicapped person seeking its services, that there is no method of complying with paragraph (a) of this section other than making a significant alteration in its existing facilities, the recipient may, as an alternative, refer the handicapped person to other providers of those services that are accessible.

304

Appendix A — Section-by-Section Analysis, Subpart C — Program Accessibility.

Several commenters expressed concern about the feasibility of compliance with the program accessibility standard. *The Secretary believes that the standard is flexible enough to permit recipients to devise ways to make their programs accessible short of extremely expensive or impractical physical changes in facilities. Accordingly, the section does not allow for waivers.* The Department is ready at all times to provide technical assistance to recipients in meeting their program accessibility responsibilities. For this purpose, the Department is establishing a special technical assistance unit. Recipients are encouraged to call upon the unit staff for advice and guidance both on structural modifications and on other ways of meeting the program accessibility requirements . . . . (Emphasis added.)

Further, it is the Department's belief, after consultation with experts in the field, *that outside ramps to buildings can be constructed quickly and at a relatively low cost.* Therefore, it will be expected that such structural additions will be made promptly . . . . . (Emphasis added.)

SECTION 504 OF THE REHABILITATION ACT OF 1973

Policy Interpretation No. 4

Subject: Carrying Handicapped Persons to Achieve Program Accessibility.

Policy Interpretation: Carrying is an unacceptable method for achieving program accessibility for mobility impaired persons except in two cases. First, when program accessibility can be achieved only through structural changes, carrying may serve as an expedient until construction is completed. Second, carrying will be permitted in manifestly exceptional cases if carriers are formally instructed on the safest and least humiliating means of carrying and the service is provided in a reliable manner.

Discussion: The section 504 regulation requires that federally assisted programs and activities be "readily accessible" to handicapped persons. A program or activity will be judged "readily accessible" only if it is conducted in a building and room that mobility impaired persons can enter and leave without assistance from others. Carrying requires such assistance and is therefore unacceptable.

Carrying may also be undependable (e.g., when college students or employees are expected to volunteer) and often hazardous (e.g., when carriers are untrained or when the carrying is to occur on poorly illuminated or narrow stairs). It may humiliate the handicapped person by dramatizing his or her dependency and creating a spectacle. Its use is therefore inconsistent with section 504's critical objective of encouraging handicapped persons to participate in programs and activities.

The Department recognizes that carrying may be necessary in the following cases:

(1) The section 504 regulation requires "program accessibility" for handicapped persons and suggests a variety of methods for attaining compliance that can be implemented within 60 days. However, if "program accessibility" can be achieved only through "alterations of existing facilities (or) construction of new facilities," the construction must be completed "as expeditiously as possible," but in no event, later than June 3, 1980. Although recipients are not required to provide "program accessibility" during the period of construction, the Department encourages recipients to develop an interim expedient that may be carrying.

306

(2) Carrying is also acceptable in manifestly exceptional cases. For example, a university has properly maintained that the structural changes and devices necessary to adapt its oceanographic vessel for use by mobility impaired persons are prohibitively expensive or unavailable. Carrying, under this exception, must be provided in a manner that attempts to overcome its shortcomings. For example, carriers must be formally instructed on the safest and least humiliating means of carrying and the service must be provided in a reliable manner.

Coverage: This policy interpretation applies to any public or private institution, person, or other entity that receives or benefits from HEW financial assistance. For further information, see definition of "recipient" at 45 CFR § 84.3(f).

Authority: Regulation issued under section 504 of the Rehabilitation Act of 1973, 45 CFR § 84.22 (a), (b) and (d).

Section 84.22:

(a) *Program Accessibility.* A recipient shall operate each program or activity to which this part applies so that the program or activity, when viewed in its entirety, is readily accessible to handicapped persons. This paragraph does not require a recipient to make each of its existing facilities or every part of a facility accessible to and usable by handicapped persons.

(b) *Methods.* A recipient may comply with the requirement of paragraph (a) of this section through such means as redesign of equipment, reassignment of classes or other services to accessible buildings, assignment of aides to beneficiaries, home visits, delivery of health, welfare, or other social services at alternate accessible sites, alteration of existing facilities and construction of new facilities in conformance with the requirements of § 84.23, or any other

307

methods that result in making its program or activity accessible to handicapped persons. A recipient is not required to make structural changes in existing facilities where other methods are effective in achieving compliance with paragraph (a) of this section. In choosing among available methods for meeting the requirement of paragraph (a) of this section, a recipient shall give priority to those methods that offer programs and activities to handicapped persons in the most integrated setting appropriate.

(d) *Time period.* A recipient shall comply with the requirement of paragraph (a) of this section within 60 days of the effective date of this part except that where structural changes in facilities are necessary, such changes shall be made within 3 years of the effective date of this part, but in any event as expeditiously as possible.

SECTION 504 OF THE REHABILITATION ACT OF 1973

Policy Interpretation No. 5

Subject: Participation of Handicapped Students in Contact Sports.

Policy Interpretation: Students who have lost an organ, limb, or appendage but who are otherwise qualified, may not be excluded by recipients from contact sports. However, such students may be required to obtain parental consent and approval for participation from the doctor most familiar with their condition. If the school system provides its athletes with medical care insurance for sickness or accident, it must make the insurance available without discrimination against handicapped athletes.

Discussion: The Department has received several complaints that students have been denied an opportunity to participate in contact sports solely because they have lost

308

an organ, limb, or appendage. The regulation's requirement that handicapped students be provided an equal opportunity to participate in physical education and athletics programs extends to contact sports. The exclusion from contact sports of students who have lost an organ, limb, or an appendage (e.g., a kidney, leg, or finger) but who are otherwise qualified is a denial of equal opportunity. It denies participation not on the basis of ability but because of a handicap.

A recipient cannot assume that such a child is too great a risk for physical injury or illness if permitted to participate in contact sports. However, a child may be required to obtain parental consent and approval for participation from the doctor most familiar with his or her condition.

If the recipient provides its athletes with medical care insurance for sickness or accident, it must make the insurance available without discrimination against handicapped athletes.

Coverage: This policy interpretation applies to any public or private institution, person, or other entity that receives or benefits from HEW financial assistance. For further information see definition of "recipient" at 45 CFR § 84.3(f).

Authority: Regulation issued under section 504 of the Rehabilitation Act of 1973, 45 CFR § 84.37(c)(1).

Section 84.37(c)(1):

(c) *Physical education and athletics.* (1) In providing physical education courses and athletics and similar programs and activities to any of its students, a recipient to which this subpart applies may not discriminate on the basis of handicap. A recipient that offers physical education courses or that operates or sponsors interscholastic, club, or intramural athletics shall provide to qualified handicapped students an equal opportunity for participation in these activities.

Section 504 of the Rehabilitation Act of 1973

Policy Interpretation No. 6.

Subject: School board members as hearing officers.

Policy Interpretation: School board members may not serve as hearing officers in proceedings conducted to resolve disputes between parents of handicapped children and officials of their school system.

Discussion: The section 504 regulation requires school districts to establish a "system of procedural safeguards" to protect against errors in the educational programs developed for handicapped students. One requirement of that system is an "impartial hearing ... and a review procedure" through which a parent may contest the evaluation and placement of his or her child.

Recipients have asked whether school board members may serve as the hearing or reviewing authority in their own school district. The Department has concluded that this practice is inconsistent with the regulation's requirement of "impartial" proceedings. School board members have a clear interest in the outcome of the hearing. For example, determinations adverse to the parents will often avoid additional expenditures by the board. Also, the school board has hired, and therefore expressed confidence in, the judgment of the professionals challenged in the hearing. Moreover, since the Department will generally not review individual placement and other educational decisions of a school district if the "system of procedural safeguards" is in place, every precaution must be taken to ensure that those procedures operate fairly.

310

This interpretation is also supported by our commitment to coordinate section 504 procedural safeguards with those established by the Office of Education under the Education of the Handicapped Act. The regulations issued under that statute, as interpreted by the Office of Education, bar school board members from serving as hearing officers in their school system.

Coverage: This policy interpretation applies to any public or private institution, person, or other entity that receives or benefits from HEW financial assistance. For further information, see definition of "recipient" at 45 CFR § 84.3(f).

Authority: Regulation issued under section 504 of the Rehabilitation Act of 1973, 45 CFR § 84.36 and Appendix A thereto.

Section 84.36: A recipient that operates a public elementary or secondary education program shall establish and implement, with respect to actions regarding the identification, evaluation, or educational placement of persons who, because of handicap, need or are believed to need special instruction or related services, a system of procedural safeguards that includes notice, an opportunity for the parents or guardian of the person to examine relevant records, an impartial hearing with opportunity for participation by the person's parents or guardian and representation by counsel, and a review procedure. Compliance with the procedural safeguards of section 615 of the Education of the Handicapped Act is one means of meeting this requirement.

Appendix A, Subpart D (Fifth Paragraph): It is not the intention of the Department, except in extraordinary circumstances, to review the result of individual placement and other educational decisions, so long as the school district complies with the "process" requirements of this subpart (concerning identification and location, evaluation, and due process procedures) . . ..

Regulations Issued Under the Education of the Handicapped Act, 45 CFR 121a.507 and Appendix A Thereto

Section 121a.507: (a) A hearing may not be conducted:

(1) By a person who is an employee of a public agency which is involved in the education or care of the child, or

(2) By any person having a personal or professional interest which could conflict with his or her objectivity in the hearing.

(b) A person who otherwise qualifies to conduct a hearing under paragraph (a) of this section is not an employee of the agency solely because he or she is paid by the agency to serve as a hearing officer . . . .

Appendix A, Subpart E ("Response" to "Comment" on Section 121a.507): [A] parent of the child in question and school board officials are disqualified under § 121a.507.

[FR Doc. 78-22612 Filed 8-11-78; 8:45 am]

APPENDIX F *

Liability Inventory, Self-Test

(Answer key at end of test)

1. Which term represents a failure to exercise the reasonable care and prudence expected of a physical educator/coach?
   A. Anti-trust
   B. Negligence
   C. Tort
   D. Liability

2. If a *spectator* at your softball class/game is injured by a ball which comes through a noticeable hole in the backstop, which condition would apply?
   A. Negligence — failure to insure the spectator's safety
   B. Negligence — failure to provide reasonably safe conditions
   C. Spectators assume the risks which are inherent to the activity
   D. Spectators assume the risk by choosing to attend the activity

3. Does the type of activity that your students participate in have any bearing on the degree of supervision required?
   A. Yes, potentially dangerous activities require closer supervision

---

* Nancy Frank, Knowledge Tests Covering Selected Liabilities of Physical Educators and Coaches, unpublished masters thesis, University of North Carolina at Greensboro, 1982.

    B. Yes, team activities require closer supervision due to the greater number of participants

    C. No, all activities are potentially dangerous and therefore should be supervised at all times

    D. No, the more dangerous the activity, the more risks the student must assume

4. Where can you find a written code that will tell you whether or not your actions are negligent?

    A. In the *Second Restatement of Torts*

    B. In your state statutes

    C. In *Sports and the Courts*

    D. No such code exists

5. When should physical examinations be administered to your student/athletes?

    A. Before the first day of practice

    B. After the first day of practice

    C. Before the first strenuous workout

    D. After the team has been selected

6. Which condition is *not* required for an interscholastic or intercollegiate athletic program to be in compliance with Title IX?

    A. Equal opportunity for all teams to use the facilities

    B. Equal opportunity for all athletes to receive adequate coaching

    C. Equal monies for overall operation of men's and women's programs

    D. Equal provision of medical and training services

7. Which statement best defines the statute of limitations?

    A. Legislation which limits the amount of a settlement

314

    B. Specified time limit for filing a law suit

    C. Behavioral expectations of a reasonable and prudent person

    D. Restrictions prohibiting a law suit from being appealed

8. What degree of training in emergency care is expected of a physical educator/coach?

    A. The completion of an advanced first aid certificate

    B. Satisfied the requirements for a first aid certificate

    C. The ability to recall and perform necessary first aid acts

    D. Knowledge required to secure immediate emergency treatment

9. A soccer player dives for a ball that is falling close to the line. The field has been lined with unslaked lime. As a result, the player suffers permanent eye damage. Which statement best describes the player's position?

    A. The player has the right to expect the field to be free from potential hazards

    B. The injury sustained was inherent in the game

    C. The player assumed the risk of injury by diving for the ball

    D. Both A and C

10. What statement best describes the status of the governmental immunity doctrine?

    A. It remains applicable in all states

    B. It is applicable unless abrogated by state legislation

    C. It is applicable for required school activities only

    D. It has been declared unconstitutional by federal legislation

11. For which activities should you be especially careful to warn of dangers and provide adequate instruction?
    A. Swimming and baseball
    B. Power volleyball and football
    C. Wrestling and gymnastics
    D. Archery and basketball

12. Where can you obtain liability insurance?
    A. Through the National Education Association
    B. From your independent insurance agent
    C. Through the American Alliance for Health, PE, Rec., and Dance
    D. From any of the above sources

13. What is the correct terminology for a condition which by its mere existence could endanger one's well being?
    A. Tort
    B. Omission
    C. Nuisance
    D. Commission

14. How does "due process" apply to student/athletes?
    A. Due process does not apply to minors
    B. School personnel have the right to abrogate due process
    C. Due process is a constitutional right guaranteed for all
    D. A consistent legal precedent concerning student rights has not been established

15. You give a small group of college physical education majors permission to observe your volleyball class/practice. During the activity, an errant spike strikes the head of a spectator who was just lifting her head from taking notes. What defense would you claim if damages were sought?

A. Act of God

B. Assumption of risk

C. Contributory negligence

D. Comparative negligence

16. Which procedure is *not* a legal responsibility of school authorities in reference to equipment and facilities?

    A. To insure the safety of the students using the equipment and facilities

    B. To periodically inspect the facilities and equipment and make needed repairs

    C. To foresee hazardous situations and forewarn students accordingly

    D. To keep premises free from hidden dangers and reckless conduct

17. What can you, as a professional, do to limit involvement in a liability suit?

    A. Avoid teaching high risk activities

    B. Conduct yourself in a prudent and professional manner

    C. Secure a liability insurance policy with appropriate coverage

    D. Consult your attorney as to what behaviors constitute negligent behavior

18. Who generally makes decisions concerning questions of fact in court cases where negligence is alleged?

    A. The jury

    B. The judge

    C. The clerk of court

    D. Any of the above depending on the situation

19. Which added precaution should be taken when using your personal vehicle to transport students?

    A. Secure written permission from parents to transfer any incurring liability

    B. Notify the school administration of the route you plan to follow

    C. Add a rider to your existing automobile insurance policy

    D. Require all passengers to have valid accident insurance

20. Do you think it is necessary to keep a written record of accidents that happen during activities you are conducting?

    A. No, a written record can be used against me in court

    B. No, if I witnessed the accident, a written record is unnecessary

    C. Yes, it should include all facts and judgments concerning the accident

    D. Yes, it should include only the facts describing the accident

21. Cases involving alleged inadequate supervision often stem from the claim that teachers/coaches act "in loco parentis." Which statement best describes this condition?

    A. The parent entrusts the child to the custody of the school and thereby waives the right to sue for any ensuing damages

    B. The school personnel have a duty to protect the student's welfare as they represent a parental replacement

    C. As a parental replacement, school personnel assume the responsibility for all student actions

    D. The parent and the school share equally the responsibility of providing the child with a safe environment

318

22. Which statement reflects the rights of a physically impaired student/athlete concerning participation in school sponsored activities, i.e., physical education, intramurals, athletics?
    A. Public Law 94-142 indicates that these students are to be permitted to participate to try out for an activity
    B. The physically impaired may participate if they have consent of both the family doctor and the school doctor
    C. The student may participate only in non-contact sports

23. What combination of factors must exist before you can be accused of being negligent?
    A. You must owe a duty to the plaintiff and a breach of this duty must occur
    B. There must be a causal relationship between your conduct and the wrong doing, and the plaintiff must suffer an actual loss
    C. Both A and B are required
    D. Either A or B would be adequate

24. Which philosophical orientation could create a potentially hazardous situation for your students?
    A. Requiring students to attempt all skills at least once
    B. Extending opportunities for students to assist in developing regulations for the class
    C. Planning activities so that each student can work independently without constant supervision
    D. Encouraging students to strive for specific skill levels

25. AAHPERD guidelines are often consulted when investigating a case involving adequacy of instruction.

319

What position does AAHPERD take concerning the use of trampolines and mini-trampolines?
- A. Offer the activity only to students with above average motor ability skills
- B. Offer the activity, but require all students to sign a form relieving you of any incurring liability
- C. Offer the activity as an elective and do not permit the somersault to be attempted
- D. Do not use this equipment at all, the risk of injury is too high

26. Which term represents a legal wrong-doing resulting in direct or indirect injury to person or property?
- A. Liability
- B. Tort
- C. Negligence
- D. Causative factor

27. Which behavior is recommended for the teacher/coach in the event of an emergency?
- A. Begin first aid treatment, then go for help
- B. Get another faculty member to supervise your students while you get help
- C. Send someone for help and begin first aid immediately
- D. Dismiss the other students at once and begin first aid

28. The courts often decide that drowning is not the result of supervisory negligence. Which factor contributes highly to water-related accidents?
- A. The possibility of bodily malfunction
- B. The victim's negligence
- C. The inherent dangers of swimming
- D. All of the above

29. A California college student was injured when he stepped on a loose basketball and crashed into an unpadded wall during intramurals. The court found the college to be 75% at fault and the student to be 25% at fault. What action allows for the proration of damages?
    A. Comparative negligence
    B. Contributory negligence
    C. Assumption of risk
    D. Misfeasance

30. If you make a quotable written statement about another member of the sport community which is false and endangers his/her reputation, what allegation could you face?
    A. Libel charges
    B. Nuisance charges
    C. Battery charges
    D. None, no wrong doing has been committed

31. Assume that proper instruction and adequate warning about the hazards inherent in the activity have taken place. What does the participant assume?
    A. All risks of injury
    B. Risks inherent in the activity
    C. Risks not covered by school insurance
    D. No risks of injury

32. What principle recognizes the fact that, even though care and proper precautions have been taken, injuries are inevitable in physical activity?
    A. Contributory negligence
    B. Act of God
    C. Assumption of risk
    D. Comparative negligence

321

33. A sixteen-year-old student comes to your class, dresses for activity, but leaves before you begin the activity. The student leaves school property, is hit by a car and seriously injured. The parents initiate a suit against you alleging inadequate supervision. What would be your best defense?
    A. Contributory negligence
    B. Assumption of risk
    C. Unforeseeable accident
    D. Act of God

34. Supervision responsibilities include seeing that the area is free from hazards. What condition best represents an attractive nuisance?
    A. A wrestling mat rolled up against the wall
    B. A folded trampoline leaning against the wall
    C. A basketball goal secured to the wall
    D. Volleyball standards stored in the corner

35. Which obligation are school personnel *not* expected to fulfill?
    A. Exercise reasonable and prudent care
    B. Insure the student's safety
    C. Indicate hazards inherent in the activity
    D. Provide adequate supervision

36. From what condition does liability insurance protect the teacher/coach?
    A. The risk of extensive loss
    B. The hazard of being sued
    C. The damage to one's profession
    D. Both A and B

37. Which method of transporting students is most desirable?

    A. Instruct student to drive his/her personal vehicle

    B. Contract a reputable common carrier

    C. Utilize school vehicles with faculty drivers

    D. Arrange for parents to transport students

38. Which defense does *not* depend on the establishment of the defendant's negligence?

    A. Governmental immunity

    B. Contributory negligence

    C. Assumption of risk

    D. Act of God

39. Which combination of factors should be most strongly considered when planning activities involving physical contact?

    A. Height and weight of participants

    B. Size and skill level of participants

    C. Age and weight of participants

    D. Height and age of participants

40. You remove a severely injured player from the field without awaiting medical assistance. What may you be guilty of?

    A. Malfeasance

    B. Misfeasance

    C. Comparative negligence

    D. Contributory negligence

41. Which statement best describes "save harmless" legislation?

    A. Legislation which states that no harm is inflicted unless permanent damage is sustained

    B. Legislation which requires public buildings to maintain hazard free conditions

    C. Legislation which permits a school district to protect teachers from large financial loss

    D. Legislation which requires administrative personnel to purchase liability insurance for employees

42. What is the intent of Title IX?

    A. To force the men's and women's physical education departments to merge

    B. To enable the more established men's athletic departments to absorb the weaker women's programs

    C. To insure equal opportunity for participation in school sponsored activities

    D. All of the above

43. An injury occurs during your absence from the activity area. Under what condition would the court hold you responsible for damages?

    A. If the proximate cause of the injury was reasonably foreseeable

    B. If the activity involved dangerous equipment

    C. If the accident was unavoidable

    D. If either conditions A or B exist

44. A student is in a position of potential danger. You recognize the peril, but fail to correct the situation. If an injury occurred, what principle would the student utilize in trying to prove your negligence?

    A. Comparative negligence

    B. Contributory negligence

    C. Attractive nuisance

    D. Last clear chance

45. What type of insurance always provides compensation for injury regardless of the negligence involved?

    A. Liability insurance

324

B. Accident insurance

C. Life insurance

D. Disability insurance

46. What degree of supervision does the court expect you to uphold?

    A. That of a reasonable average person

    B. That of a reasonable parent

    C. That of a reasonable professional instructor

    D. That of a reasonable level corresponding to the instructor's age and experience

47. Which principle expects you to alleviate as well as anticipate harmful situations for your students?

    A. In loco parentis

    B. Proximate cause

    C. Foreseeability

    D. Respondeat superior

48. Which factors become more important when high risk activities are involved?

    A. Quality of equipment and qualifications of instructor

    B. Quality of instruction and size of the activity area

    C. Quality of equipment and size of the class

    D. Quality of instruction and qualifications of instructor

49. You allow a student to use a bow string that is worn because you were not appropriated any funds to upgrade the archery equipment. The student is injured as a result and brings suit against you. Where would you stand?

    A. You could be held liable as the accident was foreseeable

    B. You could be held liable for comparative negligence

    C. You could not be held liable because no funds were appropriated to upgrade the equipment

    D. You could not be held liable because the student assumes the risk inherent in the activity

50. A spectator is injured solely due to the nature of the activity being observed. What would the defendant claim?

    A. Charitable immunity

    B. Governmental immunity

    C. Act of God

    D. Assumption of risk

Answer Key

QUESTION	ANSWER	QUESTION	ANSWER
1	B	26	B
2	B	27	C
3	A	28	D
4	D	29	A
5	A	30	A
6	C	31	B
7	B	32	C
8	C	33	C
9	A	34	B
10	B	35	B
11	C	36	A
12	D	37	B
13	C	38	A
14	C	39	B
15	B	40	A
16	A	41	C
17	B	42	C
18	A	43	D
19	C	44	D
20	D	45	B
21	B	46	C
22	A	47	C
23	C	48	D
24	A	49	A
25	C	50	D

APPENDIX G

Teacher Referral Form

GUILFORD COUNTY SCHOOL SYSTEM
Referral for Exceptional Child Services Placement

EC-1
1982

Name _____ Birthdate _____
First   Middle   Last   Nickname

Student ID Number _____ Grade ____ Age ____ Sex ____ Date of Referral _____

Referring Teacher _____ School _____

REASON FOR REFERRAL:
A. Area of Exceptionality (Check all that apply)
  1. SPEECH/LANGUAGE
    Child has difficulty in:
    _____ Speaking fluently (hesitant, halting speech, stuttering)
    _____ Understanding and/or using oral communication
    _____ Articulation (producing sounds correctly, speaking clearly)
    _____ Sequencing words in a sentence, or sequencing sounds within words
    _____ Vocal quality (hoarse, husky, nasal, denasal, inappropriate pitch and/or volume, too loud or too soft)
  2. HEARING
    _____ Appears that hearing loss is handicapping the student educationally and developmentally
    _____ Needs frequent repetitions
  3. VISUAL
    _____ Screening by classroom teacher, school nurse, or eye specialist indicates an acuity reading of 20/70 or poorer in the better eye with correction
    _____ Child exhibits unusual behaviors (i.e. rubbing eyes, excessive blinking, squinting, etc.) when performing fine visual tasks
    _____ Child has a known deteriorating eye condition with acuity presently in normal range.
  4. LEARNING
    Child has difficulty in:

_____ Oral expression	_____ Written expression	_____ Reading comprehension
_____ Listening comprehension	_____ Basic reading skills	_____ Mathematical calculation
		_____ Mathematical reasoning

  5. EMOTIONAL/BEHAVIOR
    Child:
    _____ Leaves his/her seat inappropriately (Time _____ Manner _____ - check appropriate)
    _____ Wanders within or outside classroom
    _____ Is physically aggressive or bothersome toward others
    _____ Is verbally aggressive or bothersome toward others
    _____ Talks out loud or out of turn
    _____ Is withdrawn or preoccupied
    _____ Is easily frustrated or angered
    _____ Destroys property
    _____ Daydreams
    _____ Is excessively anxious or nervous
    _____ Lacks respect for authority
    _____ Other - please describe _____
  6. GIFTED (Check all that apply)
    _____ Child shows evidence of maturity and performance beyond years
    _____ Reasons out concepts
    _____ Is willing to try new or different things
    _____ Is an independent worker

B. Strengths and how utilized in order to better meet child's needs. _____
_____

C. Behaviors which need improvement and strategies used to modify. _____
_____

D. Additional information
_____

The list of resources in Appendix H was originally published in 94-142 and 504: NUMBERS THAT ADD UP TO EDUCATIONAL RIGHTS FOR HANDICAPPED CHILDREN: A GUIDE FOR PARENTS AND ADVOCATES (Washington, D.C.: Children's Defense Fund, 1980). Copies of that publication are available from Children's Defense Fund, 122 C Street, N.W., Washington, D.C., 20001.

We are grateful to the Children's Defense Fund for granting permission to print this list of resources in this publication.

APPENDIX H

Resources—State and National Organizations

6.1. State and Local Advocacy Groups.

Alabama
Alabama Developmental Disabilities Advocacy Project
918 Fourth Avenue
Tuscaloosa, AL 35401
205/348-4928

Alabama Council on Human Relations
P. O. Box 1632
Auburn, AL 36830
205/821-8336

Alaska
Protection and Advocacy for Developmental Disabilities, Inc.
600 University Avenue
Fairbanks, AK 99701
907/479-6940

Arizona
Arizona Center for Law
112 N. 5th Avenue
P. O. Box 2783
Phoenix, AZ 85002
602/252-4904

Legal Services for the Developmentally Disabled
Arizona ARC
5610 S. Central Avenue
Phoenix, AZ 85040

Central Arizona Regional Epilepsy Society
P. O. Box 33638
Phoenix, AZ 85607

Arkansas
Arkansas Developmental Disabilities Advocacy System
Governor's Office
Capitol Building, Room 011
Little Rock, AR 72201
501/371-2171

California
Youth Law Center
693 Mission Street
San Francisco, CA 94105
415/495-6420

Public Advocates, Inc.
1535 Mission Street
San Francisco, CA 94103
415/431-7430

Disabled Paralegal Advocate Program
Center for Independent Living
2539 Telegraph Avenue
Berkeley, CA 94704
415/841-4776

Legal Aid Foundation of Los Angeles
1550 West Eighth Street
Los Angeles, CA 90017

Western Center for Law
849 S. Broadway, Suite 206
Los Angeles, CA 90014

Protection and Advocacy Panel
150 Grand Avenue
Oakland, CA 94612

Sonoma County Citizens Advocacy, Inc.
P. O. Box 4449
Santa Rosa, CA 95402

Colorado
Colorado Migrant council
7905 W. 44th Avenue
Wheatridge, CO 80033
303/425-1532

Legal Center for Handicapped Citizens
1060 Bannock Street, Suite 316
Denver, CO 80202
303/575-0542

Connecticut
Office of Protection and Advocacy for Handicapped and
    Developmentally Disabled Persons
1380 Asylum Avenue (Rear)
Hartford, CT 06105
203/566-7303

United Cerebral Palsy
1 State Street
New Haven, CT 06511
203/772-2080

Delaware
Community Legal Aid Society, Inc.
913 Washington Street
Washington, DE 19801
302/575-0660

District of Columbia
Information Center for Handicapped Children
1619 M Street, N.W.
Washington, D.C. 20036
202/347-4986

Neighborhood Legal Services Program
635 F Street, N.W.
Washington, D.C. 20001
202/628-9161

One America Educational Service, Inc.
1750 Pennsylvania Avenue, N.W.
Suite 418
Washington, D.C. 20006
202/628-2216

Florida
Governor's Commission on Advocacy for Persons With
  Developmental Disabilities
Division of State Planning
Carlton Building
Tallahassee, FL 32304
904/488-9070

Georgia
American Friends Service Committee
Southeastern Public Education Program
P.O. Box 56JJ
Macon, GA 31208
912/742-3335

334

Georgia Advocacy Office, Inc.
1447 Peachtree Street, Suite 811
Atlanta, GA 30309
404/885-1447

Hawaii
Kahua Ho'omalu Kina, Inc.
P. O. Box 939
Honolulu, HI 96808
808/538-6631

Idaho
CO-AD, Inc.
100 Scout Lane
Boise, ID 83702
208/336-5353

Illinois
American Friends Service Committee
Midwest Regional Office
407 S. Dearborn Street
Chicago, IL 60605
312/427-2533

Illinois Developmental Disabilities Advocacy Authority
222 South College Street
Springfield, IL 62706
217/782-9696

Legal Assistance Foundation of Chicago
343 South Dearborn Street
Chicago, IL 60604
312/341-1070

Indiana
National Center for Law and the Handicapped
1235 N. Eddy Street
South Bend, IN 46617
219/288-4751

Protection and Advocacy Project
Community Service Council
445 N. Pennsylvania
Indianapolis, IN 46204
317/634-4311

Iowa
Iowa Protection and Advocacy System, Iowa Civil Rights
  Commission
418 Sixth Avenue
Liberty Building, Room 340
Des Moines, IA 50319
515/281-4121

Kansas
Kansas Advocacy and Protection Services for the
  Developmentally Disabled, Inc.
513 Leavenworth Suite 2
Manhattan, KS 66502
913/776-1541

Kentucky
Kentucky Protection and Advocacy Program
Department of Justice
Office of Public Defender
625 Leawood Drive
Frankfort, KY 40601
502/564-3754

Louisiana
Louisiana Advocacy System
New Orleans Legal Assistance Corporation
226 Carondelet Street, Suite 716
New Orleans, LA 70130
504/522-2357

Advocates for Juvenile Justice
344 Camp Street, Suite 1101
New Orleans, LA 70130
504/586-8835

Maine
Maine Coalition for Children With Special Needs
163 Lisbon Street
Lewiston, ME 04240
207/784-1558

Advocates for the Developmentally Disabled, Inc.
Cleveland Hall
Winthrop Street
Hallowell, ME 04347

Maryland
Disabilities Law Project University of Maryland Law
  School
500 W. Baltimore Street
Baltimore, MD 21201
301/528-6307

Maryland Advocacy Unit for the Developmentally
  Disabled, Inc.
201 W. Preston Street
13th Floor
Baltimore, MD 21201
301/383-3358

Employment Security Administration/DHR
1100 N. Eutaw
Baltimore, MD 21201
301/383-5070

Anne Arundel County Association for Retarded Citizens
937 Spa Road
Annapolis, MD 21401
301/268-8805

Massachusetts
Massachusetts Advocacy Center
Two Park Square
Boston, MA 02111
617/357-8431

Center for Law and Education
Guttman Library — Third Floor
6 Appian Way
Cambridge, MA 02138
617/495-4666

North Shore Parents and Friends of the Handicapped
3 Elnew Avenue
N. Beverly, MA 01915

Center for Law and the Developmentally Disabled
c/o Massachusetts Association for Retarded Citizens, Inc.
381 Elliot Street
Newson Upper Falls, MA 02164
617/623-2876

Office for Children
120 Boylston Street
Boston, MA 02116
617/727-8900

Michigan

Michigan Protection and Advocacy Service for
Developmentally Disabled Citizens
Michigan Association for Retarded Citizens
416 Michigan National Tower
Lansing, MI 48933
517/487-1755

Student Advocacy Center
202 E. Washington, Room 300
Ann Arbor, MI 48104
313/995-0477

Minnesota

Developmental Disabilities Advocacy Project
501 Park Avenue
Minneapolis, MN 55415
612/338-0968

Minnesota Developmental Disabilities Protection and
Advocacy System
200 Capitol Square Building
550 Cedar Street
St. Paul, MN 55101
612/296-4018

Legal Aid Society of Minneapolis
Legal Advocacy for the Developmentally Disabled
501 Park Avenue
Minneapolis, MN 55415
612/332-1441

Mississippi

Children's Defense Fund
Mississippi Project
Box 1684
Jackson, MS 39205
601/355-7495

Mississippi Mental Health Project
Box 951
Jackson, MS 39205
601/948-6752

Mississippi System of Protection and Advocacy for
 Developmentally Disabled Individuals, Inc.
235 Watkins Building
510 George Street
Jackson, MS 39201
601/354-6520

Missouri
Missouri Developmental Disabilities Protection and
 Advocacy Services, Inc.
420 A Brooks Street
Jefferson City, MO 65101
314/636-8113

National Juvenile Law Center
St. Louis University School of Law
3701 Lindell Boulevard
St. Louis, MO 63108
314/533-8868

Bootheel Legal Aid Society
300 Ward Avenue
Caruthersville, MO 63830
314/333-4076

Montana
Montana Developmental Disabilities Advocacy Program,
 Inc.
8000 Dark Horse Road
Missoula, MT 59801
406/549-4848

Nebraska
Nebraska Developmental Disabilities Protection and
  Advocacy System
301 Centennial Mall South
Box 95007
Lincoln, NE 68507
402/471-2981

Nevada
Developmental Disabilities Advocacy Office
Governor's Office of Planning Coordination
Capitol Building — Room 45
Carson City, NV 89701

New Hampshire
New Hampshire Association for Retarded Citizens, Inc.
110 North Main Street
Concord, NH 03301
603/224-7322

New Jersey
Education Law Center
605 Broad Street
Newark, NJ 07102
201/624-1815

New Jersey Department of the Public Advocate
Advocacy for the Developmentally Disabled
234 East Hanover Street
Trenton, NJ 08625

New Mexico
New Mexico Developmental Disabilities Protection and
  Advocacy System
State Human Rights Commission
303 Bataan Building
Santa Fe, NM 87503
505/827-5681

Legal Advocacy Project
Community Services for the Handicapped
122 La Veta, NE
Albuquerque, NM 87108

New York
Public Education Association
20 W. 40th Street
New York, NY 10018
212/354-6100

Advocates for Children
29-28 41st Avenue
Room 508
Long Island City, NY 11101
212/786-9100

New York Civil Liberties Union
84 Fifth Avenue
New York, NY 10011
212/924-7800

Protection and Advocacy System for Developmental
  Disabilities, Inc.
175 Fifth Avenue
Room 1308
New York, NY 10010
212/982-1140

Mayors' Office for the Handicapped
250 Broadway
New York, NY 10007
212/566-0972

Center on Human Policy
216 Ostrom Avenue
Syracuse, NY 13210
315/423-3851

North Carolina
North Carolina Protection and Advocacy System
Department of Administration
Howard Building, Room 107
112 W. Lane Street
Raleigh, NC 27611
919/733-3111

North Dakota
North Dakota Protection and Advocacy System
Governor's Council on Human Resources
State Capitol — 13th Floor
Bismarck, ND 58505
701/224-2972

Ohio
Ohio Protection and Advocacy System
4554 Coe Avenue
North Olmstead, OH 44070
216/777-4683

State Parent Involvement Network
3505 LaRue Prospect Road South
Prospect, OH 43342

Oklahoma

Protection and Advocacy Developmental Disabilities Agency
P.O. Box 14452
Oklahoma City, OK 73114
918/743-6453

Oregon

Oregon Developmental Disabilities Advocacy Center
718 West Burnside Street
Room 301
Portland, OR 97209
503/228-6571

Pennsylvania

Public Interest Law Center of Philadelphia
1315 Walnut Street
Philadelphia, PA 19107
215/735-7200

Developmental Disabilities Advocacy Network, Inc.
1607 City Towers
301 Chestnut Street
Harrisburg, PA 17101
717/278-0474

Education Law Center
2100 Lewis Tower Building
225 South 15th Street
Philadelphia, PA 19102
215/732-6655

Rhode Island

The Rhode Island Protection and Advocacy System for Developmentally Disabled Persons, Inc.
65 Wild Street
Providence, RI 02904

South Carolina
South Carolina Protection and Advocacy System
P. O. Box 1254
Charleston, SC 29402
803/723-2518

South Dakota
South Dakota Advocacy Project, Inc.
111 West Capitol Avenue
Pierre, SD 57501
605/224-8294

Tennessee
Tennessee State Planning Office
Division of Advocacy
660 Capitol Hill Building
301 Seventh Avenue North
Nashville, TN 37219

Texas
Advocacy, Incorporated
5555 N. Lamar Street, Suite K-109
Austin, TX 78711
512/475-5543

Utah
Legal Services for the Developmentally Disabled, Inc.
141 East First South
Salt Lake City, UT 84111
801/532-3333

Vermont
Vermont Developmental Disabilities Advocacy Project
Vermont Legal Aid, Inc.
180 Church Street
P.O. Box 562
Burlington, VT 05641
802/863-2881

Virginia
Virginia Developmental Disabilities Protection and
   Advocacy Office
Ninth Street Office Building — Suite 100
Richmond, VA 23219
804/786-4185
800/552-3962 (toll free from outside Richmond)

American Civil Liberties Union of Virginia
Student Rights Project
1000 One East Main Street
Suite 515
Richmond, VA 23219
804/644-8022

Washington
Troubleshooters
1600 W. Armory Way
Seattle, WA 98119

West Virginia
West Virginia Advocates for the Developmentally
   Disabled, Inc.
922 Quarrier Street
Embleton Building, Room 309
Charleston, WV 25301

346

Wisconsin
Wisconsin Association for Retarded Citizens
2 West Mifflin, Suite 200
Madison, WI 53703
608/831-3444

Wyoming
Developmental Disabilities Protection and Advocacy
Systems, Inc.
508 Hynds Building
Cheyenne, WY 82001
307/632-3496

Puerto Rico
Protection and Advocacy System of Puerto Rico
Consumer Affairs Dept.
Box 13934

Minillas Gubernamental Center
North Building
Santurce, PR 00908

Guam
Advocacy and Protective Services for the Developmentally Disabled
P. O. Box 10C
Agana, GU 96910

6.2. National Organizations for the Handicapped.

Note: Most of these organizations have state and local chapters which you can contact for assistance. This list was provided by the Closer Look Information Center for the Handicapped

All Disabilities
American Coalition of Citizens with Disabilities
1346 Connecticut Avenue, N.W.
Suite 1124
Washington, D.C. 20036

Autism
National Society for Autistic Children
169 Tampa Avenue
Albany, NY 12208

Blind
American Council for the Blind
1211 Connecticut Avenue, N.W.
Washington, D.C. 20006

American Foundation for the Blind
15 West 16th Street
New York, NY 10011

National Federation of the Blind
1346 Connecticut Avenue, N.W.
Suite 212, Dupont Circle Building
Washington, D.C. 20036

Cerebral Palsy
United Cerebral Palsy Association
66 East 34th Street
New York, NY 10016

Deaf
Alexander Graham Bell Association for the Deaf
3416 Volta Place, N.W.
Washington, D.C. 20007

348

National Association of the Deaf
814 Thayer Avenue
Silver Spring, MD 20910

Deaf-Blind
National Association for the Deaf-Blind
2703 Forest Oak Circle
Norman, OK 73071

Emotionally Disturbed
Mental Health Association, National Headquarters
1800 North Kent Street
Arlington, VA 22209

Epilepsy
Epilepsy Foundation of America
1828 L Street, N.W., Suite 405
Washington, D.C. 20036

Learning Disabilities
National Association for Children with Learning
  Disabilities
4156 Library Road
Pittsburgh, PA 15234

Mental Retardation
National Association for Down's Syndrome
P. O. Box 63
Oak Park, IL 60303

National Association for Retarded Citizens
2709 Avenue E East
P.O. Box 6109
Arlington, TX 76011

National Down's Syndrome Congress
528 Ashland Avenue
River Forest, IL 60305

Physically Handicapped
National Easter Seal Society for Crippled Children and
   Adults
2023 W. Ogden Avenue
Chicago, IL 60612

National Paraplegia Foundation
333 North Michigan Avenue
Chicago, IL 60601

Spina Bifida Association of America
343 South Dearborn Street, Room 319
Chicago, IL 60604

Speech Impaired
American Speech and Hearing Association
10801 Rockville Pike
Rockville, MD 20852

6.3. National Advocacy and Service Organizations.

Center for Law and Education
Guttman Library
6 Appian Way
Cambridge, MA 02138
617/495-4666

Center on Human Policy
216 Ostrom Avenue
Syracuse, NY 13210
315/423-3851

Children's Defense Fund
1520 New Hampshire Avenue, N.W.
Washington, D.C. 20036
202/483-1470

Closer Look Information Center for the Handicapped
P. O. Box 1492
Washington, D.C. 20013

Council for Exceptional Children
1920 Association Drive
Reston, VA 22091
703/620-3660

Mental Health Law Project
1220 Nineteenth Street, N.W.
Washington, D.C. 20036
202/467-5730

Mexican-American Legal Defense Fund
28 Geary Street
San Francisco, CA 94108
415/981-5800

National Association for the Deaf, Legal Defense Fund
Florida Avenue & 7th Street, N.E.
Suite 311
Washington, D.C. 20002
202/447-0503

National Center for Law and the Handicapped
c/o University of Notre Dame
South Bend, IN 46617
219/288-4751

National Juvenile Law Center
St. Louis University School of Law
3701 Lindell Boulevard
St. Louis, MO 63108
314/533-8868

Native American Rights Fund
1506 Broadway
Boulder, CO 80302
303/447-8760

Youth Law Center
693 Mission Street, Second Floor
San Francisco, CA 94105

6.4. National and Regional Offices of Federal Agencies.

Office for Civil Rights National Office:

Director, Office for Civil Rights
Department of Health, Education and Welfare
330 Independence Avenue, S.W.
Washington, D.C. 20201

Bureau of Education for the Handicapped
400 Maryland Avenue, S.W.
Donohoe Building
Washington, D.C. 20202

Region I:

Connecticut, Maine, Massachusetts, New Hampshire, Rhode Island, Vermont

HEW
Office for Civil Rights
140 Federal Street, 14th Floor
Boston, MA 02110

Region II:

New York, New Jersey, Puerto Rico, Virgin Islands

HEW
Office for Civil Rights
Federal Building
26 Federal Plaza, Room 3908
New York, NY 10007

Region III:

Delaware, District of Columbia, Maryland, Pennsylvania, Virginia, West Virginia

HEW
Office for Civil Rights
P. O. Box 13716
3535 Market Street
Philadelphia, PA 19101

Region IV:

Alabama, Florida, Georgia, Kentucky, Mississippi, North Carolina, South Carolina, Tennessee

HEW
Office for Civil Rights
101 Marietta Street
Atlanta, GA 30323

Region V:

Illinois, Indiana, Minnesota, Michigan, Ohio, Wisconsin

HEW
Office for Civil Rights
300 South Wacker Drive, 8th Floor
Chicago, IL 60606

Region VI:

Arkansas, Louisiana, New Mexico, Oklahoma, Texas

HEW
Office for Civil Rights
1200 Main Tower Building, 19th Floor
Dallas, TX 75202

Region VII:

Iowa, Kansas, Missouri, Nebraska

HEW
Office for Civil Rights
12 Grand Building
1150 Grand Avenue
Kansas City, MO 64106

Region VIII:

Colorado, Montana, North Dakota, South Dakota, Utah, Wyoming

HEW
Office for Civil Rights
Federal Building
1961 Stout Street, Room 11037
Denver, CO 80294

Region IX:

Arizona, California, Hawaii, Nevada, Guam,

American Samoa, Trust Territory of Pacific Islands, Wake Island

HEW
Office for Civil Rights
100 Van Ness, 14th Floor
San Francisco, CA 94102

Region X:

Alaska, Idaho, Oregon, Washington

HEW
Office for Civil Rights
1321 Second Avenue
Room 5041, M/S 508
Seattle, WA 98101

6.5. State Special Education Departments.

Alabama

Mr. Cecil Bobo
Coordinator
Exceptional Children and Youth
State Department of Education
Montgomery, AL 36104

Alaska

Dr. Tom Brown, Director
Division of Educational Program Support
State Department of Education
Pouch F
Juneau, AK 99801

Arizona
Mr. Don Johnson, Director
Department of Special Education
1535 W. Jefferson
Phoenix, AZ 85007

Arkansas
Dr. Larry L. Rogers
Division of Instructional Services
Arch Ford Education Building
Little Rock, AR 72201

California
Mr. Leslie Brinegar
Director, Office of Special Education
State Department of Education
Sacramento, CA 95814

Colorado
Special Educational Services Unit
State Department of Education
201 East Colfax
Denver, CO 80203

Connecticut
Mr. Robert I. Margolin
Bureau of Pupil Personnel and Special Educational
    Services
State Department of Education
Hartford, CT 06115

356

Delaware
Dr. Carl Halton
Director of Instruction
State Department of Public Instruction
John G. Townsend Building
P. O. Box 1402
Dover, DE 19901

District of Columbia
Dr. Doris Woodson
Assistant Superintendent
Special Education
Division of Special Educational Programs
Presidential Building, Suite 602
415 12th Street, N.W.
Washington, DC 20004

Florida
Dr. Landis M. Stetler, Chief
Bureau of Education for Exceptional Students
Florida Department of Education
Tallahassee, FL 32304

Georgia
Mr. Herbert D. Nash, Director
Special Education Program
Division of Early Childhood & Special Education
State Department of Education
Atlanta, GA 30334

Hawaii
Mr. Miles Kawatachi, Director
Special Education Branch
State Department of Education
1270 Queen Emma Street, Room 120
Honolulu, HI 11206

Idaho
Dr. Judy Schrag
Director of Special Education
Len Jordan Building
State Office Building
Boise, ID 83720

Illinois
Joseph Fisher, Assistant Superintendent
Department of Specialized Educational Services
100 North First Street
Springfield, IL 62777

Indiana
Mr. Gilbert A. Bliton, Director
Division of Special Education
Department of Public Instruction
229 State House
Indianapolis, IN 46204

Iowa
Mr. J. Frank Vance
State Director, Division of Special Education
State Department of Public Instruction
Grimes State Office Bldg.
Des Moines, IA 50319

Kansas
Mr. James E. Marshall, Director
Division of Special Education
State Department of Education
120 East Tenth Street
Topeka, KS 66612

358

Kentucky
Bureau for Education of Exceptional Children
Capital Plaza Tower, 8th Floor
Frankfort, KY 40601

Louisiana
Dr. Henry L. Smith, Director
Assistant Superintendent
Special Educational Services
State Department of Education
Capital Station
P. O. Box 44064
Baton Rouge, LA 70804

Maine
Mr. John T. Kierstead, Director
Division of Special Education
State Department of Educational & Cultural Services
Augusta, MA 04333

Maryland
Dr. Linda J. Jacobs
Assistant State Superintendent
Division of Special Education
State Department of Education
P. O. Box 8717, Balt-Wash International Airport
Baltimore, MD 21240

Massachusetts
Mr. Roger Brown
Division of Special Education
State Department of Education
Park Square Building
31 St. James Avenue
Boston, MA 02116

Michigan
Mr. Murray O. Batten, Director
Special Education Services
State Department of Education
P. O. Box 30008
Lansing, MI 48909

Minnesota
Mr. John C. Groos, Director
Special Education Section
State Department of Education
Capitol Square
550 Cedar Avenue
St. Paul, MN 55101

Mississippi
Dr. Walter H. Moore, Assistant Director
Special Education Section
State Department of Education
Jackson, MS 39205

Missouri
Mr. Roland J. Werner, Jr.
Director of Special Education
Dept. of Elementary and Secondary Education
P.O. Box 480
Jefferson City, MO 65101

Montana
Shirley M. Miller, Director Special Education Unit
Office of Public Instruction
State Capitol
Helena, MT 59601

Nebraska
Mr. Gary Sherman, Administrator of Special Education
Special Education Section
233 S. 10th Street
Lincoln, NE 68509

Nevada
Mr. Frank South
Exceptional Public Education
Nevada State Dept. of Education
Capital Complex
400 West King Street
Carson City, NV 89710

New Hampshire
Mr. Robert Kennedy
Director, Special Education Section
State Department of Education
105 Loudon Road
Concord, NH 03301

New Jersey
Mr. Paul Parado
Acting Deputy Assistant Commissioner
Branch of Special Operations and Pupil Personnel
  Services
State Department of Education
225 West State Street
Trenton, NJ 08625

New Mexico
Mr. Elie S. Gutierrez, Director
Division of Special Education
State Department of Education
State Educational Building
300 Don Gaspar Avenue
Santa Fe, NM 87503

New York
Dr. Louis Brumet
Office for the Education of Children with Handicapping
   Conditions
State Education Department
55 Elk Street
Albany, NY 12234

North Carolina
Mr. Theodore R. Drain, Director
Division for Exceptional Children
State Department of Public Instruction
Raleigh, NC 27611

North Dakota
Mr. Robert Miller, Director
Special Education
State Department of Public Instruction
Bismarck, ND 58501

Ohio
Mr. S. J. Bonham, Jr. Director
Division of Special Education
State Department of Education
933 High Street
Worthington, OH 43085

362

Oklahoma
Dr. Maurice, P. Walraven
Director of Special Education
State Department of Education
2500 N. Lincoln
Room 263
Oklahoma City, OK 73105

Oregon
Dr. Mason D. McQuiston
Director of Special Education
Oregon Department of Education
942 Lancaster Drive N.E.
Salem, OR 97310

Pennsylvania
Dr. Gary J. Makuch
Bureau of Special and Compensatory Education
P. O. Box 911
Harrisburg, PA 17126

Rhode Island
Mr. Charles Harrington, Director
Special Education
State Department of Education
Roger Williams Building
Providence, RI 02908

South Carolina
Mr. Robert S. Black
Office of Programs for the Handicapped
State Department of Education
Room 309, Rutledge Building
Columbia, SC 29201

South Dakota
Dr. George Levin, Director
Section for Exceptional Children
Office Building #3
Pierre, SD 57501

Tennessee
Mr. Vernon Johnson, Director
Division for the Education of the Handicapped
State Department of Education
102 Cordell Hull Building
Nashville, TN 37219

Texas
Mr. Don Weston, Director
Division of Special Education
Texas Education Agency
201 East 11th Street
Austin, TX 78701

Utah
Dr. Elwood Pace, Coordinator
Pupil Services
Utah State Board of Education
250 East, 500 South
Salt Lake City, UT 84111

Vermont
Ms. Jean S. Garvin, Director
Special Educational and Public Personnel Services
State Department of Education
Montpelier, VT 05602

Virginia
Mr. James T. Micklem, Director
Division of Special Education
State Department of Education
Richmond, VA 23216

Washington
Mr. Floyd M. Jackson, Director
Special Services Section
Old Capitol Building
Olympia, WA 98504

West Virginia
Mr. Keith Smith, Director
Division of Special Education
West Virginia Department of Education
Building 6, Room B-315
State Capitol
Charleston, WV 25305

Wisconsin
Victor J. Contrucci, Admin.
Division for Handicapped Children & Assistant State
    Superintendent
State Department of Public Instruction
126 Langdon Street
Madison, WI 53702

Wyoming
Mr. Lamar Gordon, Jr., Coordinator
Office of Exceptional Children
State Department of Education
Cheyenne, WY 82002

APPENDIX I

Sports Organizations

American Athletic Association of the Deaf, Inc.
3916 Lantern Drive
Silver Spring, MD 20902

American Wheelchair Bowling Association
6718 Pinehurst Drive
Evansville, IL 47711

American Wheelchair Pilots Association
Dave Graham
P. O. Box 1181
Mesa, AZ 85201

Disabled Sportsmen of America
P. O. Box 26
Vinton, VA 24179

Handicapped in Sports
United States Olympic Committee
Colorado Springs, CO 80901

National Association of Sports for Cerebral Palsy
66 E. 34th St.
New York, NY 10016

National Foundation for Wheelchair Tennis
3855 Birch Street
Newport Beach, CA 92660

National Wheelchair Athletic Association
2607 Templeton Gap Road.
Suite C
Colorado Springs, CO 80907

National Wheelchair Basketball Association
110 Seaton Building
University of Kentucky
Lexington, KY 40506

National Wheelchair Softball Association
P. O. Box 737
Sioux Falls, SD 57101

North American Riding for the Handicapped Association
Box 100
Ashburn, VA 22011

Paralyzed Veterans of America
4350 East-West Highway, Suite 900
Washington, DC 20014

Special Olympics, Inc.
1701 K. Street, N.W.
Suite 203
Washington, DC 20006

The National Spinal Cord Injury Foundation
369 Elliot Street
Newton Upper Falls, MA 02146

United States Association for Blind Athletes
55 West California Avenue
Beach Haven Park, NJ 08008

Wheelchair Motorcycle Association, Inc.
101 Torrey Street
Brockton, MA 02401

GLOSSARY OF TERMS
Legal Terms

Abrogate: To annul or repeal a law or an order.

Appellant: The party who initiates the appeal to an appellate court.

Appellate Court: A court which reviews trials of lower courts for errors of law, to be distinguished from a trial court where the case is originally heard.

Appellee: The party against whom the appeal is taken; the party on the other side from the appellant.

Charitable Immunity: The freedom of a charitable institution, such as a hospital, from being held liable for certain actions rendered in pursuit of its charitable undertaking.

Defendant: The person defending against or denying a claim; the person against whom relief is sought; in a criminal case, the person against whom a criminal charge is brought.

Governmental Immunity: Usually called sovereign immunity; a limitation upon an individual or institution's right to sue the government for those functions which are held to be governmental in nature.

In Loco Parentis: In the place of a parent; someone who stands in the place of a parent and is charged with the same rights, duties, and responsibilities.

Injunction: An order of the court normally requiring a party or institution to cease taking certain actions which are alleged to be harmful or to take certain actions to alleviate harm.

> Temporary Injunction — An injunction issued for a set period of time and which will expire upon the passage of time.

> Permanent Injunction — An injunction issued which will stay in effect indefinitely from the date it is entered.

Judgment: In the legal sense, the official decision of a court of record.

Liability: In a legal sense, the responsibility for an action; in civil cases, most often expressed in terms of fault with an accompanying responsibility to pay money damages to an injured party.

Litigation: The filing and trial of a lawsuit between two or more parties for the purpose of enforcing an alleged right or recovering money damages for a breach of duty.

Moot: An undecided point not settled by courts but concerning some matter which has, as a practical matter, already been decided by the happening of an event prior to a court's determination.

Nuisance: Anything which reasonably interferes with enjoyment of life or property to the detriment of another.

Plaintiff: A person who brings a civil action against another person or institution.

Remand: Action by a higher court to send a matter back to the same court from which it came, with directions as to what must be done in the lower court.

Remittur: The process by which a judge can reduce by subtraction an award for damages made by a jury considered to be excessive.

Res Ipsa Loquitur: Latin meaning the thing speaks for itself; a theory of negligence arising when an injury happens, which ordinarily would not happen in the absence of negligence, and which requires the instrumentality which caused the injury to be under the exclusive control of the negligent party.

370

Respondeat Superior: Latin meaning let the master answer; a theory whereby a master is held liable for the wrongful acts of his servant or employee if the servant or employee is acting within the legitimate scope of this authority.

Summary Judgment: A judgment entered by a court without a trial because there is no genuine dispute about the facts; judgment is entered as a matter of law as applied to undisputed facts.

Tort: A theory of negligence involving a wrongful act or a violation of a duty; there must be a legal duty to the person harmed, there must be a breach of that duty, there must be damage to the person wronged as the usual (proximate) result of the breach.

Terms Relating to Handicapped Conditions

Cerebral Palsy (CP): Any one of a group of conditions characterized by paralysis, weakness, uncoordination, or any other aberration of the motor function of the body due to pathology of the motor control centers of the brain.

Deaf (D): A term to denote hearing impairment which is so severe that the child is impaired in processing linguistic information through hearing, with or without amplification, which adversely affects educational performance.

Deaf-Blind (DB): A term to denote concomitant hearing and visual impairments, the combination of which causes such severe communication and other developmental and educational problems that they cannot be accommodated in special education programs solely for deaf or blind children.

Diabetes: Inability to metabolize carbohydrates as a result of failure of the pancreas to secrete insulin.

Epilepsy: A cerebral disorder manifested by transient disturbance in motor and/or sensory function.

Hard of Hearing (HH): A term to denote hearing impairment, whether permanent or fluctuating, which adversely affects a child's educational performance but which is not included under the definition of "deaf" in this section.

Hemophilia: Hereditary disease of the blood characterized by delayed clotting; inherited by males maternally.

IEP: Individualized Education Program.

Leukemia: A disease of the blood forming organs characterized by an increase in the white blood cells in the body.

372

Mainstreaming: Education of handicapped children with their nonhandicapped peers.

Mentally Retarded (MR): A term to denote significantly subaverage general intellectual functioning existing concurrently with deficits in adaptive behavior and manifested during the developmental period, which adversely affects a child's educational performance.

Multihandicaps: A combination of handicapping conditions.

Orthopedically Impaired (OI): A term to denote severe orthopedic impairment which adversely affects a child's educational performance. The term includes impairments caused by congenital anomaly; impairments caused by disease, and impairments from other causes.

Other Heath Impaired (OHI): A term to denote limited strength, vitality or alertness, due to chronic or acute health problems such as a heart condition, tuberculosis, rheumatic fever, nephritis, asthma, sickle cell anemia, hemophilia, epilepsy, lead poisoning, leukemia, or diabetes, which adversely affects a child's educational performance.

Paraplegia: Paralysis or involvement in two body parts; usually the lower limbs.

PEOPEL: Physical Education Opportunity Program for Exceptional Learners.

Physical Education: The development of physical and motor fitness; fundamental skills and patterns; and the skills in aquatics, dance and individual and group games and sports (including intramural and lifetime sports). The term includes special physical education, adapted physical education, movement education and motor development.

Public Law 94-142: The Education for All Handicapped Children Act of 1975.

Quadriplegia: Involvement or paralysis of all four limbs.

Section 504: Section of the Rehabilitation Act of 1973.

Seriously Emotionally Disturbed (ED): A term to denote a condition exhibiting one or more of the following characteristics over a long period of time and to a marked degree, which adversely affects educational performance.

Specific Learning Disabilities (LD): A term to denote a disorder in one or more of the basic psychological processes involved in understanding or in using language, spoken or written, which may manifest itself in an imperfect ability to listen, think, speak, read, write, spell or do mathematical calculations. The term includes such conditions as perceptual handicaps, brain injury, minimal brain disfunction, dyslexia, and developmental aphasia. The term does not include children who have learning problems which are primarily the result of visual, hearing or motor handicaps, of mental retardation, or of environmental, cultural, or economic disavantage.

Speech Impaired (SI): A term to denote a communication disorder, such as stuttering, impaired articulation, a language impairment, or a voice impairment, which adversely affects a child's educational performance.

Visually Handicapped (VH): A term to denote a visual impairment which, even with correction, adversely affects a child's educational performance. The term includes both partially seeing and blind children.

INTERPRETATIONS OF SECTION 504 AND PUBLIC LAW 94-142

The following questions and answers are a brief example of questions asked regarding the federal mandates. The Unit on Programs for the Handicapped American Alliance for Health, Physical Education, Recreation, and Dance (AAHPERD) and the federal agency offices who administered these laws: Health, Education, and Welfare Office for Civil Rights (section 504) and HEW Bureau of Education for the Handicapped (Public Law 94-142) have attempted to interpret these laws. (It must be pointed out, however, that the questions and answers are individual interpretations and do not necessarily reflect HEW's official policy statements).

Physical Education

Question: Physical education is mentioned by many special educators as a related service. How is this interpreted by law?

Answer: Physical education is the only curricular area mentioned in the definition of special education; it is *not* a related service. It is a law that children who receive special services in special education also receive physical education.

Question: Many regular classroom teachers use perceptual motor, recreational and other motor activities in their classroom instruction; does this meet the requirement of physical education?

Answer: No. These activities are good and should be used in addition to the physical education program.

Question: Is there a difference between psychomotor skills and physical education?

375

Answer: Psychomotor skills are not included in the definition of the law whereas physical education is defined specifically. Physical education is a more encompassing term than psychomotor skills.

Question: Aquatics is included in the definition of physical education; does this mean that each handicapped child must be provided an aquatics program?

Answer: No. If in the opinion of the individualized planning committee the child would benefit from an aquatics program and this program is necessary to meet specifically determined annual goals then an aquatics program must be provided, regardless of the availability through the education agency.

Question: If aquatics is deemed necessary by the individualized planning committee and the educational agency does not have a swimming facility how is this problem solved?

Answer: The local education agency must make arrangements through private contracting or other public services to provide this service. This service is at no cost to the parents.

Question: Must every child with a handicapping condition receive recreation as a related service?

Answer: If the individualized planning committee deems it necessary to include recreation to meet specifically determined annual goals then the child must be provided this service.

Question: Must community services offering recreational programs provide programs for individuals with handicapping conditions?

Answer: Yes! Section 504 prohibts discrimination or exclusion on the basis of handicap. Any agency receiving federal funds either directly or indirectly is governed by section 504.

Question: Who is responsible for providing intramural and extramural programs to individuals with handicapping conditions?

Answer: The local educational agency is responsible.

Question: If a student receives physical therapy, does this meet the requirements of physical education?

Answer: No. Physical therapy is considered a related service and does not meet the requirement of physical education.

Question: If a special education child is mainstreamed into a regular physical education class, must he have an IEP written for physical education?

Answer: If the child is not in need of specially designed physical education then physical education does not have to be included in the individualized education program.

Question: Must physical education be included in every handicapped child's individualized education program?

Answer: Only if the child has special physical education or motor needs. Physical education must be dealt with by IEP planning committees, but if regular physical education is all that is needed then that takes care of it.

Question: Must physical educators be a part of the individualized planning conference?

Answer: Only three people are required to take part in the individualized planning conference. They are: (1) a representative of the public agency; (2) the child's teacher; and (3) one or both parents of the child. Other individuals may attend at the discretion of the parents and/or local education agency.

Question: What are some ways in which physical education teachers can get extra help to provide additional assistance to handicapped children with special needs who are in their classes?

Answer: First of all, one must understand that individualized education and one-to-one teaching are not necessarily synonymous. A child's individual needs can be met in a number of different settings including: (1) peer tutoring, (2) a buddy system which pairs handicapped individuals with able-bodied students, (3) contract teaching, (4) circuit or station teaching, (5) team teaching, (6) resource rooms, (7) assistance from para-professionals, to mention a few.

Question: Who is responsible for the physical education of students who receive homebound instruction?

Answer: The local education agency.

Question: What options do parents have if they disagree with the placement of their child in physical education or any other areas?

Answer: Procedural due process is guaranteed to the parents. An informal hearing is held at the local level; if the problem is not resolved it goes to regional, state and ultimately to the Supreme Court if necessary.

Question: By what date must facilities and programs be made accessible for the handicapped?

Answer: Those agencies receiving federal funds must have had programs accessible by August 3, 1977. Structural changes of facilities must now be completed by June 3, 1980.

Question: What can be done about students who have been completely excused from physical education because there is no adapted physical education program?

Answer: No student should be excused from physical education under the requirements of Public Law 94-142 and section 504 which mandate a free appropriate education for every handicapped child.

Question: If a handicapped child brings a note from a physician saying he is to be excused from physical education, how is this handled?

Answer: Excuses like these are technically and legally against the law. Unfortunately many physicians do not understand physical education and all the possibilities available for students. It may be necessary to contact the physician and explain what opportunities are available in today's physical education.

Question: Who should be involved in the evaluation of architectural barriers?

Answer: The most logical persons to be involved are those who face architectural barriers daily: individuals with handicapping conditions.

Question: What if physical education is not a requirement in a particular state? Does this mean that the special education children of that state will not receive physical education?

Answer: Physical education for special education students must be provided by the local educational agency.

Question: What questions should be asked of school administrators and school boards regarding Public Law 94-142 and physical education compliance?

Answer: It is important that school administrators help teachers and program leaders understand the legal mandates of section 504 and Public Law 94-142. In this way they can become important resource and information sources about physical education and related provisions for administrative personnel.

379

Question: May a physician waive physical education for a special education student? May the physician specifically prescribe physical or occupational therapy?

Answer: Physicians cannot supersede the law in either Public Law 94-142 or section 504. Physicians can recommend that a student receive physical and/or occupational therapy. However, the final decision is made by the individualized education committee according to the physical and motor needs of the child. (A physician may be invited to meet with the committee, as can other specialists that the members of the committee feel are needed.)

Question: If swimming instruction or any other single activity is offered to some special education students in a facility, must it be offered equally to all special education students in the facility?

Answer: Services are to be provided children in special education facilities based on their needs, not availability of services. It is possible for one or some students in special education to have swimming or any other single activity on their individualized education program while other students in the same facility do not have the same activities on their individualized education program.

Question: If the state requirement begins services to children at the age of six, is physical education required for children with exceptional educational needs below age six?

Answer: Under Public Law 94-142 requiring a free appropriate education for every child three to twenty-one years of age with a handicapping condition, an exclusion provision mandates that states need not provide special opportunities for these students if education is not required for able-bodied students.

Funding

Question: Where is all the money coming from to translate the law into action?

Answer: Although section 504 provides no financial assistance, Public Law 94-142 authorizes funds to both state and local education agencies within specific guidelines: (1) no more than twelve percent of school-age children can be counted for basic allocations, (2) local education agencies must be able to generate a minimum of $7,500 to be eligible for pass-through funds from the state.

Question: How can colleges and universities obtain funds under Public Law 94-142?

Answer: Colleges and universities can be contracted by state and/or local education agencies to provide specific services within this framework. Two possibilities for colleges and universities to receive funds are through Title D funds administered by the Bureau of Education for the Handicapped. Personnel preparation programs are available from the Division of Personnel Preparation, Bureau of Education for the Handicapped (400 Sixth St., S.W. Washington, D.C.). Research and demonstration project funding information can be obtained from the Division of Innovation and Development Bureau of Education for the Handicapped (same address above).

Question: Where does the money come from for these added services?

381

Answer: All state and local education agencies are expected to support educational services for these children just as they do for nonhandicapped children. Funds under Public Law 94-142 are to be used to assist in meeting additional costs required for providing necessary services. Public Law 94-142 funds cannot be used to supplant or replace state or local support now being given to special education.

Question: Where are funds available to purchase special equipment needed by students with different handicapping conditions participating in senior high school physical education programs?

Answer: In cases where special equipment is needed, pass or flow through funds coming from the Bureau of Education of the Handicapped through the state agency to the local agency should be used for such purposes.

Question: If a child is referred by a local education agency for a medical evaluation, who is responsible for payment?

Answer: The local education agency is responsible for the payment of such evaluations.

Question: What happens if a state decides not to take Public Law 94-142 funds?

Answer: A state that does not accept funds under Public Law 94-142 is not governed by or bound to provisions of this law. However, if any federal funds are used in the programs of that state, it is governed by section 504.

Question: If the county or city recreation department receives no federal funds directly, must it comply with section 504?

Answer: Yes. Any arm or segment of a state organization must comply with at least section 504.

Placement

Question: Does a hearing-impaired child who is mainstreamed into a physical education class need an interpreter?

Answer: If a physical education teacher is able to communicate with a child, the use of an interpreter would be neither required nor appropriate.

Question: What steps are required for a child with a handicapping condition to be assured a free appropriate education?

Answer: The following steps must be followed:
1. Identify the child as defined by law,
2. Refer the child for assessment and evaluation,
3. Assess the child,
4. Determine the eligibility of the child for special services,
5. Convene the individualized planning committee to develop and implement an individualized education program for the child.

Question: May an entire special education class consisting of students homogeneously grouped according to specific handicapping conditions be sent as a group to physical education?

Answer: *Emphatically no!* This practice is exactly what Public Law 94-142 is designed to stop and prevent. Every child is programmed and placed according to individual, not group needs.

Question: When would a regular physical education program not be appropriate for a student receiving special education and related services?

383

Answer: When the regular physical education program cannot meet the child's needs.

Question: Can a traditional adaptive physical education program suffice for special education in a student's individualized education program?

Answer: Yes and no. If the student is placed in the adaptive program based on his/her individual needs, the answer is yes. If a group of students are labeled and categorically cast in an adaptive physical education class, the answer is no.

Question: What placement is necessary for children who are obese, malnourished, or possess low levels of physical fitness?

Answer: These children can find help in special education under the category of "other health impaired conditions." The conditions must limit strength, vitality and alertness in such a way as to adversely affect the child's performance in the classroom.

Question: Do the laws apply only to formal educational environments such as private or public schools?

Answer: No. Any organization, whether it be school, municipality, or industry receiving federal funds, either directly or indirectly, must adhere to Public Law 94-142 and section 504.

Question: Once a student has been placed in a special physical education class, what procedure, if any, can be used to transfer the student back to a regular environment?

Answer: When the student meets all of the short and long term goals as prescribed in his/her individualized education program, and no other special instruction is necessary, an automatic release can be made and the student can attend regular classes.

384

Question: What procedure would be available to a physical education instructor or coach if he/she suspected that a student was impaired?

Answer: Local education agencies have developed referral forms to use for alerting school personnel that a potential problem exists. Once the physical education instructor or coach makes the situation known, the principal should assign experts to evaluate the student after securing parental permission. (Samples of a referral form can be found in Appendix G).

Due Process

Question: Suppose an impasse occurs between the local education agency and parents regarding recommendation services or placement?

Answer: After informal hearings, the procedure includes provisions for formal hearings at local, regional and state levels. If the issue is still unresolved, the case can be taken to the courts with the United States Supreme Court being the potential terminal point.

Question: If parents object to a specific placement or program of the individualized education program, what can be done?

Answer: The child remains in his/her present placement and program. Both the parents and local education agency are guaranteed the same right of appeal and due process.

Question: How are placement differences or disagreements about programs resolved?

Answer: Initial appeal (by either party) is to a hearing officer not affiliated with the local education agency at the local level. If not satisfied by the results, a similar appeal can be forwarded to the state education agency and then to civil suit action.

Question: Should a disruptive child be permitted to remain in a regular physical education class or should he/she be removed during that particular class period?

Answer: If the handicapped student's behavior is so disruptive that it impedes the learning progress of other students or *his/her* own, then he/she should not remain in a regular physical education class. In this case, "the least restrictive environment" is not the regular physical education class.

Question: What rights does a teacher have in regard to self protection when attacked by a severely emotionally disturbed student?

Answer: The teacher has the same rights of self protection whether the child is handicapped or able-bodied; however, excessive force may not be used.

Individualized Education Programs

Question: Do individualized education programs have to be written for children who are mainstreamed in regular physical education classes?

Answer: No. A child with no special physical and motor needs and for whom only expected and required accommodations are necessary does not need an individualized education program.

Question: The individualized planning committee agrees that an individual child needs a service that is not available through the local education agency. Must this service be added to programs sponsored by the local education agency?

Answer: The local education agency is responsible for seeing that provisions of the individualized education program are fulfilled.

Question: Must local education agencies provide summer programs as part of individualized education programs?

Answer: If an individualized planning committee recommends summer programs and opportunities, including day or residential camping, in an individualized education program, the local education agency is responsible for making sure it is provided.

Question: Must physical education be included in every child with a handicapping condition's individualized education program?

Answer: Yes, when the student needs a specially designed physical education program.

Question: Should physical educators be on the team that develops a child's individualized education program?

Answer: Physical education teachers can be but they are not required to be a part of the team.

Question: May union representatives accompany teachers to individualized planning meetings?

Answer: No. Their presence would violate Public Law 94-142 which protects the confidentiality of information about the children.

Question: What can teachers be held accountable for regarding individualized programs?

Answer: For not following or implementing outlined procedures as agreed for the individualized education program.

Sports Programs

Question: Must a group of students who want to play wheelchair basketball be provided opportunities?

Answer: Section 504 requires that activities such as wheelchair basketball must be provided at levels of activities similar to those open to non-handicapped students when sufficient interest is shown by students with handicapping conditions.

Question: A group of students in wheelchairs are attending schools in different locations in the same local education agency area. None of the individual schools has enough players to form a team. What is the local education agency's responsibility in such situations?

Answer: The local education agency has the responsibility to see that these students have the same opportunity to participate in intramurals, extramurals and interscholastic sports as do the nonhandicapped students. The responsibility is on the local education agency rather than the individual school.

Question: If a student needs a special wheelchair or other special equipment to participate in special sports programs, who is responsible for the purchase of this equipment?

Answer: Section 504 states that individuals with handicapping conditions must be provided an equal opportunity for participation. Lack of equipment is not an acceptable rationale for denying this participation. Public Law 94-142 states that if special equipment is needed to meet the goals and objectives of the individual's program then the local education agency is responsible for providing this special equipment.

Question: We have difficulty getting funds to purchase equipment, uniforms, and other necessary supplies for our special school intramural or

388

interscholastic athletic programs. What can we do to obtain funds?

Answer: If a local education agency or school board funds the intramural or interscholastic programs in the regular junior and senior high schools, similar support must be provided for comparable programs in special schools.

Question: If a group of handicapped students want to form a sports team and do not have enough participants, what alternatives do they have?

Answer: It is the responsibility of the local educational agency to provide an equal opportunity for participation. If the individual school is unable to provide enough participants then they may have to look within their entire educational setting.

Question: Is a ruling discriminatory if it results in a student who required special education services early in his school career exceeding the maximum age for participation in interscholastic sports?

Answer: It is the opinion of personnel in the Office of Civil Rights that no discrimination is evident in this situation. While they agree that the age cutoff is arbitrary, ways in which this rule is administered are not discriminatory since it is applied to everyone concerned. The route that must be followed is an individual appeal which is ruled upon according to merits of the specific case through procedures administered by the state high school activities/athletic associations.

Question: Are Little League baseball, Pop Warner Football, bitty basketball, age group swimming, junior hockey, youth soccer, and similar youth sports programs governed by section 504?

Answer: If any youth sports program receives direct federal assistance, it cannot discriminate. Similarly, a program which does not receive direct financial assistance but is funded or sponsored by a recipient cannot discriminate. In addition, a recipient of federal financial assistance may not in any way sponsor or assist any program, even if privately funded, that discriminates.

Question: A high school student with only one kidney has been denied the opportunity to participate in interscholastic football. Is this a discriminatory practice under section 504?

Answer: In this instance, he is being denied the opportunity to play football because his condition is perceived to be a handicap. He is therefore protected from exclusion under section 504.

Question: What are examples of specific sports rules that may have to be modified?

Answer: Rules barring sideline signals and other mechanical devices in football games between teams of hearing-impaired players competing against hearing players have to be modified. Starting procedures in track and swimming have to be reviewed so that the deaf athlete is not placed at a disadvantage against his opponents. However, handicapped individuals are not to be given unfair advantages through these rule modifications. Separate or different treatment can be permitted only where necessary to ensure equal opportunity.

Question: A high level single upper arm amputee competes in the butterfly stroke with opponents having both arms. He rotates his arm, stub, and head in ways that approximate a crawl or freestyle stroke. Is it discriminatory to disqualify him because of improper execution of the stroke?

390

Answer: While rules committees must make sure that rules are not discriminatory, they are not intended to give the handicapped participants unfair advantages. In this situation the amputee appears to be gaining a definite advantage. It would not appear to be discriminatory if he/she could not perform this particular stroke without gaining an advantage. This person could compete in the freestyle event, however.

Question: A university has an official team representing wheelchair basketball. It also sponsors a basketball team for men and women for which athletic scholarships are given. Does the university have to provide athletic scholarships for players who represent it in wheelchair basketball?

Answer: An unofficial clarification from the Office of Civil Rights suggests that athletic scholarships do not have to be provided for wheelchair sports just as they do not have to be provided for any officially recognized intercollegiate sport. If scholarships are given for specific sports, however, individuals with a handicapping condition cannot be denied such scholarships because of their handicapping conditions. An individual with a handicapping condition can be denied an athletic scholarship in such sports when decisions are based on comparative skills and abilities in those sports.

Question: Are academic eligibility requirements that require students to pass three (or sometimes more) subjects discriminating against mentally retarded students in special education programs?

391

Answer: Many states have made special provisions for such situations. Those states which still maintain rigid academic requirements based on passing a given number of subjects or Carnegie Units that make it impossible for mentally retarded students to gain eligibility for interscholastic sports would appear to be operating in a manner potentially contrary to the letter and intent of section 504.

Question: Can students with handicapping conditions be denied opportunities to participate in physical education, recreation, or sports activities because insurance policies do not cover them?

Answer: Recipients of federal funds (i.e., local education agencies) cannot enter into contracts or do business with companies or corporations that discriminate.

Question: Can a state or local education agency prohibit an individual with one eye/kidney or who is deaf/epileptic from taking part in athletics in general or specific sports in particular for their own health, welfare, and safety?

Answer: While there is no indication of how higher courts might rule, conflicting judgments reveal the complexity of these situations and how unpredictable and inconsistent resulting rulings can be.

Question: Is the interscholastic football rule that bars anyone with an artificial hand, arm, or leg discriminatory?

Answer: The 1978 Football Rule Book of the National Federation of State High School Associations contained the following change:

Each State Association may authorize the use of artificial limbs which in its opinion are no more dangerous to players than the corresponding human limb and do not place an opponent at a disadvantage.

392

The case book interprets the rule change in more detail.

Question: A male paraplegic qualified for a weight-training class in a senior high school but was denied the opportunity to participate. Can this be done?

Answer: The student cannot be denied the opportunity to take part in the weight training program. Weight training is a sanctioned sport in competitions for paraplegics, cerebral palsied and quadriplegics at every level, including international and national games.

Question: May an individual be carried physically into a swimming pool for instructional or recreational activities?

Answer: The Office of Civil Rights extending rules and regulations for section 504 prohibits physically carrying or lifting individuals so that they can participate in activities. Carrying an individual circumvents facility and program accessibility under section 504. It also encourages dependence rather than independence and compromises an individual's dignity.

Question: A blind student ran cross country last year and wants to participate again. A change of coaches has resulted in a situation where there is resistance toward this student's participation. Please comment.

Answer: In the case mentioned, the school and local education agency are not complying with section 504's regulations.

Question: In the case above, the school principal does not want the boy to participate in indoor track because of safety reasons. Please comment.

393

Answer: Accommodations are required for indoor track as well as outdoor track. No assumptions should be made about safety. The few statistics available about accident rates of blind individuals in physical education and sports activities show a safer rather than more hazardous population.

Question: When differences of opinion exist between school and personal physicians, whose recommendation shall be final?

Answer: Policy interpretations from the Office of Civil Rights stipulate that the doctor most familiar with a student's condition is the one who provides approval for participation in contact sports.

Index

A

B

I

J

M

MALPRACTICE.
Educational malpractice, p. 226.

MAYOR AND CITY COUNCIL V. MATTHEWS, p. 127.

MCKART V. UNITED STATES, p. 127.

MEDICAL DISQUALIFICATIONS.
Eligibility rules for sports participation, p. 154.

MEDICAL EXAMINATIONS.
Preparticipation medical exam, p. 188.

MILLS V. BOARD OF EDUCATION OF DISTRICT OF COLUMBIA, p. 48.

N

NATIONAL BANK OF COMMERCE V. MARSHALL, p. 129.

NATIONAL WHEELCHAIR ATHLETIC ASSOCIATION.
Established, p. 37.

NATIONAL WHEELCHAIR BASKETBALL ASSOCIATION.
Established, p. 37.

NEGLIGENCE.
Assumption of risk, p. 186.
Comparative negligence, p. 185.
Consent.
  The need to inform, p. 224.
Contributory negligence, p. 184.
Defenses, p. 183.
Elements, p. 182.
Equipment and facilities, p. 243.
Instruction, p. 242.
Inventory for liability, appx. F.
Proximate cause, p. 182.
Self-test for liability, appx. F.
Supervision, p. 242.
Who is responsible for negligence, p. 189.

NOTICE.
Acceptance of risk, p. 188.
Injuries to participants.
  The need to inform, p. 224.

INDEX

O

P

R